ALSO BY WILLIAM POLLACK

Real Boys' Voices

Real Boys: Rescuing Our Sons from the Myths of Boyhood

In a Time of Fallen Heroes: The Re-creation of Masculinity (coauthor)

A New Psychology of Men

New Psychotherapy for Men

ALSO BY KATHLEEN CUSHMAN

The Collected Horace: Theory and Practice in Essential Schools

Schooling for the Real World (coauthor)

REAL BOYS WORKBOOK

WILLIAM S. POLLACK, PH.D.

REAL BOYS WORKBOOK

AND KATHLEEN CUSHMAN

VILLARD

NEW YORK

All rights reserved under International and Pan-American Copyright Conventions. Published in the United States by Villard Books, a division of Random House, Inc., New York, and simultaneously in Canada by Random House of Canada Limited, Toronto.

VILLARD BOOKS is a registered trademark of Random House, Inc. Colophon is a trademark of Random House, Inc.

The "Bill of Rights for Young Athletes" on page 265 is reprinted from *Parents Complete Guide to Youth Sports* with permission from the National Association for Sport and Physical Education (NASPE), 1900 Association Drive, Reston, VA 20191-1599.

Library of Congress Cataloging-in-Publication Data is available.

Villard Books website address: www.villard.com

Printed in the United States of America on acid-free paper

2 4 6 8 9 7 5 3

First Edition

This book is dedicated

to Marsha and Sarah—
who have genuinely listened and "worked" with me

to my parents and the memory of my grandparents—
who heard and sustained the inner meaning of this boy's life

and

to the boys themselves—and all who love them—
they open up their inner lives to us, courageously baring their
hearts and souls daily, waiting for our understanding and response
Let us not disappoint them in their yearning for a better life

—W.S.P.

For Eliza

—K.C.

ACKNOWLEDGMENTS

Boys' lives, struggles, and their need for unswerving support from all who love them in this complex modern world have only recently found themselves the limelight that they so richly deserve. The publication and response to *Real Boys* and *Real Boys' Voices* have led to a groundswell of interest and change in this challenging area, and also to a clamor for an interactive volume in which readers could "put their hands around" some of the most pressing issues for the boys in their lives. Throughout the country, wherever I have traveled on behalf of making this a better world for boys and helping boys to fit better into our culture, in the countless letters, e-mails, and telephone calls from around the world there has been a constant request for a workbook, a volume like this one that incorporates the central concepts of the Real Boys research and philosophy in a model that allows parents, teachers, coaches, clergy, mentors, and boys and girls themselves to tackle the issues essential to understanding boys' experience—a book not only to read but to "write for oneself," a book in which to record essential feelings and new insights, prodded by new information, special tips, and important suggestions. I have designed this workbook to be not just for one narrow group, but for many—for use in homes, schools, churches, synagogues, youth facilities, and sports arenas—in the hands of both adults and young adults who yearn to better understand the lives and voices of the boys among us, from childhood through adolescence and beyond. It is a book meant to offer practical suggestions and opportunities for self-discovery, and ultimately to create both profound change and great joy for all boys and for those of us who love them. It is important to note, however, that in creating such a volume, careful thought was also given to girls' lives, how intertwined girls are with the boys I've studied and with whom I've worked and how much the workbook is meant to affect their lives positively as well.

Such a project cannot succeed without the creative intelligence of a team of dedicated people who bring their efforts together in support of both the book and its authors. The insight of these colleagues and their contributions to the work—both individually and collectively—inevitably make it stronger, more meaningful, and ultimately better able to shape its message. Therefore, I'd like to take this opportunity to offer my sincerest gratitude to some of the people who helped make the *Real Boys Workbook* possible:

Kate Medina, my editor at Random House, whose sagacity, energy, intellectual support, and critical thinking have been essential components of all my work, must receive the first acknowledgment here. Without her there would not have been a *Real Boys Workbook.* From her earliest connection with my work and then her thoughtful guidance in the creation of this book's older brothers, *Real Boys: Rescuing Our Sons from the Myths of Boyhood* and *Real Boys' Voices,* Kate has helped to make an important difference in how we think about and raise boys in America and throughout the world. Her editorial comments and suggestions are reflective of the highest order of professional excellence, and her "magical" eye and guidance in organizing, shaping, and polishing this workbook made all the difference. Her skill, sincere dedication to this enterprise, and faith in my work with boys cannot be too deeply praised. Bruce Tracy's willingness at Villard to "adopt" our boys series and his creativity in bringing these ideas to workbook form must be praised. Others at Random House have also been unceasingly supportive. Most especially, I'd like to acknowledge the support of Frankie Jones, Ms. Medina's assistant, who made everything happen, providing the "glue" among the authors and publishing house while forestalling all emergencies. Random House's remarkable publicists, Carol Schneider, Tom Perry, Liz Fogarty, Frances Yue, and Jynne Martin, deserve my praise as well for bringing this work to the public's attention, even before its pages were complete. I am grateful also to Caroline Cunningham, Steve Messina, Richard Elman, Keith Goldsmith, and Dan Rembert.

Next, I would like to convey my deep appreciation for the invaluable assistance and support that I received from my agent, Todd Shuster. Todd has truly become a "fellow traveler" in the world of understanding and caring about boys. His literary skills are outstripped only by his passion, indefatigable enthusiasm, and depth of concern for the themes raised in this book. I greatly appreciate all he has done for this workbook, for me personally, and for boys everywhere. I would also like to convey my deep thanks to his colleagues Lane Zachary and Esmond Harmsworth at the Zachary Shuster Harmsworth Agency for all the support they have provided me.

I am grateful to the countless parents, boys, educators, coaches, guidance counselors, and youth workers who have shared their ideas, sorrows, and joys with me. I hope you will see your inspiration in the pages that follow. Although it would be most fitting to mention, by specific reference to their significant institutions, the educators, superintendents, school heads, counselors, organizational leaders, grassroots organizers, and union leaders who on behalf of boys contributed so much to the success of this project, the process would take a volume in itself, so this partial list in alphabetical order will need to suffice. Please understand that any omission in no way reflects the level of my gratitude or diminishes the meaningfulness of your contribution: Gary Baker, Jeff Bleich, Irwin Blummer, Cindy Bouvier, Kay Donovan, Pam Eakes, Dale W. Emme, Dar Emme, Robin Finegan, Krystan Flannigan, Shari Hobson, Laurie Hoffner, Peter Holland, Tony Jarvis, Michael Jenkins, Matthew King, Carleton Land, Barbara Macgillivray, Rena Mirkin, Bill Modzeleski, Gail Revis, Richard Riley, Pat Ruane, Thomas Scott, David Sherman, Pam Stinson, Elizabeth Twomey, Robert Vitalo, David Weston, Ken Wilson, and Jeffrey M. Young.

The International Boys' Schools Coalition has long recognized the need for a new psychology of boys and has also been generously supportive of my work. I would like especially to thank John Farber, Rick Melvoin, Rick Hawley, Brewster Ely, Brad Gioia, and Diane Hulse as well as the other members of the coalition's board and research committee for their unrelenting faith in my projects.

Although the work on this project was carried out independently under the auspices of the Real Boys Education Program™, I would still like to acknowledge the gracious input and emotional support of my colleagues at Harvard Medical School and McLean Hospital in general, and particularly Drs. Bruce Cohen, Joseph Coyle, Philip Levendusky, and Paul Barreira for their support for the Center for Men and Young Men and their recognition of the psychology of boys and men as a legitimate field of specialization. I am grateful for the spiritual support of the Department of Continuing Education at McLean, as well as my coworkers, past and present, Carol Brown and Cathy Toon.

I would also like to express my unending gratitude to Dr. Shervert Frazier, psychiatrist in chief, emeritus, of McLean Hospital, who has been an incredible mentor, helping me to develop my "voice" in a field of psychological study that was once largely overlooked. No one else has provided me the opportunity to absorb such sagacity about the inner lives of boys and men.

I must acknowledge how much I have learned from my colleagues in gender and adolescent studies in general, in particular from my friends at the Society for the Psychological Study of Men and Masculinity, Division 51 of the American Psychological Association; my colleagues at the National Campaign Against Youth Violence, Mothers Against Violence in America, and the Yellow Ribbon Program; and my friends and collaborators at the National Threat Assessment Center of the U.S. Secret Service— Bryan Vossekuil, its director, and Dr. Robert Fein—who have greatly increased my knowledge about boys and violence.

The struggle to help boys develop into healthy, happy men clearly has much in common with the struggles in the lives of girls—more than we often like to believe. Although my research derives from many years of work with boys and men, it is important to recognize the important influence that the "new" psychology of girls and women has had on this field. I would like to mention my particular appreciation of the seminal work of Carol Gilligan and that of the core faculty of the Stone Center at Wellesley College, all of whom have helped to shape a concept of a "connected self" in women that bears much relevance to my own theories of the development of boys. Dr. Judith Jordan, my colleague, collaborator, and friend, has had a tremendously positive impact on my thinking in this field. Her deep intelligence and creative inspiration may be felt throughout my work. Dr. Mary

Pipher has generously supported my endeavors, and I hope that the many stimulating conversations we have had will lead to greater collaboration and understanding between boys and girls in the future.

Researching and writing this work would have been impossible without the love, understanding, and unyielding patience of my family. I am deeply indebted to my wife, Dr. Marsha Padwa, for her invaluable insights about children, adolescents, and their families and school environments as well as her critical input on earlier drafts of this work, and to both Marsha and my daughter Sarah F. Pollack, for their intelligent suggestions as well as their unwavering love and care—juggling schedules, tolerating crises, and sustaining my spirits during times of distress.

To the boys who inspired this workbook and their parents and teachers, who have opened their lives to us and who have taught me so much through their struggles, I extend my personal gratitude and thanks.

Real Boys Workbook has been a work of love, and I hope it will help us all to discover and nurture the love boys themselves have been struggling to convey—along with assuaging their angst, longing, and uncertainty. I hope it will help us all to change for the better. Of one thing I can be certain: This book itself was enhanced through the collaboration of my educationally sophisticated coauthor, Kathleen Cushman. I thank her for her dedication to this project and to the many boys' lives I anticipate it will improve.

William S. Pollack

Kathleen Cushman gratefully acknowledges the help of the dozens of parents, teachers, and boys who shared with her their experiences during her research for this book. Special thanks to Lynnwood Andrews, Celia and John Bohannon, Barbara Cervone, Connie Cushman, Cynthia and Ted Cushman, Nancy Cushman, Amy MacDonald, Montana Miller, Rosa Miller, John O'Grady, Laura Rogers, Justin Samaha, and Adria Steinberg. The stamina, tolerance, and sometimes even surreal humor of my three children also provided crucial support. Most important, Eliza Miller's critical contribution at every stage throughout the writing and editing process cannot be overstated. My deepest gratitude to all of you.

CONTENTS

INTRODUCTION

UNDERSTANDING REAL BOYS: UNCOVERING THE MYTHS, FACING THE BOY CODE

In those first moments when they look up, and really look at us, boys catch our interest, our attention, our hearts.

A boy may be out on the playing field, hot and dirty, about to throw the ball at the instant it matters most—and his eyes reveal that he fears the scorn of those who wait and watch.

Or he may be hunched over his homework, tangled in something he doesn't quite get—and in his brief, tense glance we see his worry that he'll *never* get it the way the others do. But he often doesn't say anything.

Or he may be leaving his mother at the door of day care, and as she pries away his hand, his eyes fill up with tears he tries to hide.

Or he may come in from the school dance, and the look of excitement he left with has turned into some private pain impossible to forget.

We know boys need something in these moments—but usually we don't quite know what. Should we say something—and what? Should we wait for them to give us a signal?

Steeped in the ways our culture has taught us from childhood, we have a lifetime of images to instruct us in how boys should look and act. The boys we brag about are natural athletes, good in school, popular with girls. They don't cry when their mothers leave, and they don't allow anything to defeat them. We *want* them to be that way.

And yet, when we meet the eyes of a boy in such moments, some other instinct also stirs within us.

We don't want to ignore, be silent about, and therefore deny boys their feelings just because they don't fit the popular mold. We know it's worse if we encourage them to hide their real selves from the world in order to gain some imagined place as a man. But how to avoid this? How to respond in a way that will draw out and confirm boys?

For those of us with boys in our lives, the crucial questions of how we should raise and teach our male children arise every day.

There's never been a time when it mattered more to do this right—for boys themselves, for the girls they'll work and live with, and for a society that depends more than ever on the emotional strength of the young people we're bringing up today.

And it's never been more difficult. This workbook exists, in fact, because so many people—after reading *Real Boys: Rescuing Our Sons from the Myths of Boyhood* and *Real Boys' Voices*—are asking for practical coaching about how to work through the challenges they face as parents, teachers, coaches, youth workers, or friends and relatives of boys. Boys, too, are reaching out for help.

As the research presented in *Real Boys* and *Real Boys' Voices* shows, many boys—however normal they may be—struggle every day with silent crises, internal conflicts difficult for even the most informed and caring adult to identify and deal with.

The boy on the playing field fears that if his throw doesn't reach second base, he will have lost not just the game but a critical part of his self-esteem. He fears what boys fear most—shame. He knows that boys are supposed to throw hard and well—and that if he fails, he must conceal his shame behind a stoic mask.

The boy tangled in his homework has picked up somehow that asking for help is not something a boy does. And the little boy at the door of day care already senses, at the moment his mother pushes him away, that if he were a big boy—a little man—he wouldn't be needing or going to his mother for the solace for which he so yearns.

Whether we're parents, teachers, coaches, or others who work with youngsters, none of us wants our boys to suffer from these stereotypes. But without our even knowing or wanting it, we can make those painful issues worse for them. What we want, though, is to make things better—and this book is about how to do that.

There are no easy answers. Even though we want nothing but the best for the boys we care about, often we're not quite sure what "the best for them" actually looks like.

Just when we need peace and order, our boys may be creating a ruckus we can't control. Just when they need to be learning most in the classroom, they may stop doing their homework or caring about whether they succeed in school. Bombarded with violent images from mass media, they gravitate toward games and movies that make our hair stand on end.

Our little boys may be crying and clinging when we have to leave them. The older boys may constantly be picking fights, hitting, and shoving. Our moody teenage boys often won't talk to us at all, even when we know something's bothering them.

Are boys somehow hardwired to be this way? Or are we part of making it happen—and if so, can we change it?

Real Boys has called society's set of expectations for boys the **Boy Code**. A whole society has learned it well; we act on it every day, in ways we may not even realize. We're caught, ourselves, by a set of myths that we grew up thinking were the truth. Here's what the myths tell us:

1. **Boys will be boys.** Nature wins out over nurture. Boys' testosterone levels will always defeat their potential for sensitivity, making them "naturally" more aggressive. (In truth, though, a boy's behavior is shaped more by loved ones than by nature.)

2. **Boys *should* be boys.** They must hide "weak" emotions like fear, hurt, or shame behind a stoic mask. Except for the anger that counts as a man's only acceptable feeling, they should always stay cool and in control. (Actually, as we know, there are many diverse ways to express oneself as a male.)

3. **Boys are toxic.** Unless they are kept under strict controls and punishment, they are dangerous to society. (In fact, boys are empathic and caring, with a strong desire for fairness and justice.)

WHAT THE BOY CODE TELLS BOYS—AND SHOULDN'T

➤ Stand on your own two feet. Always be independent.
➤ Separate from Mom and all things female as quickly as possible, or you'll be a "sissy" or "wuss."
➤ Never show any feelings (except anger). Fear and vulnerability are for wimps and you will be teased or shamed for revealing them. Keep the "code of silence."
➤ Stay on top and in the limelight.
➤ "Give 'em hell" through macho behavior, cruelty, bravado, and banter.
➤ Sex is conquest.
➤ Bullying and teasing are just "normal" boy talk.
➤ Never give in or really listen.
➤ Don't show your fear of violence.
➤ Don't "rat" or let anyone else know when another boy does something harmful.

In human terms alone, the Boy Code perpetuates a terrible injustice. Afraid of appearing less than fully masculine, boys defend themselves by taunting others with hurtful terms like "fag." But just as girls need the freedom to act with boldness and courage, to display their physical and intellectual prowess, so do boys deserve the freedom to express their full range of emotions and capabilities. Freeing them from the gender straitjacket of the Boy Code, the work we undertake in this workbook, is one of the most important things adults can do for the boys—and the girls—they care about.

SUGGESTIONS ON HOW TO USE THIS BOOK

If you want immediate help, you can go straight to the particular topics you're most interested in. If your boys—by which we mean the boys you parent or teach or coach or care for in other ways—are caught up in violent video games, you'll find ways to intervene. If you know a boy who's being bullied, you'll learn strategies to defuse and stop the situation. If you're wondering whether your rambunctious boy is hyperactive, you'll get practical help assessing this. Boys themselves may want to try some of the exercises here; indeed, many are designed just for that purpose.

But as you use the exercises to explore your own thoughts and feelings, this book can also shed light on how you see and relate to the boys in your life.

We'll use everyday situations and exercises as windows into what society unfairly demands from our boys. And as we go through these exercises, together we'll come up with ways that our attitudes and actions can help counteract those cultural strictures, so that our boys can grow into the men they'd be if they could choose freely.

Whether you are a teacher or a parent, you probably face comparable dilemmas every day. Working through this book can help you reflect on your own habitual responses—and perhaps reexamine your beliefs about boys.

In any one of the situations you encounter every day, you may begin to stop and ask yourself, "Is this happening not because I mean it to, but because of something I didn't quite realize before—and may not even believe in anymore?"

As you try these exercises and strategies, we hope you may answer that question and find ways to adjust your actions so you *do* act according to what you believe in.

The exercises won't tell you what you ought to think. Instead, we'll help you work through your own ideas, coaching you about new possibilities that could make things better for both you and your boys. We hope you'll be writing in this book, as you think out the dilemmas of raising and teaching boys.

Sometimes that process will create new struggles for you. What if your ideas differ from those of other important people in your boy's life—whether that be a parent, a teacher, a coach, a relative, or someone else whose opinion matters to him or to you?

You may not always be able to resolve these different points of view. But this book aims, at the very least, to start a discussion about them that allows for differences.

Countless parents and teachers have shared their stories and questions with us since the research into these topics that culminated in *Real Boys* and *Real Boys' Voices*. They've struggled with how to help boys through the jungle of playground teasing and bullying. They've watched as the boys they care about move from friendships to adolescent crushes to falling in love for the first time. They've wondered how to deal with disruptive or defiant behavior without depriving a boy of his dignity.

Perhaps similar things have happened to you in your experiences with boys—or maybe you went through them in your own youthful years. Maybe you're preparing for the next challenges that your growing boy will hand you—or maybe you juggle these situations all day long at your job working with kids.

As a caring adult—or maybe as a boy or girl yourself—you're already committed to changing boys' lives for the better. This book will help you put your best ideas to work with "real boys."

REAL BOYS
WORKBOOK

1

SOME DOS AND DON'TS WITH BOYS

SHAMING AND HOW TO AVOID IT • TALKING AND LISTENING TO BOYS: ACTION TALK AND TIMED SILENCE • HOW TO TELL WHEN SOMETHING'S WRONG • LIFE WITH BOYS: ADULT SURVIVAL STRATEGIES

"I treated my two kids exactly the same," said Marianne. "But by the time my little boy was three years old, he acted so different from his older sister at that age!" Her daughter, Evie, always loved playing in a corner with a friend, "pretending" complex stories that they made up as they went along. Her son Gregory's play relationships, on the other hand, didn't seem to go any farther than knocking down towers of blocks and running around the house screaming like wild men.

As Gregory got older, Marianne said, the differences between her children only became more pronounced. "I always swore that my son would be an exception, but I've learned my lesson," she laughed. "You know that rhyme about what little girls and little boys are made of? Well, at seven, Gregory's pretty much all nails and puppy-dog tails. He'd rather wrestle on the rug with his dad than talk to me about his problems at school. I know he needs my support just as much as Evie does, but it's so much easier for me to relate to Evie! I think I end up letting Gregory fend for himself more than I should."

Boys *are* different from girls—partly because their biology is different, but more often because we unwittingly treat them differently from their earliest infancy in what we have described as the Boy Code. (See pages xxi–xxii.) Although there are important exceptions, as a group they tend to be more action-oriented, more confrontive, less quick to communicate verbally and more likely to hide their feelings of tenderness, hurt, or shame.

Of course, boys are different from one another, too, as are girls. In fact, many girls share traits with some of the boys described in this book, or some boys may act in the same way girls might act. But as things stand right now in our culture, these patterns describe the ways many boys in fact behave and feel.

It's normal that the boys in our lives often present us with problems we may not know how to handle. But there's also something very wrong. Our culture has developed a rigid code of behavior for boys—the Boy Code. If we fall into line with it and enforce it, we lose out on the pleasure of close connections with our boys, and they lose their own crucial rudder through life.

The world we live in expects our boys to prematurely *disconnect* from other people and from their own feelings, in order to "stand on their own two feet." And even if we aren't the ones enforcing the unspoken rules, boys hear them everywhere—on television and on the playground, in school and at camp.

But as caring adults—like Marianne—we can find ways to *connect* with our boys and give them the support they need to negotiate the hurdles of growing up. We can understand boys' developmental process, and know what a boy needs at each stage. We can listen and talk to boys without shaming them. We can create family rituals and school and sports programs that foster connection, trust, and supportive relationships. Knowing the difference between action and aggression, we can search for ways to encourage the positive and productive expressions of a boy's energy.

Most of all, we can discover ways to relate to a boy so that he isn't left to "fend for himself," as Marianne put it. This chapter will introduce some key concepts in the *Real Boys* approach, along with some practical exercises to make those ideas work effectively for parents and teachers.

SHAMING AND HOW TO AVOID IT

"Should I worry that my little boy, Franklin, seems to need me so much?" asked Harriet. "He's afraid of the dark, and even with the light on, he cries at bedtime. I have to sit in his room until he falls asleep." At four, Franklin clings to his mother when she leaves him at day care, when she introduces him to friends, and even when he goes to visit his father on weekends. "My sister told him he'd better stop acting like a baby, or they'll gang up on him when he gets to kindergarten."

In her heart, Harriet said, she feels that Franklin really does need her right now. "This has been a tough year for him, with his father leaving," she said. "He'll grow up in his own time." But she worried that her sister might be right. "Am I setting him up to be the one everybody picks on?" she asked.

Harriet's sister is only trying to help: She doesn't want to see people looking down on her nephew. But her words may echo in Franklin's ears in the years ahead, making him ashamed of his normal need for loving shelter and emotional support in times of trouble. At the scary times in his life, he might think he needs to take on a stance of bravado. He might feel shame about his true feelings of vulnerability and sensitivity, and may learn to shut them out altogether.

As she talked through the situation, Harriet became more certain that Franklin's fears at bedtime and other times of separation, or his anxiety around strangers, were a reaction to his father's recent departure. "If his father can just leave," she asked, "how does he know his momma won't leave, too?" She decided to keep giving Franklin what her instinct told her he needed—"plenty of hugs and love whenever he wants it."

AVOIDING SHAME: DOS AND DON'TS

➤ **Do** trust your instincts that tell you to reach out to a boy in emotional pain. *Example:* Harriet spent extra time sitting with her son when he couldn't get to sleep, even though she worried about his neediness. Her heart told her that her boy needed her, even though her culture was telling her he shouldn't.

➤ **Don't** be afraid of what "everyone else" will think of you or him. *Example:* Harriet told her sister, "I think Franklin will do just fine in kindergarten. He just needs a little extra from me right now." When you stick up for what you feel, it encourages other people to reexamine their own attitudes.

➤ **Do** encourage the expression of a full range of emotions. *Example:* Harriet asked Franklin, "When I leave you with the baby-sitter, do you sometimes feel really scared?" When you use a broad range of emotion words—happy, sad, tired, disappointed, nervous, lonely—you teach boys that anger isn't the only emotion a male is allowed to feel. If he won't talk to you, try reaching out to him through action instead of words. (See the section on "Action Talk.")

➤ **Don't** discourage a boy from expressing vulnerable feelings. *Example:* Don't tell a teenager whose girlfriend just dumped him to "cheer up, there'll be other girls." Instead, ask him if he'd like to talk about it, and try to "mirror back" the feelings he expresses in an empathetic way. (See the sections on listening in this chapter and in chapter 2, pages 9 and 27–28.)

➤ **Do** give your boy your undivided attention at least once a day. *Example:* Sit with your little boy as he goes to bed, as Harriet did. Or leave the radio off when you drive him to soccer practice. Knowing that you've got time for him gives him the message that you're there and that you care.

➤ **Don't** use shaming language. *Example:* Rather than asking "How could you do that?" when a boy gets sent to the principal, ask "What's going on?" or "What happened here?" This suggests that you haven't formed a judgment about the situation.

(continued)

> **Do** express your love and empathy openly and generously.

Example: Tell your boy you're proud of him when he comforts a crying baby or stands up for someone in trouble. No matter what you may hear, there's no such thing as giving a boy too much affection, love, and positive attention.

> **Don't** tell your boy to "be strong" or "act like a man."

Example: When your six-year-old is scared to jump off the diving board, don't send him back to face the terrors of the leap. Instead, tell him how you used to get scared, too, and let him play in the shallow end with you. Show him that even the strong people he looks up to, like you, express vulnerability openly.

> **Do** create a model of masculinity for your boy that is broad and inclusive.

Example: Point out interesting examples of men you know who work in traditionally female fields, like nursing, elementary-school teaching, or dance. Show him that real men cook dinner, change diapers, sing lullabies, cry when they're sad, and generally act in caring and expressive ways.

Think about the boys in your life. Looking through the "Dos" in the above list, can you think of situations where you could put these ideas into action? Describe one of them here:

_____

_____

_____

_____

_____

_____

CREATING THE "SHAME-FREE ZONE"

Boys face shame in so many places—in locker rooms and school cafeterias, on street corners and even in classrooms. Adults can't protect their boys from the entire culture, and until the society as a whole changes, many boys will continue to wear the "mask of masculinity" that shields them. But creating what *Real Boys* calls a "shame-free zone" can ensure that boys can take off that mask when they want to.

What is a shame-free zone? It's a safe space or time in which everyone agrees to listen to one another without making judgments or shaming one another for expressing feelings. A shame-free zone could be a particular classroom ritual, an after-school club, or a time in the week when a boy and his parent share an activity. Explicitly stating—and demonstrating—that this time and place is safe for emotional expression can help reassure boys that here, at least, they will not be shamed for being themselves.

➤ *Mr. Gunner begins and ends his third-grade class each day with personal "connections" and "reflections." He and his students have agreed that nobody will argue with, ridicule, or gossip about what people share during that special circle time.*

➤ *After every season, Coach Thorpe gathers his soccer team at his house for pizza. It's not an awards ceremony or a time to criticize technical plays, but a time to talk about the ways each boy has supported the team, and how they feel about their season together. Each boy also says something that he wishes he could do better, and the team agrees on ways to help him work on that in the next season.*

➤ *Anna's son, Eric, is in the high-school drama club, and he often needs her to help him memorize his lines. They've agreed that when they read through plays together, Eric is free to try any interpretation he wants, even if he's afraid it will be silly or overdone. "It's amazing how much faster he remembers his part after saying the whole thing in a fake French accent!" marvels Anna.*

TALKING AND LISTENING TO BOYS:
ACTION TALK AND TIMED SILENCE

As boys move away from their closest caregivers and into the world, they'll be under tremendous pressure to conform to the Boy Code. They'll be desperately afraid to look babyish on the playground, to look dumb (or too smart) in the classroom, to look inept on the playing field, to look awkward on a date—in short, to make any wrong step that would humiliate or shame them in the eyes of others.

We adults can give boys safe ways to express their real feelings as they take these important and scary steps toward independence. We can spend time with them daily, simply joining them in activities they enjoy. We can share our own stories, opening the way to listening with empathy to theirs. By staying connected to our boys, we can help them stay connected to their own true selves.

ACTION TALK: HOW TO TALK TO A BOY

Many parents and teachers worry about how to get boys to talk to them at all. "His sister is always ready to hang out with me and gab," said one mother. "But my boy's always on the go. Even if I can get him to sit for a minute, I can tell he'd really rather be doing something else."

But "doing something else" can actually provide just the opportunity this mother is looking for. Many boys feel more comfortable expressing their feelings of closeness and affection through actions rather than words. He may not actually speak the words "I love you," but you'll see his face light up when you invite him to help check out a problem under the hood of your car.

Once you join a boy in *doing something,* you'll find that the two of you establish a comfort level that leads naturally to better communication. If he has something else to focus on as he talks, he can protect himself from shame he might experience as he shares his worries and fears. This kind of "action talk" provides a potent technique for breaking through the mask that boys so often wear.

Here are just a few examples of "action talk":

Most days, when he gets home from work, Bob goes out in the driveway to shoot hoops with his ten-year-old son, Curtis. "The exercise feels great," he says. "But the best part of it is getting some time alone with Curtis. Sometimes we take a break for water and end up talking about both our days." He laughs. "Sometimes it's actually more break than basketball."

Rachel and her fourteen-year-old son, Sebastian, make pancakes every Sunday morning for the rest of the family. "We try out different recipes," she says. "He likes to put in different ingredients, like chocolate chips or nuts. And he likes to make complicated shapes out of the batter. We call it Rachel and Sebastian's Creative Pancake Jamboree."

Last summer, when his father had a stroke, Barry had to travel to Florida to help arrange his care. "I decided to make the trip by car," he says, "and to ask my teenage son, Jared, to come along. We've never spent such a long time alone together, and at first it was a little uncomfortable—I was pretty upset about my dad, I guess. But Jared and I ended up talking about it a lot. Once I even kind of cried in front of him."

Tom, a high-school math teacher, stays after school every Tuesday to offer extra help to students. "One boy, Stanley, has been coming this whole semester," he says. "At first we stuck to geometry, but as he got more comfortable he told me about his hopes for college and his dream of being a writer. I sometimes bring him a book I think he'd like, and after he reads it we talk about it."

Bob, Rachel, Barry, and Tom haven't done anything expensive or complicated here. They weren't lecturing or correcting their boys. They've simply made time to share their lives and emotions with their boys. They didn't worry about winning or losing the shot, about botching a pancake, about shedding tears, or about stepping outside their area of expertise. Making yourself vulnerable in ways like this teaches a boy that it's safe for him to do it, too. And you'll be giving him memories of closeness with you that will last his whole life.

When you were young, did you ever share time with an adult who mattered to you? Who was it, and what did you do?

_____

_____

_____

_____

_____

Can you think of ways that you already share time and talk with boys in your life? Make some notes about it here:

_____

_____

_____

_____

_____

Do you have a story about your own hopes or experiences that you can imagine sharing with a boy you care about? Make a note about it here:

_____

_____

_____

_____

_____

TIMED SILENCE

"I really want to talk with my boy when something upsets him," Rebecca said. "Like last week, when Gabriel failed his algebra test, I sat down with him right away to find out what had gone wrong. I told him how hard algebra used to be for me, and I offered to help him study for a retest. But he just acted really hostile and told me to leave him alone. How can I be a supportive mother if he won't ever talk to me about his problems?"

Rebecca did everything right to support her boy. But her timing was off—Gabriel just wasn't ready to receive her empathy and open up in response. It's not unusual for children to need their space. But many boys especially have a particular timing pattern before they can share what they are feeling. When they are hurting and angry, boys often need a period of "timed silence," in which they are not under pressure from adults to communicate.

WHAT IS "TIMED SILENCE"?

➤ Giving a boy the time alone he needs to recover from an upsetting experience, especially one that was humiliating in some way.

➤ Waiting for him to give a signal that he's ready to talk. He may not bring up the subject directly, but he'll let you know that your presence is not unwelcome. It could be something as simple as coming in and sitting by you as you're watching TV.

➤ Noticing his signal, and *then* giving him your undivided attention. Turn down the TV, put down the newspaper, and show him you're interested in listening. (For tips on how to be a good listener, see pages 27–28 in chapter 2.)

Timing is everything. If an adult pushes a boy to talk before he's ready, he experiences the attention as an intrusion and will respond defensively. Boys are so shame-phobic that they are exquisitely sensitive to possible humiliation. Directly after a boy has a bad experience, calling attention to it only adds to his shame.

(continued)

Let your boy know that you still care about him, but give him the time to retreat and recover his balance. He'll be ready to emerge eventually and reconnect with family, friends, or teacher. Then it's time to engage in "action talk." (See page 16.)

If you've given a boy plenty of time and he still hasn't shown any signs of talking, try creating the opening yourself. Sometimes bringing up the experience of a friend or acquaintance, or even a news article, can help.

"Mr. Fletcher was telling me that his students were really stressed about their college applications," one teacher said to a boy who had recently received very low SAT scores in the mail. "How do you think he could help?"

Sometimes a boy just won't communicate, no matter how many openings you give him. If a boy's withdrawn behavior goes on too long, you'll want to check out the possibility that the boy is experiencing not just hurt and anger but a clinical depression, whose signs a trained professional will recognize.

HOW TO TELL WHEN SOMETHING'S WRONG

How do you know when a boy's behavior is normal for his particular temperament and stage of development, and when you ought to be concerned? What are the signals of trouble? The answer lies in a combination of trusting your instincts, gathering information, and keeping the lines of communication open.

"Pete's always been a reader," said Cathy about her thirteen-year-old son. "But this year I notice that he's more reclusive than ever. He spends every day after school holed up with his science-fiction collection, and he never seems to have any plans. He's not exactly giving us trouble, but his father and I still worry a little. Our friends tell us we're lucky, but he seems so antisocial! I almost wish he'd get in a little normal trouble."

At thirteen, Pete may simply not want to spend much time with his family. Carving out his private space and having time with friends his own age typically has far more appeal at this stage. Pete's always had a quiet nature, so it's possible that his solitary behavior is fine, especially if he's working out for himself some of the important life changes that adolescence brings.

Yet if he has no close connection with even one other boy, girl, or adult, there may be cause to worry that he is depressed or in serious emotional trouble. He doesn't have to have a whole crowd of friends. Even having one person he's close to—such as a grandparent, a special teacher, or the girl he's known forever—shows that he can make emotional connections. But if Pete is totally isolating himself—or if his only "connections" are the impersonal ones in Internet chat rooms—his behavior may signal that he's in trouble. His parents are wise to want to find out.

Given Pete's introspective temperament, one of his parents might succeed in simply finding a quiet time to sit down for a gentle talk about how he's feeling. Otherwise, they can turn to "action talk," as described above. For example, his dad could invite him to go see a science-fiction movie together, and then go out for a snack afterward.

Desmond, at age seven, is giving his teacher fits. "He stomps around the classroom like a crazy man, yelling at the top of his lungs," she complained. "He has tantrums whenever I don't choose him for chalk monitor, or if his sandwich is in squares instead of triangles. I know this is normal for some boys, but maybe his behavior is a signal that there are problems. Do I need to refer him for psychological screening?"

Something is clearly going on with Desmond—his behavior is a symptom that he's in distress. His teacher is right to be concerned, although from just these symptoms, she can't tell either the level of severity or the nature of that distress. Before recommending a psychological evaluation, she needs to gather some more information—by talking with Desmond herself, or by calling his parents in to talk.

While teachers don't have a lot of time for individual counseling with their students, an occasion for action talk might present itself. If possible,

Desmond's teacher should pick one of his "good days" to do this, and then join him in something he enjoys, either in class or outside. She can offer him the opening he needs to say what's bothering him, whether it's at home or at school.

If Desmond's teacher chooses to call the parents, she should take special care to ally herself with them in the initial conversation. Rather than telling them their son has a problem, she might say things like, "I've noticed that Desmond seems upset in class. Have you noticed a change in his behavior at home?" She can ask them what their concerns are, and perhaps gently prompt them: "Is there anything happening in his life that might be upsetting him? Does he talk to you about school at all?" The key here is for teacher and parents to stay connected in their mutual caring for the boy. It's important to help the parents not take sides—either with the teacher or with their son against the teacher.

If the parents and teacher agree that something seems wrong, they can ask for further evaluation by a school counselor. It's possible that Desmond is suffering from some problem like depression or a learning disorder, and that treatment could alleviate the problem.

If you are worried about a boy:

➤ **Trust** your instincts. Caring adults usually have a sense when a boy's behavior is expressing a deeper need.

➤ **Gather** information. Consult with other people who know him, like teachers, friends, and relatives. Especially with a teenage boy, his friends (or even his friends' parents) may know more about how a boy is doing than his parents do.

➤ **Compare** his behavior to previous patterns. Ask yourself, "Has he always been like this? When did this behavior begin? What else was happening around that time?" Did the change coincide with the anniversary of some loss, like a divorce or death, or the loss of a friend or pet?

➤ **Communicate** with your boy. Use "action talk" to help him open up about his feelings. Be a good listener. Don't assume you know what's wrong or how to fix it. Just talking with your boy will help him feel less alone.

➤ **Stay alert to warning signs** that something more serious may be wrong. He may be depressed (see chapter 8) or be struggling with a bully (see chapter 6).

LIFE WITH BOYS: ADULT SURVIVAL STRATEGIES

All of us with boys in our lives—at home, at school, and elsewhere—know that life with a boy can be a challenge. And boys themselves are struggling more and more with their lives these days. Some simple, practical steps can make these challenges an everyday pleasure instead of a trial. We can create some predictable rituals and routines, at home or in school, that stabilize the normal ups and downs of daily life. And we can plan our time to include space in our lives for boys and for ourselves.

RITUALS: PLANNING TIME FOR YOUR BOYS

➤ Family meals can be an important ritual. Try to sit down together for one meal a day, even if it's just ten minutes at breakfast. A daily meal together provides an opportunity to check in with your boy, share a little discussion about the news from your own life and the outside world, and wish one another well in your various pursuits. But don't bring disputes between family members to the table. Establish mealtime as a time of pleasure and connection that everybody can look forward to.

➤ Provide plenty of safe, structured, and creative outlets for the energy that boys have in such abundant supply. Make a regular time to visit the playground or the playing field. "We go Rollerblading every Sunday when the park is closed to car traffic," said one New York father. Another family volunteers at a local soup kitchen once a month. Setting aside time for energetic activities helps a boy feel appreciated for his love of action.

➤ Establish family traditions for holidays and other special occasions. "We always go up to the amusement park after school closes on the last day," one boy said. A city family makes a custom of strolling past the decorated windows of the big department stores every year on the day after Thanksgiving. Birthday boys might get to specify the dinner menu and the flavor of cake; or a family might adorn its windows with paper snowflakes as winter arrives.

➤ Simple gestures—an evening story or a good-night kiss—can form part of your family's ritual heritage. One boy wouldn't go to sleep until he had hugged every member of the family, including the two cats. Another boy liked to fix his father's thermos of coffee for the morning commute. Make your boy an indispensable part of the daily routine, and praise his participation generously. He'll know that he's needed and appreciated in the family, which helps to keep him connected.

➤ Even homework can have a ritual nature to it, if you set aside a time and place where it always happens. Especially if your boy resists sitting down to his assignments, it can help to have a regular custom that doesn't get negotiated. (For example, "Homework first, TV after," is the rule in many homes.)

FINDING YOUR OWN SUPPORT

For adults, it's also very important to set aside some time for yourself, in addition to the time you spend caring for boys. Adults need emotional support, just as much as children do. Raising boys takes a lot of hard work and commitment. As caring mothers, fathers, teachers, and youth workers, we need to regularly give voice to our own feelings, so that difficult issues don't build up and interfere in our relationships with our boys.

Support can be a telephone call, a hug from your mother, a kid down the street baby-sitting for a few hours so you can take a break. No one person can be everything to you, but different people offer different kinds of help: money, time, friendship, love, back rubs, or help at work.

Who Makes Up My Support Network?

My Household Supporters
Name anyone regularly in your house, other than your children, to whom you feel comfortable going for support.

_____

_____

_____

My Local Supporters
Name people within an easy drive, bus ride, or even walk of where you live, to whom you feel comfortable going for support. (Within your own area code is essential; within your local calling area is better.)

_____

_____

_____

Supporters in My Extended Family
Name any members of your extended family whom you feel comfortable calling "just to talk." (A sibling in a distant city? A godparent? A favorite aunt?)

_____

_____

_____

Professional Supporters
Name any physicians or nurses, counselors, therapists, members of the clergy, or social workers with whom you have relationships.

_____

_____

_____

Oldies but Goodies

Name any old and close friends you haven't already written down. Even if you haven't talked for years and aren't sure where they're living, write them down anyway.

_____

_____

_____

Other Supporters

Name any supporters you haven't mentioned yet. (Your secretary? Your family doctor, who's watched all the kids grow up? The nice college kid who helps you out with odd jobs?)

_____

_____

_____

The people on this list form your support network. With which ones do you feel most comfortable discussing your troubles? Circle them. They are the people you can turn to when you feel overwhelmed.

2

WHAT DO BOYS NEED MOST?

CONNECTING WITH BOYS • HOW TO BE A GOOD LISTENER • SUPPORTING BOYS THROUGH ACTION • HOW THE FAMILY CAN HELP • WHAT DOES A BOY NEED LEAST? • BREAKING THE BOY CODE

"This has got to be the busiest time of our lives," said Carla, a head nurse on the cardiology ward of a suburban hospital. "My husband, Dan, is an insurance appraiser and he's on the road from morning till night. Our two older boys are in middle school and they have sports practice pretty much every day—on different teams! The little boy is in elementary school at last, and my schedule lets me get home just in time to meet his bus, but then I usually have to rush right out the door again for something. I try to check in with how the kids are doing, but we hardly ever have a chance to really talk. What can Dan and I do to make sure they're getting what they need?"

With three boys and two full-time careers, Carla and Dan face an extremely challenging situation—yet it's not uncommon these days. Even families in which there are fewer children and more time often feel that life is rushing by them at breakneck speed. They want to share strong connections with their boys, but between children's busy schedules and the demands of adult life, they don't know where to start.

But, in fact, it doesn't take a major life makeover to meet the needs of the boys we care for. In small moments throughout our days, we can find ways to stay in touch with boys and their feelings, and support them in the difficult business of growing up.

The *Real Boys* approach involves what we call *connection through action*. This means that rather than nudging a boy to sit down and share his feelings with us, we begin by simply joining him in an activity that he enjoys. Often by simply *doing* something with boys—going out for ice cream, playing catch, working on the car, cooking out on the grill, or even straightening up the classroom—we forge a connection that then enables them to open up.

And once we've connected with them, we can actively listen to our boys, establishing relationships of trust and creating a web of support so that they won't feel alone. This chapter's exercises aim to help adults find new ways to connect with, listen to, and support boys.

CONNECTING WITH BOYS

Like Carla and Dan, many adults have a hard time identifying when in their busy lives they can find moments to connect with a boy. And when the boy doesn't seem to want to connect with the adult, it can seem even harder.

But there may be more opportunities to connect with your boy than you think. Try this exercise to find out how to open up spaces for connection in your particular situation:

My Boy and I Have Nothing in Common

AN EXERCISE FOR PARENTS

How much unstructured "free time" does your boy have on an average weekday (when he is not in school, practice, lessons, job, chores, or "family time" such as dinner)?

____ Less than an hour

____ One to three hours

____ Three to five hours

___ More than five hours

___ None (only on weekends/holidays)

___ I don't know

When exactly are these "open times"?

___ Mornings

___ Afternoons

___ Before dinner

___ Evenings

___ Other_____

Where does your boy spend his free, unstructured time? Check all that apply.

___ His bedroom

___ Living room

___ Den/TV room

___ Outside, near house (back- or front yard)

___ Outside, public space (park, basketball courts, playground, mall)

___ I don't know

___ Other_____

What does your boy choose to do in his free time?

___ Read

___ Draw/paint

___ Watch TV

___ Build models (or anything else)

___ Play computer games

___ Sleep

___ Internet/e-mail

___ Listen to (or play) music

___ Talk on the phone

___ Hang out with a parent and "help"

___ Play inside, alone (with toys or games)

___ Play inside, with other children (siblings or friends)

___ Play outside, alone

___ Play outside, with other children

___ I don't know

___ Other_____

_____

_____

Looking at this list, I see that my boy usually chooses:

___ Energetic, physical activities

___ Quiet, sedate activities

___ Social activities involving a lot of talk and other communication

___ Solitary activities

___ All of the above, depending on his mood

___ I'm not sure—I'm not around much when he has free time

Now look over your responses to these lists. Imagine that you had never met this boy before. Write a few sentences describing how and where this boy likes to relax and spend his free time. Try to stay away from judgments or assessments of his character; just state the facts. (For example: "Tommy spends a lot of his free time in the living room, playing on the family computer," not "Tommy is a loner and never plays normal games with the other kids.") See if you can put the sentences in the positive ("Joe likes . . ." "He makes . . ."). Be honest; if you're not sure what your son does in his free time, just say what you do know ("He spends hours in his room with the door closed").

_____

_____

_____

_____

_____

_____

Now think about your own average workday.

How much free time do you have in a day—time when you really get to choose what to do?

___ Less than an hour

___ One to three hours

___ Three to five hours

___ More than five hours

___ None (only on weekends/holidays)

List the exact times of day that you have free (for example: 10:00–11:00 A.M.—baby's nap, or 5:30–6:00 P.M.—after work, before dinner):

_____

_____

_____

_____

_____

_____

What kinds of things do you do in your free time?

___ Read

___ Watch TV

___ Internet/e-mail

___ Exercise

___ Sleep

___ Talk on the telephone

___ Cook

___ Listen to/play music

___ Shop

___ Go to movies/rent videos

___ Individual sports (golf, tennis, swimming)

___ Team sports

___ Play with children

___ Hang out with adults (spouse, friends, family)

___ Other_____

Where do you spend your free time (bedroom, living room, garage, outside)?

_____

_____

Now try writing the same kind of description for yourself that you wrote for your boy. Remember, stay away from judgments of character and stick to neutral facts.

_____

_____

_____

_____

_____

Now look back and read both descriptions. Compare the kinds of activities you and your boy enjoy. Where are the similarities? Where are the differences? Think carefully. Sometimes things that look different on the surface are actually quite similar—for instance, the boy who loves collecting frogs and leaves in the woods, and the father who spends all his free time on the golf course. Both probably love walking and studying the landscape around them, looking for unusual features.

My boy and I both enjoy_____

_____

_____

_____

_____

Something my boy enjoys that I don't know much about is_____

_____

_____

_____

Something I enjoy that my boy doesn't know much about is_____

_____

_____

_____

Now go back and look carefully at your boy's and your own schedule. Are there any times of day (or days of the week) that you both have free? List them here:

_____

_____

_____

Making time to do things together will open up chances for your boy to talk when he's ready, and give him a safe setting in which he can explore his feelings—what *Real Boys* calls a "shame-free zone." Shame-free zones offer time and space where you and your boy are together in an atmosphere free from judgments, criticisms, and fear.

A list of things to do with the boy you care about might include:
➤ Fixing a bicycle
➤ Making music together
➤ Minor carpentry projects
➤ Volunteering for a political campaign
➤ Going fishing
➤ Working at the soup kitchen
➤ Going for a walk or a bike ride
➤ Climbing a mountain
➤ Exploring an unfamiliar part of the city

Based on the answers I wrote down before, I think that some activities my boy and I could share are:

_____

_____

_____

_____

_____

_____

What you do together doesn't matter so much as that you do it *together.* Let him choose the activity at least as often as you do. And even if your boy doesn't start spilling his soul to you right away, don't worry. Just giving him your full attention will help establish trust and a sense of security and safety.

HOW TO BE A GOOD LISTENER

Adults might worry that they won't know what to say when a boy shares a complicated or upsetting problem with them. But when it comes to listening, less is more. In fact, boys don't need anything complicated from a good listener. It's enough for a caring adult to listen with empathy, saying almost nothing in response. If they do want you to say something, here are some possibilities that will help a boy get through a difficult moment:

- ➤ I'm so sorry that happened.
- ➤ You must feel so terrible.
- ➤ That sounds like it really hurt.
- ➤ It makes sense that you're so angry/sad/worried/upset.
- ➤ You're really doing the right thing by talking about it.
- ➤ I know what you mean.
- ➤ It really takes courage to be able to share your feelings like this.
- ➤ I'm so proud of you for the way you're handling this.

WHAT MAKES A GOOD LISTENER?

Pay attention. Keep your ears and eyes open and direct all of your attention to what your boy is saying. Don't assume you know what he's going to say.

Never interrupt. Wait for a boy to finish his thoughts, even if he's taking a long time.

Arms open, mouth closed. Good listeners give hugs or praise, not advice or criticism. Don't be afraid to show a boy how much you care for him—even if he doesn't seem to want that.

Reflect, don't react. If what a boy is saying makes you feel angry, sad, guilty, worried, or defensive, put aside those feelings for the time being. You can talk about them later. Right now it's important to let your boy know you heard what he said. This can be done with just a simple "Hmm," or "Oh," or by restating what he has just said: "I see. You thought . . ." or "It sounds like you feel . . ."

Don't try to "fix it" right away. The object of listening is to let the boy open up and talk, not to solve the problem. But after you've had a chance to really listen, he might really appreciate some practical suggestions, as long as you don't force him to accept them.

Be patient. If a boy isn't ready to talk, don't push or goad him with questions. Let him know this isn't going to be his last opportunity to have your ear.

SUPPORTING BOYS THROUGH ACTION

We naturally want to help and support the boys we care about—not just at times of crisis, but in their day-to-day lives. Yet sometimes we're unsure how to do it. Although connecting with boys and listening to them with empathy is support in itself, sometimes we need to take practical action to help a boy who's in a difficult situation.

The key is to stay sensitive to what a boy is feeling, and to take supportive action without humiliating him or detracting from his independence.

The following stories illustrate some successful ways of supporting boys without intruding on their autonomy and self-respect. As you read them, reflect on what the adults in the stories did to support their boys.

When his son, Louis, entered his teens, Jonathan noticed with chagrin that the boy had inherited the family tendency toward adolescent acne. "I remembered how miserable my skin condition made me feel," he said, "so I didn't even want to mention it to Louis." But before his son was scheduled for his preseason sports physical, Jonathan thought to give the doctor a call. "On the way home from the appointment, Louis asked if we could stop at the pharmacy," he recalled. "I didn't ask any questions, but in a month or so I could see that his skin was clearing up." Now Louis is more comfortable asking his father to refill the prescription for him, and Jonathan has even said to him, "I wish they had had this stuff when I was a kid."

Jonathan avoided making his son feel as if his dad were ashamed of him for his skin problems. By instead coming up with a private and effective way for Louis to get help without drawing undue attention, he established a sense of trust between them that will extend to other matters as they arise.

Eight-year-old Jeremy spoke with a serious stutter, and though they took him regularly to a speech therapist, his parents, Roy and Hillary, were aware that the boy faced considerable teasing at school. Rather than ignoring the issue, Roy and Hillary shared with Jeremy's teacher the information they had learned about stuttering, and asked her to comfortably address this disability with the other students. "It was great," said Hillary. "She ended up reading aloud to the class a book that we had also read to Jeremy, about a child with a stutter. Now his whole class knows to be patient with him and not to interrupt when he's trying to finish a sentence. The teacher told us she's heard some of his classmates sticking up for him on the playground when kids from other classes make fun of him."

Jeremy's parents could see that he needed them to stand by him, yet they knew it would make him feel even more conspicuous if his parents tried to defend him from the teasing of his peers. Instead they made an ally of the teacher, whose understanding and authority could go far to affect the attitudes of Jeremy's classmates.

When their daughter was seven and their son, Gilbert, was nine, the Randall family took them to the city ballet's production of The Nutcracker *as a special holiday treat. "We thought that little Sandra would be the one to come home demanding ballet lessons," said Gilbert's father, Troy. "I admit I was taken aback when it was Gilbert who said he wanted to learn to dance." The Randalls decided to give their son a twelve-week ballet course for Christmas. "In the spring his teacher told us that he had exceptional talent," Troy said, "but Gil told us he wanted to stop the lessons because the kids at school were teasing him." Troy told Gilbert that ballet dancers were among the greatest athletes in the world, and that he would be proud if his son kept on dancing. "I could see him relax as soon as I said it," he remembered several years later. "He went back to the lessons and hasn't stopped since. Now we go as a family to all the city ballet's productions, and sometimes his friends will even come along, too."*

By expressing an immediate and unconditional positive attitude toward Gilbert's choice, Troy freed his son to pursue his interest in dance without shame, despite how others might react. At a crucial moment he let Gilbert know that he was proud of him, and the effects of that lasted for years.

Parents exert one of the most powerful influences on a boy's life. Showing your son that you approve of him will help counteract the shame he might feel about being "different"—whether it's a physical difference like bad skin or a stutter, or a love for ballet that brands him a "sissy" in some people's eyes. When he steps out of the Boy Code to act according to his real feelings, your approval gives him strength. And your small but practical gestures of support can ease any situation—from his new glasses to his needing a ride to pick up a date—that otherwise would make him feel uncomfortable.

Can you recall a time when you supported your boy either with specific actions or with emotional support? If so, describe the problem you noticed he was having:

_____

_____

What specific action(s) did you take to support him?

_____

_____

How did you support him in emotional ways?

_____

_____

Do you think your boy might currently need support in facing a particular problem? If so, describe the situation:

_____

_____

What specific action(s) might you take to support him?

_____

_____

How could you support him in emotional ways?

_____

_____

HOW THE FAMILY CAN HELP

Parents aren't the only family members who can weave this strong web of emotional and practical support for a boy. His siblings, for example, often provide important support in situations where adults are rarely present, at school or in neighborhood play. A boy may also find models and support in his aunts, uncles, and older cousins. Without the anxiety about "good parenting" that mothers and fathers often feel, they can comfortably offer help with sensitive subjects like sexuality, peer pressure, and academic worries. It's good for a boy to feel that there's an extended community of relatives to whom he can turn without fear of shame. Don't be afraid to go up a generation further, too—your favorite uncle could turn out to be as supportive to his grand-nephew as he was to you.

And grandparents, of course, often take a special place in a boy's upbringing. Doting grandparents may be a cliché, but that extra dose of love and attention can create a priceless intergenerational bond. Grandparents can provide essential guidance to boys, and they can sometimes influence a boy's decisions and behavior, even when he isn't interested in listening to his parents. Of course, teachers, coaches, and other nonrelatives who are invested in boys' lives can also use these techniques in their own special ways.

How Does Your Family Help Your Boy?

List the members of your boy's immediate family and caretakers in the space below.

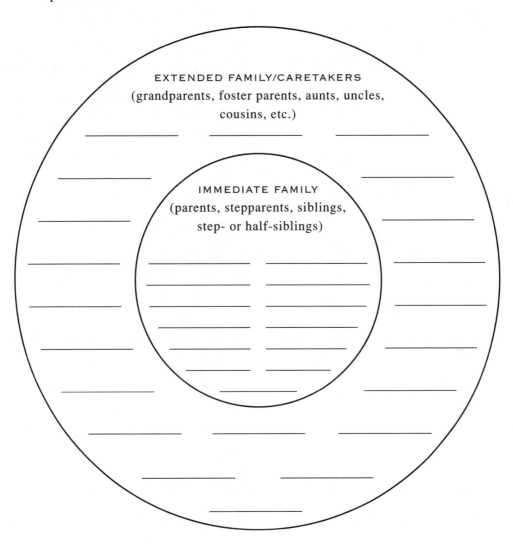

List a few of the ways that these people support him already.

_____

_____

_____

_____

_____

_____

_____

_____

_____

WHAT DOES A BOY NEED LEAST?

Glenn started worrying about his son, Andrew, when the boy, at fifteen, still had the slight build and short stature of a younger child. "Let's build you up," he told Andrew cheerfully that summer, bringing home a two-month supply of athletic power drinks and setting up a weight-training and exercise center in the basement. Every day, when Glenn got home from work, he would supervise Andrew's workout, and in a chart on the wall he recorded his weight, height, and endurance every week. "It's great!" he told his neighbor. "We're spending more time together than we ever did—and he's showing a lot of improvement in his upper-body strength. The girls aren't going to recognize him when he goes back to school."

What messages might Andrew's father want to give his son by his actions? Write your ideas here:

_____

_____

_____

What messages might Andrew get from his father's push to build him up?
Write your ideas here:

_____

_____

_____

Glenn only wants the best for his son. And by spending extra time with Andrew, he is showing his love in a very concrete way. But what if Andrew's physique and stature never do match up to his father's hopes? Though he wants only to bolster Andrew's confidence through the nutritional supplements and the exercise regimen, Glenn may be handing his boy a painful burden of shame about his appearance.

We don't know what Andrew is feeling here. But we do know that no boy needs additional pressure to conform to a single image of masculine success. Surrounded every day by society's expectations, he needs a refuge of love and acceptance by the people he admires most.

As caring adults, we must be careful to counteract the straitjacket of the Boy Code, not to reinforce it implicitly through what we appear to value and devalue in our boys.

Some of the messages that boys need least *to hear:*
- Big boys don't cry.
- If you're not sure of the answer, don't raise your hand.
- Chin up; tough it out.
- If you can't play well, maybe you shouldn't be playing.
- Real men are big and strong.
- Boys don't play with girls.
- Give 'em hell.
- Be cool.
- Stay in control.
- Don't break the code of silence.
- Don't ask for help.

Parents and teachers don't want to restrict boys' individuality through messages like these. But many of us pass on the code without realizing it, because we ourselves were taught the same things as children. One father, whose own childhood was spent on military bases, remembered how his dad, a colonel, made "Zero Defects" the family slogan. "It's one thing to do that with a brigade in wartime, where one mistake can cost a lot of lives," he said. "But as little boys, it just made us afraid that we might mess up." Now this father is careful to praise his own sons for trying new things, even if they make mistakes.

Becoming conscious of our own ingrained patterns can help us when we have boys of our own to raise. Use the next exercise to think about your own upbringing and the messages you may have internalized about masculinity.

Finding My Buried Beliefs About Masculinity

AN EXERCISE FOR PARENTS, TEACHERS, YOUTH WORKERS, AND BOYS OR GIRLS

1. Fighting Back

Walking past the playground in the park, you see a bigger boy push a smaller boy off his swing. The smaller boy picks himself up and goes at the big one, hitting him with his fists.

Do you approve of the smaller boy's behavior? Why or why not?

_____

_____

Two preschool girls are playing in the sandbox when one throws sand in the other's face. The smaller one screams at her, then gets up and kicks her in the shins.

Do you approve of the smaller girl's behavior? Why or why not?

_____

_____

Do you feel differently about a child's fighting back when the children involved are boys, not girls? Explain.

_____

_____

Did anything like this ever happen to you as a child? If so, how did other people react?

_____

_____

_____

Many of us have learned from our earliest experiences that boys are supposed to fight back when someone acts aggressively toward them, not let themselves be pushed around. We might worry when we see girls getting into physical fights, but shrug off the same behavior with boys, assuming that's just a normal way for boys to work things out.

Boys do often respond physically to aggression, and so do girls in many cases. But both boys and girls need a repertory of nonviolent ways to deal with an attacker. By letting them know they can solve problems like this with words, adults can help break old patterns and start rewarding boys for asserting their rights without coming to blows.

2. Winning

It's the last quarter of the basketball game and you're watching from the sidelines as your team struggles to pull ahead. With seven seconds to go, losing by one point, another player passes the ball to one of your boys, and he dribbles it down the court unimpeded. But unbelievably, when he reaches the basket the boy misses what should have been an easy layup.

How do you think you would feel about this boy's blunder? Explain why.

_____

_____

You're watching as the junior varsity girls softball game winds to a close, with your favorite player in left field. With players on second and third base and two outs, the opposing team's batter lofts an easy fly to left field. One girl somehow isn't paying attention, though. She moves too late and misses the ball, allowing the two base runners to score and ending the game.

How important is this girl's mistake? Why?

_____

_____

Do you feel differently about the importance of winning when the players involved are boys, not girls? Explain.

_____

_____

Did anything like this ever happen to you? If so, how did other people react?

_____

_____

_____

Our society typically sees winning at sports as an important way for a boy to prove his strength and manhood. But few girls grew up with the feeling that their self-worth depended on whether they won the game. "It's only a game," we might tell a girl who missed the crucial play. But for a boy, it's more than a game—his masculinity is on the line.

Competition can be healthy and fun, as boys and girls strive for a "personal best" or work together with a team to try to outperform their rivals. Help your boy stay focused on the positive aspects of sports, whether he's winning or losing. Highlight what he does well, and comfort him when he's disappointed. Above all, don't shame him for making mistakes on the playing field.

All of us are shaped by the different experiences we had as we grew up, as the previous exercise may remind us. Recognizing this can help you to take a new approach with your own boys, rather than following old patterns that can limit your boy's growth.

Some other situations where boys might be treated differently because of old expectations and beliefs about masculinity:

➤ A toddler who refuses to share toys
➤ A child who clings to Mommy in the early school years
➤ A child who doesn't develop physically at the same time as others do
➤ A child who doesn't like to read
➤ A youngster who has no interest in sports
➤ An adolescent who acts aggressively with peers of the opposite sex
➤ A teenager who obsesses about hairstyles and fashion

We all have buried feelings about how boys and girls "should" act, and it's good to identify them and know where they come from. If they don't line up with how you would like to be treating your boy, you can take special care in situations like these to counteract the ways your own past may have conditioned you to respond.

BREAKING THE BOY CODE

If boys are going to grow up free to be themselves, not only individual families will have to change, however. We can band together and put pressure on all our institutions—schools, churches, print and broadcasting media, political parties, and government bodies—to break through the Boy Code and support the diverse ways that boys and men choose to express their individuality.

SOME WAYS TO BREAK DOWN BOY CODE STEREOTYPES

Opportunities to change society's attitudes about boys come up every day, once we start looking for them. Find other parents who are concerned, and group together for support and strength. Among the possibilities:

➤ Sponsor school or PTA workshops where parents and teachers can discuss gender issues. Review the data for patterns of which gender dominates what courses or activities, and discuss why that might be occurring.

➤ Speak up in public when you see gender stereotyping take place. (*Examples:* Write letters to the editor, speak up at meetings, ask questions of candidates for election to local or state office.)

➤ Suggest constructive changes to existing patterns. Sometimes a small adjustment to the status quo can make a big difference. (*Examples:* Create an outdoor exercise break at school; let boys try out for the cheerleading team.)

➤ Set up or participate in community mentoring programs for boys.

➤ Provide peer support or discussion groups at school, where boys can talk about their emotions safely in a facilitated setting.

➤ Join to support other parents whose boys are breaking gender stereotypes, such as parents of boys who reject violence, or parents of gay children.

BOYS AND THEIR MOTHERS, BOYS AND THEIR FATHERS

**A MOTHER'S INSTINCTS • FIRST SEPARATIONS • MOTHERS
AND TEENAGE SONS • SINGLE MOMS • THE SPECIAL ROLE
OF A BOY'S FATHER • FATHERS AND ACTION LOVE
• REAL FATHERS: MEN EMPATHIZING WITH BOYS
• LIVING APART AND STAYING CONNECTED
• DADS WHO RAISE THEIR SONS ALONE
• PREVENTING "FATHER HUNGER"
• THE MOTHER-FATHER PARENTING TEAM**

"Even though my parents are divorced," said twelve-year-old Ethan, "in some ways I'm kind of lucky. I mean, my mom's the best. When my dog broke his leg, she let me stay home from school the first day to take care of him, 'cause she knew how worried I was. She always gets how I feel about stuff." He paused. "My dad, though, he's always thinking up these cool things to do, like take apart an old computer his company was getting rid of. We had this idea we could turn it into a robot or something. It didn't really work— it made like a little explosion and sparks came out. My mom would freak out if she saw that happen, but my dad was into it."

Ethan has close, caring relationships with both of his parents. But he himself agrees that those relationships are very different.

When Ethan's mother lets him stay home with his injured dog, she's encouraging his natural urge to love and nurture others, especially when they're in need. She's also being sensitive to his feelings, not requiring him to endure his worry and pain stoically. Mothers like this one help boys grow up to be tender, caring, and emotionally strong men.

Ethan's father shows him other ways of making close connections. By taking time for an experimental project, even one that doesn't work, Ethan's dad lets him see the pleasure and fun of creating something with another person. As Ethan grows up, he'll be able to laugh about his mistakes rather than thinking of them as shameful. And he'll be secure in the knowledge that his dad understands his enthusiasm, energy, and appetite for action.

What are the particular strengths of mothers and fathers? How can parents use their strengths to build the kind of strong connections that Ethan has with his mom and dad? In this chapter, we'll explore the special nature of mothers and fathers. We'll learn what a boy needs from each of his parents, and how we as parents can give it to him.

A MOTHER'S INSTINCTS

In today's world, many mothers of boys feel themselves caught in a bind. They want to nurture and encourage their son's sensitive and empathetic sides. They know their boy is loving and caring at heart. In fact, very often a mother is the only person who gets to experience her boy when he shows his "sweet" side. Most mothers want to bring out that part of their boy's personality, and to express the love they feel with lots of physical affection and tender words.

But our culture warns mothers away from those instincts. Mothers fear that their boy won't be able to survive in the harsh masculine world if he gets "spoiled" by too much maternal closeness. In a century when psychological theories derived from Freud's early ideas have infiltrated popular thought, mothers worry about "smothering" their boy children, or even stripping them of their masculinity.

When Sarah gave birth to her first baby, Joey, she received a deluge of presents and advice. "Boys are tough," her neighbor sympathetically told an exhausted Sarah, who had walked her screaming baby through much of a colicky night. "I can see already he's going to be a handful. If I were you, I'd just let him holler in his crib—he can handle it." But when Sarah tried this, she ended up in tears for an hour herself, until she gave in to her instincts and picked Joey up to comfort him again. "I just couldn't leave him to suffer alone that way," she said. "But people tell me I'm spoiling him."

Sarah's instincts are right on target. By screaming with pain, infant Joey is expressing his desperate need for comfort and help. Even if holding him won't alleviate his colic, Sarah is teaching him that he's not alone with his misery. There's no such thing as "spoiling" an infant boy with too much holding.

Likewise, a mother should not fight her natural urge to encourage her baby boy's expression of a wide range of emotional states. Research has shown that infant boys are actually more emotionally expressive than girls, but that parents, worried by their sons' vulnerability, unwittingly reinforce only "positive" expressions of emotions like smiling. In her heart, Sarah knew Joey was suffering—she even shed her own tears of empathy. By holding him close while he's crying, and recognizing his distress, she's allowing him to feel his painful emotions in the safe haven of her arms.

On nights when her husband works late, Barbara and her thirteen-year-old son, Will, have a special ritual. "I make us hot cocoa after dinner," she said, "and we curl up together on the couch and read out loud to each other from a book one of us picks out. It makes me feel so close to him, but I always feel a little twinge of guilt. Is it perverted for a mom and son of that age to be cuddling?"

Definitely not! At thirteen, Will may feel starved for the close physical affection he knew as a little boy with his mother. Reading together on the couch re-creates that warmth and closeness between them. It also lays the groundwork for a trustful relationship between mother and son, at an age when boys often find it hard to put words to their feelings. That trust will serve Barbara well in the next years, as Will navigates his way through adolescence.

What's more, Barbara is teaching Will that men and women can have close, affectionate, and even physical connections without sex being involved. Boys like Will grow into caring and affectionate teenagers who can have friendly physical contact with girls, but don't jump into having sex before they're ready.

Barbara's instincts will tell her loud and clear if the physical connection she and Will experience goes too far. As long as it doesn't, they should enjoy their evening reading ritual. In fact, it might be nice to bring Barbara's husband into the tradition—he may be craving that kind of connection as well.

Are there times that you, as the mother of a boy, have felt torn between nurturing your son and the constrictions of the Boy Code? Describe one such time here.

_____

_____

_____

_____

Do Sarah's and Barbara's stories shed any light on the situation you described? Write your thoughts here.

_____

_____

_____

_____

FIRST SEPARATIONS

Even when boys have a healthy sense of masculine gender identity, they still identify strongly with their mothers, research makes clear. This begins in babyhood, when their mothers are often the ones whose nurturing care helps them build an identity as an individual. And it continues much longer than most of us assume.

Of course, boys need plenty of contact with their fathers from an early age. But if we want them to grow into the kind of men we hope they will be, boys also need to stay very close to their mothers—not just in infancy but throughout their childhood years. This is a boy's natural desire. But our whole society—the media, their toys, their families, teachers, and older playfellows—gives him the message that he should hide it as shameful.

The Boy Code tells boys to perform a constant acting job—to pretend to be confident when they may feel afraid, sturdy when they may feel shaky, independent when they may need love, attention, and support. As they start day care or school, society's gender stereotypes permit girls to linger with their mothers, while little boys are urged out of their comfort zones and into a premature separation.

Separating from home—and from mother, in particular—can be extremely traumatic for young boys. How we treat that separation makes a crucial difference to boys—a difference that can affect the rest of their school careers and even beyond. If adults stay connected and empathetic with their feelings throughout the difficult transition from home to school, boys do much better in their later classroom experiences.

School had started almost a month ago, and Alice was already tearing her hair out trying to get her four-year-old son, Andy, out the door to preschool. "At first he seemed eager to be a big boy and start school—but now he'll try anything to put off going," she complained. "First he dawdles getting dressed, and when I get after him for that he starts hitting his little brother, Bobby, until they both are screaming bloody murder. I try to give him 'time out,' but by the time everything calms down he's missed the bus and we're late getting him to school. I can't figure out if it's just a bad habit or if there's something really wrong."

Ms. Franken, Andy's young preschool teacher, expressed her worry, too. "Andy mopes around after he gets here late," she said. "He hangs back in the corner when we do group activities, and on the playground he tends to isolate himself, too. Maybe we should have him screened by a psychologist."

Four-year-old Andy is taking his first steps to separate from his mother without losing their loving connections. Just like girls, when boys have to separate, they deal with painful emotions of abandonment, fear, and vulnerability.

But whereas girls typically receive empathic support in these situations, adults frequently send boys the message that these vulnerable feelings are shameful. This begins the repressive process of hardening boys—enforcing the Boy Code, which requires them to act tough and stoic, no matter how sad they might feel. The following exercise will help you imagine the kind of feelings that a little boy experiences during his early separations from his mother.

Saying Good-bye

AN EXERCISE FOR PARENTS AND TEACHERS

Imagine that your spouse has been asked to take on an important new job in a distant city, and you have agreed to live separately for the next few months. You know you'll see each other occasionally, and of course you'll talk frequently by phone, but when you drive to the airport you suddenly feel how much you're going to miss your spouse. You pull up to the airport departure area, and your eyes fill up with tears. How would you feel if you received the following responses?

1. "Just drop me off here at the curb, sweetie. I'll be in touch with you when I get there. Bye—have a great day!"

    You feel:

    _____

    _____

    _____

2. "Come on, don't get all emotional. Lots of people go through these separations these days. What are you so worried about?"

You feel:

_____

_____

_____

3. "Listen, my plane doesn't leave for another hour and a half. Why don't we park the car and go in together. You can always leave if you need to, but we can at least spend some of this time together."

You feel:

_____

_____

_____

Saying good-bye to someone you love and depend on stirs up difficult emotions for both people, and so we shouldn't dismiss it as unimportant. Now that you've thought about it from another perspective, let's explore a parent's feelings about separating from a boy as he goes off to school for the first time.

PARENTS HAVE SEPARATION ANXIETY, TOO

Sometimes parents who rush their boys through their first experience of being on their own may actually be trying to avoid their own painful feelings, not just those of the boy. Don't be afraid to let your boy know that you, too, have mixed emotions about his starting day care or school. This not only makes him feel loved and supported, but it also gives him a model of expressing all kinds of feelings openly and safely.

The following statements describe how parents often feel when they place their little boys in day care or send them off to school. Do any of these apply to you? (Check as many as you want.)

___ I feel tearful at the thought that his baby years are over.

___ I feel liberated from having to take care of him all day long.

___ I feel afraid that he doesn't need me anymore.

___ I feel worried that I can't protect him.

___ I feel lonely for his company.

___ I feel excited to see him starting a whole new stage of life.

___ I feel nostalgic about my own childhood.

In the space below, try writing a short good-bye letter to your boy, telling him how you feel as he goes off for day care or to school. If you want, you can read it to him, but you don't have to. Just putting it down on paper will free you up to tell him what he needs to know.

_____

_____

_____

_____

_____

_____

You will find that if you take the time to go through this process slowly, you'll end up feeling closer to your boy and not as if you've lost him to the care of strangers. And he will feel more confident about leaving you, knowing that you remain connected and close by in case he needs you.

EARLY SEPARATIONS: DOS AND DON'TS

➤ **Do** treat a boy's close bond with his mother as normal and natural.

➤ **Do** give little boys extra time to make the developmental leap toward being their own person, while remaining in the safe context of supportive family relationships.

➤ **Do** offer boys plenty of empathy and attention when it comes time for them to leave their mothers and go to school.

➤ **Do** allow mothers to stay in the classroom for the first few days of school, to help their boys gain confidence in the new environment.

➤ **Do** give little boys the chance to express the pain, longing, and sadness they feel on separation. Girls may reveal their vulnerable emotions relatively quickly, but boys typically do so more slowly. Give a boy time to process what he feels, then make easy, private opportunities for him to share that at his own pace.

➤ **Do** share with your boy your own experiences of separation anxiety from the past.

➤ **Do** talk to other parents about their experiences, and what worked well for them.

➤ **Do** arrange for the support you need in order to help your boy through this transition. For example, you might need someone to watch the baby for an hour in the morning so you can stay on in the classroom.

➤ **Don't** let anyone put down your boy for having and expressing his feelings. If you hear terms like "sissy," "crybaby," and "acting like a girl," start a conversation about what those terms mean and why we use them.

➤ **Don't** shame boys for having what are very human emotions at this age.

ESPECIALLY FOR TEACHERS . . .

➤ Find ways for boys and girls to talk together about their anxieties and sadness when they separate from parents. Read aloud books with that theme.

➤ Address stereotypes directly. Say, "Big boys, just like big girls, love their mothers and fathers and feel sad when they leave." Remind him that big boys—even men—sometimes cry, and that's okay.

➤ Mothers or fathers can take a special place in the classroom in the first few weeks of school, as children get used to leaving them. They might help with classroom tasks, sit in on small-group activities, or just stay quietly on the side with a book of their own. Have a few clear and simple procedures to help parents stay connected in the classroom in the morning without disrupting the activities.

What to avoid: Don't try to rush or diminish the boy's first experience of being out on his own. Children need a more gradual period of adjusting to taking on new situations without their caregivers being so close by.

Three questions for teachers to ask themselves:
What do I say or do with little boys when they have a hard time with the feeling of separation at the start of school?

_____

_____

_____

What do I say and do with their caretakers, and why?

_____

_____

_____

Is anything about my response different when it's a boy, not a girl, who's involved?

_____

_____

_____

MOTHERS AND TEENAGE SONS

When boys reach their teenage years, their mothers often wonder if they should back off from the closeness they shared in the years before. Especially as a boy develops physically and begins to look like a man, his mother may experience emotional conflict, associating him with other men she's loved—her father, present or past partners, or the like.

As a result of society's pressures, she may feel confused about whether to hug him as much. She may find herself feeling hostile toward him for reasons she doesn't understand. She may discover that she wants him to take care of her, instead of the other way around.

But while a teenage boy may look and even act like a man, he isn't. Even though he too may experience very mixed emotions in his mother's presence sometimes, he still desperately needs to feel that his mother is there for him, in the important supportive role she has always taken. Teenage boys look to their mothers as mentors, just as they do to their fathers, as they try out the roles and decisions of young adulthood. They need their mothers' sympathetic ears, and they count on their mothers' loving acceptance.

"Ian and I used to have a lot of chances to talk when I picked him up from the hockey rink," said Charlotte. "But when he got his license, he started taking the old station wagon to school and driving himself everywhere. I started to feel really out of touch with him, but I knew he needed his independence."

But one January afternoon, Charlotte got a call from the local emergency room, where a badly shaken Ian had ended up after skidding on ice and hitting a telephone pole. "He said he was okay and I didn't need to come, but I headed right over," Charlotte said. "We had to wait for hours to get a couple of stitches in his forehead, and we had a long time to talk. I could have gotten mad—he'd promised me he wouldn't drive when it was snowing. But I knew how scared he was, and he really needed me to just listen while he talked through what had happened. He was really being hard on himself over not using good judgment, and he was terrified of what his father would do—the car was totaled. But I called my husband and explained the situation and how Ian was feeling. By the time Skip joined us, Ian was a little more calm, and he could see how glad we were that he wasn't hurt worse."

Over dinner that evening, Ian and his parents discussed what to do about the car and Ian's driving privileges. Before Ian went to bed, he came to Charlotte and kissed her on the cheek. *"Thanks, Mom,"* he said. *"I don't know what I would have done without you today."*

What Did Charlotte Do Right?

➤ She let her son have the space to develop that he craved, but still was there for him when he needed her.

➤ She trusted her instincts, and went to the emergency room right away even though Ian said he was okay without her.

➤ She didn't shame her son for making a mistake.

➤ She put aside her own mixed emotions of anger and worry, in order to listen to Ian's feelings.

➤ By calling her husband and alerting him to Ian's worries, she helped pave the way toward good communication between Ian and his father about the accident.

➤ She showed Ian how much he mattered to her, and how glad she was that he was okay.

➤ She treated him with respect, giving him a voice when the time came to discuss the consequences of his accident.

Because Charlotte was sensitive to her son's emotions, the family put off discussing consequences with Ian until after the crisis was over and they were home safe. When they did talk about it, everyone was calm and Ian's parents could work with him to think through what was fair. Ian went to bed feeling respected, understood, supported, and loved by both his parents.

Teenage boys will make mistakes—it's a normal part of trying out the responsibilities and decisions that come with adulthood. Let boys know that you trust them to act on their own. When they do make mistakes, don't withdraw your trust and confidence in them. Knowing his mother still loves him and approves of him helps a teenage boy face up to the consequences of decisions he may regret.

When your teenage boy makes a big mistake, you could say:

➤ What happened?

➤ How are you feeling?

- ➤ What do you think led you to make that decision?
- ➤ I'm glad you're talking with me about this.
- ➤ It sounds like you feel pretty bad/upset/worried about this.
- ➤ It's okay that you made a mistake.
- ➤ How do you want to deal with this?
- ➤ How can I help?

Here again, action talk can help open up the dialogue.

Many teenage boys will turn to their mothers before any other adult when they're in trouble. Instinctively, they may trust their mothers to understand their emotions even when they are afraid of how others will react.

SINGLE MOMS

The mother who is raising her son without his father faces special challenges. How will she provide that key ingredient of her son's upbringing—whether it be how to use the men's room or how to throw a fastball—that we often assume a father's steady presence contributes? How will she keep her own mixed feelings about men (which may include hurt, anger, or disappointment) from negatively affecting her son? How can she keep from unduly relying on her son to play the part of the man in her life, when he is still a child himself?

YOU'RE NOT ALONE

The majority of boys of divorce who live in single-family households live with their mothers, and the vast majority of those are in the sole custody of their mothers, many with little or no contact with their fathers.

Yet many single mothers successfully overcome these challenges, providing stable, caring guidance to their son in the absence of a male partner. Their ability to parent their boys well puts the lie to the myth that only a man can teach a boy to be a man.

As you read this section, did anything stand out as a special challenge in your own life? Describe it here:

_____

_____

_____

If your boy's father is absent, think about what positive things about him you might share with your son. Write a few of them here:

_____

_____

_____

Think about men in your life whom you admire. Which of their positive traits would you want your son to know about? Identify a few of these here:

Name: _____ Positive trait: _____

Name: _____ Positive trait: _____

Name: _____ Positive trait: _____

THE SPECIAL ROLE OF A BOY'S FATHER

Just like mothers, fathers have special qualities that support a boy's emotional health and development. A man's style of caring for a boy stands out for its qualities of action, playfulness, and zest. Research shows that right from the start, fathers tend to arouse their babies' emotions and stimulate them, while mothers tend to want to soothe their boy children and shield them from too much stimulation.

Although a mother may be taken aback when her husband tosses the baby playfully, bounces him around, or pretends to gobble up his little feet, this kind of extra stimulus is actually good for a boy's emotional development. While interacting like this with his father, a close caregiver, a baby boy learns to experience and tolerate a wider range of emotions. A father's rough-and-tumble action play encourages a boy to express fear, surprise, excitement, and upset when he feels them—as long as his father remains sensitive and stops when his son shows him that he's had enough.

These early father-son lessons help a boy later on. He will be better equipped to manage frustration, explore new circumstances, and handle academic challenges. When he gets into a conflict, he'll be more likely to work it out cooperatively. Playing "rough" with his dad—so long as it never gets dangerous and remains loving—actually teaches a boy the aggression management tools he'll need throughout his life.

What's Going Too Far?

In the following situations, small differences in the father's interactions with his boy make the difference between action play and going too far:

A father "plays horse" on all fours with his two-year-old boy, occasionally bucking the toddler off his back onto the grass. The boy shrieks when he falls off, then runs to get back on.

A father holds down and tickles a two-year-old boy whose laughter is mixed with screams and struggling.

In the first example, the boy is clearly enjoying pushing the limits of his fears, while the father knows that his son will not be hurt on the grass. In the second case, the father isn't noticing his son's signals that he wants the tickling to stop. The key difference is that the boy in the first example can control his own level of fear—he decides when to get back on the "horse." The second boy feels powerless to put a stop to his discomfort and fear.

A father throws his five-year-old son into the swimming pool to "teach him" to sink or swim. "I won't let you drown—just kick and paddle!" he calls to his flailing boy.

Standing in the surf, a father lets his five-year-old son jump up and down vigorously with him in the waves. The boy comes up sputtering and coughing, and runs to his father to be picked up.

In both cases, the boys are confronting their fears of the water with their fathers standing by. But the first boy has no choice or control over his situation. Though the second boy may be scared, too, he knows that his dad isn't making him jump, and that he's there to comfort him when he gets water up his nose. The first boy, forced into the water before he's ready, may feel that he can't trust his father, even though his dad assures him that he won't drown.

Have you ever witnessed a scene like this? If so, describe it:

_____

_____

_____

Do you think the parent involved was going too far? Explain why or why not:

_____

_____

FATHERS AND ACTION LOVE

"Starting when I was about six years old, my father used to take me with him on his Saturday rounds in the hospital," remembered Tarik, the son of a New York City surgeon. *"As long as there wasn't anything too upsetting, I got to stand at his side while he talked with each of his patients. He would introduce me, and even let me ask them questions about what had happened to them. I was always so impressed with how he cared about every little detail of how they were feeling. And they liked it, too—the older patients used to say how it cheered them up just to see me. My dad used to call me his little intern. He even gave me a white jacket to wear when I was at the hospital."* Tarik grew up to be a teacher himself, but he often thinks of his father's bedside manner when faced with a classroom situation. *"I think I got the gift from him,"* he said. *"Nobody listens as well as a good doctor."*

To Tarik, his father is a hero—not because he is strong and tough, but because of his caring and attentive manner with people in need. He admires his father's competence and skill as well, of course. But the best part is that his dad felt that Tarik was important enough to include on his rounds.

Whether a father delivers newspapers or removes appendixes for his living makes no difference to a boy. A father who includes his son in his important work is showing his love through action.

This "action love" is an important gift a father can bring to his boy. As a man, his expression of caring may differ from the mother's role in particular ways. Where often she might provide an emotional sounding board, he can show his son through their shared activities the traits of understanding and caring. He can model tenderness and strength, empathy and competence. And he can join his son in the action they both like so well.

A Dad's Example

AN EXERCISE FOR FATHERS

Can you remember aspects of your own father's life that you shared as a child? If so, list them here:

_____

_____

Were there qualities about your father that you particularly admired? How did you observe those qualities in action?

_____

_____

_____

_____

Were there qualities about your father that you did not admire? If so, why?

_____

_____

_____

_____

If you are a father, can you think of any work activities that you might share with your son? Describe them here:

_____

_____

Are there hobbies you enjoy in which you might include your boy? List them here:

_____

_____

Are there activities your boy particularly likes (sports, music, etc.) that you might enjoy sharing with him? List them here:

_____

_____

Although you may not realize it, your boy probably thinks of you as a hero. Imagining yourself through his eyes, can you think of some of the qualities he might especially notice and admire?

_____

_____

_____

_____

REAL FATHERS: MEN EMPATHIZING WITH BOYS

Contrary to the myths of the old Boy Code, men relate to boys with just as much empathy and sensitivity as do women. But because of their societal conditioning, a man may not express his empathic side the same way a woman does. In addition, he may show his boy he understands through action, like the men in these stories:

When ten-year-old Nick's cat was run over, he was devastated. While his father, Rob, took away the body and cleaned up the accident scene, Nick cried in his mother's arms. Later that afternoon, Rob came to his son with a toolbox and some cedar planks. "I think we should make a coffin to bury Shadow in the backyard," he said. "Want to help?" Nick's eyes filled with tears, but he nodded. They spent the whole evening on the project, constructing a small box, lining it with soft material, and digging a grave. The next morning the family gathered for a burial ceremony.

Bill went to all his fifteen-year-old son Matthew's baseball games, and afterward they always dissected the plays over hamburgers at a fast-food restaurant. On the way to the big semifinal game, they discussed the other team's reputation—especially one very good pitcher. With his son's team down by one point in the ninth inning, Bill watched from the stands as Matthew struck out, ending the game and the season. Afterward Bill walked to the car with his arm around the shoulders of a silent Matthew. "You played a great game, Matt," he said. "That was a tough situation at the end." He hesitated. "Are you still up for burgers?" he asked. "'Cause I'm starving!" Matthew smiled wanly. "Yeah, me too," he said.

Rob and Bill both understand instinctively what their sons are feeling. But rather than talking it through at first, they use action to show empathy for their sons. When Rob takes a whole afternoon and evening with his son to prepare for his pet's burial, he's affirming that Nick's grief is legitimate and that he'll be there to support him through it. When Bill invites Matthew for their traditional after-game treat, he's showing his boy that he won't withdraw his love and approval just because Matthew couldn't save the game for his team.

A DAD UNDERSTANDS THE HARD TIMES

Fathers also have a special understanding of the feelings of shame that boys experience. As a man, a father can especially empathize with his son's terrible fears of failure—or even worse, of being seen as "not masculine enough." If he's in touch with the experiences he had growing up, a father may have an instinct about what's bothering a boy, where a mother sometimes feels at a loss.

"I couldn't understand why Trevor was acting so belligerent all the time," said Louisa about her nine-year-old son. *"It's like all of a sudden he went from being this sweet, loving kid into some kind of little Rambo—getting into fights at school, yelling and even swearing at his sister! I wanted to ground him the last time he swore, but Mark, my husband, told me to hold off until he'd talked to him."* Mark took Trevor for a "man-to-man" after-noon of minigolf. Between holes, Louisa explained, he found out some crucial information. *"It turned out that a couple of kids at school had been calling Trevor a 'girl' because he walked his sister and her best friend to school every day. My husband told him those kids were all wrong—that protecting and helping people you care about was one of the most manly things a guy could do."* After the talk with his father, Trevor's angry behavior toward his sister ceased. *"He told us those boys at school still tease him,"* added his mother, *"but he doesn't listen anymore—he's proud of his job guarding the little kids."*

In this case, Mark had an instinct that there was something behind Trevor's aggressive behavior. By inviting the boy to do something fun with him—away from the crowd, his peers, and the "girls"—Mark helped Trevor let go of his defensive anger and talk about what was really bothering him. Once he found out more information, Mark reassured his son that what he was doing was perfectly "manly." Knowing his father approved of him allowed Trevor to ignore what the kids at school were saying and be proud of doing something good for his sister.

DON'T BUY THE MYTH OF THE MACHO FATHER

Some fathers are haunted by worries that if they don't display tough, macho behavior, their sons will turn out effeminate or gay. Nothing could be farther from the truth. Modeling masculine behavior that includes the full range of human responses—from toughness to tenderness—offers boys the security they need to grow into their own individual personalities, whatever they may be like. Ideally, a boy, rather than feeling distance and judgment, feels loved and accepted by the most important man in his life, his father.

Most often, when a father feels worried about whether his son is "manly" enough, it's because of shame he himself suffered as a boy. These leftover feelings of shame can fester painfully. He may unconsciously act out with his son the same scenarios he endured as a boy.

Cliff grew up cowering in corners as he watched his father abuse his older brother, calling him a "fairy" and even hitting him. Now Cliff finds himself biting back critical remarks about his oldest son, Paul. "I love Paul so much and I want the best for him," Cliff says. "But I just got crazy when I heard last week that he got the lead in the school musical. I told him that no son of mine was going to sing and dance in front of hundreds of people. Now he won't even talk to me."

Cliff needs help coming to terms with the traumas of his own childhood. Without realizing it, he has imposed his abusive father's value system on his own boy. Wishing to prevent the pain he saw his brother suffer, Cliff will do anything to stop Paul from stepping over the line of his father's rigid code of behavior.

Breaking the Silence of Shame

AN EXERCISE FOR FATHERS

Especially when they've had a more traditional Boy Code upbringing, fathers benefit from working through their issues before they start to repeat them with their boys. Sometimes simply writing in a journal can help men get in touch with the humiliation they may have experienced or witnessed as children.

Did you ever witness or experience humiliation for behavior that wasn't "manly"? Describe what happened here.

_____

_____

_____

_____

_____

_____

Do you think it's easier for a boy to be himself in today's world than it was when you were growing up? Why or why not?

_____

_____

_____

Is there anything you wish a man had told you when you were a boy that would have made things easier for you?

_____

_____

_____

LIVING APART AND STAYING CONNECTED

Although many fathers do head single-parent households, the vast majority of children of divorce live primarily with their mothers. We've all heard reports about "deadbeat dads" who don't pay child support. Or we've seen fathers who, after a divorce, provide monetary support but aren't there for their children in emotional ways—becoming depressed themselves, or "deadpan dads."

But the truth is, most fathers who live apart from their children desperately yearn to stay connected to them. Many just may not know how to do it. Some fathers—especially after a long, painful divorce or separation process—may feel that contact with their families only causes more hurt. Others feel so sad and depressed after a separation that they're unable to reach out emotionally to their children. And others, separated by long distances from their families, find that it's very difficult to stay in as close touch as they would like.

While nothing can protect a boy from the pain of his parents' separation, a caring father can help a boy through that pain and reassure him of his continuing love and attention. Although this process can be difficult for everyone, the payoff is well worth it: a close connection between father and son that sustains both in hard times.

"When my dad moved out two years ago," said sixteen-year-old Christian, "I thought I'd never see him again, since we live in Nebraska and he took a new job in Chicago. He called pretty often, but I didn't even want to talk to him usually—I didn't know what to say. I guess that was the worst winter of my life."

That summer, Christian's father invited him to come to Illinois and go fishing with him at a friend's place on a lake for a week. "At first it was really weird," remembered Christian. "We were both being superpolite to each other. But after a few days on the lake, my dad started telling me how lonely he'd been for me and how he wished we could just hang out like we used to. I got pretty mad at him when he said that—I told him it was his own fault we weren't close anymore. But he didn't get angry at me for saying that, and we ended up getting a lot of stuff out in the open that we'd both been thinking."

Since that trip, Christian said, the two of them have been writing to each other often on e-mail. "We've been talking about me maybe going to college in Illinois," he added. "I'm really interested in the University of Chicago, and it would be great to have him right there when I needed a place to get away from school and relax."

How did Christian's father bridge the gap?

➤ He kept calling his son to check in, even though Christian didn't seem to want to talk.

➤ He took what time he could to spend alone with Christian, inviting him on a special fishing trip.

➤ He stuck it out through the discomfort and awkwardness they both were feeling.

➤ He shared his feelings with his son, letting him know that he missed him.

➤ He let Christian get angry with him, keeping the lines of communication open even when things got tough.

➤ He followed up on their good experience together by writing to his son.

➤ He helped Christian think of ways they could be near each other that would fall into line with his boy's own plans.

Many fathers find that communication with their sons is especially difficult during the period right around the separation, because there are so many sad and angry feelings on everyone's part. If your boy is old enough to read, writing to him can be a good way to open up a connection with him, which you can follow up with talking. In addition, letters and pictures you send can give him something to hang on to during those lonely times when he especially misses your presence.

If you're a father living apart from your boy, practice writing a letter to him in the space below. The following questions may give you some ideas about what to write:

➤ *What were some "special times" that I used to have with my boy when we lived together?*

➤ *What qualities do I especially appreciate in my boy's personality?*

➤ *Are there times of day when I particularly miss my boy, or think about him a lot?*

➤ *Do I have ideas about things my boy and I could do together, or times we could spend together?*

_____

_____

_____

_____

_____

_____

_____

_____

You don't have to show your letter to your boy. Just writing out some of your feelings about him helps you to stay emotionally connected—preventing the "deadpan dad" syndrome.

DADS WHO RAISE THEIR SONS ALONE

Ever since his divorce six years ago, Elias, a college professor, has had primary custody of his now seventh-grade son, Jonathan. They have a regular routine that includes cooking dinner together every night, and Elias shows up as often as he can at school events. But Jonathan's mom, a corporate lawyer for a multinational firm, spends most of her time traveling and can't see the boy as often as they would both like. "I'm worried that he's getting the message that he's not important to her," Elias admits. "And I wonder what my boy is missing because he doesn't have a mother in the house."

Elias is doing everything he can to give his son a stable upbringing and a strong role model of a caring father. His active involvement in Jonathan's life is the most important thing he can provide. And he is showing his boy that things like cooking dinner and helping with school matters are just as much a man's domain as a woman's.

Still, it's important that Jonathan have plenty of chances to interact with caring women, including his own mother, wherever possible. And because Elias's own attitudes about women will come through to his son, he could set a positive tone in a number of practical ways. For example:

➤ He could speak regularly in a positive way about his boy's mother, reminding him of the ways she cared for him when they lived together and avoiding blaming her for their separation.
➤ He could acknowledge his son's emotions toward his mother, both the happy and the unhappy ones.
➤ He could facilitate Jonathan's regular visits to his mom, making extra efforts because he knows it may be difficult on her part.
➤ He could create opportunities for himself and Jonathan to interact with other caring women, such as friends, relatives, or teachers.

Just as when single moms raise their sons without a father, single dads have the challenge of striving for a mutually respectful relationship with the absent parent. If the relationship is a difficult one, it's even more important not to lay blame, either on the mother or on women in general. Giving a boy reliable information on whatever led to the separation, without taking sides, is a good first step.

At the same time, Jonathan has to be able to speak openly with his father about his own feelings of loss. His dad needs to create plenty of chances for the boy to express his vulnerable feelings without shame. If Elias can share some of his own experiences and fears with his son as they go about some of their mutual activities, Jonathan will see that it's okay for him not to always be stoic and strong about his worries.

A single father who goes on to have other romantic involvements will also feel his boy's eyes on him. This may be uncomfortable, but it also gives

Dad a new chance to model the kind of behavior and attitudes he hopes to see as his son starts to show an interest in romance and sexual activity.

A single father who is involved with a woman may be hoping that his boy will form a close bond with her, receiving some of the nurturing that he may be missing. Rather than count on this, though, it's best to let any relationship evolve gradually, through shared actions over time. A new woman in a single father's life may need to understand a boy's need for "timed silence" before he can open up, and his preference for "action talk" during what can be an awkward period when trust is not yet established.

As you read this section, did anything stand out as a special challenge in your own life? Describe it here:

_____

_____

_____

If your boy's mother is absent, think about what positive things about her you might share with your son. Write a few of them here:

_____

_____

_____

Think about women in your life whom you admire. Which of their positive traits would you want your son to know about? Identify a few of these here:

Name: _____ Positive trait: _____

Name: _____ Positive trait: _____

Name: _____ Positive trait: _____

Can you think of specific activities you and your son could share with a caring woman? Write a few of them here:

_____

_____

_____

STAYING IN TOUCH: TIPS FOR PARENTS LIVING APART

Many divorced or separated parents might find some of our exercises painful, as they realize how little time they have with their sons, or even how little they might know about them. But remember that the quality of your experience with your child is just as important as its quantity. Here are some ideas that can bring you together, even if you live apart most of the time:

➤ Call your son midweek—don't wait for your "regular" times to find out how he's doing.

➤ Set up e-mail accounts for your son and yourself, and then send him messages.

➤ Take snapshots when the two of you are together, and send copies to him.

➤ Clip newspaper articles that you think would interest *him* (not just you) and put them in the mail.

➤ Use the time you do have together to do special things you know he's interested in (basketball games, theater, camping, bike trips, skateboard exhibitions).

➤ Go to every school conference and as many school events as you possibly can (games, plays, performances, open houses, graduations).

➤ Put aside animosity toward your ex-spouse to model a cooperative parental relationship for your son. Always be co-parents.

➤ Volunteer at your son's school (help out on field trips, chaperone dances, help on cleanup projects).

➤ Get to know your son's friends. Invite them to come with him on visits. Keep in touch with their parents, too.

Remember: *Never* try to connect with your son by putting down the other parent. That will just confuse and hurt him by forcing him to "take sides." If he complains about the other parent to you, be a good listener, but don't let your own issues intrude.

Some fathers find it hard to get close to their children because they had no close connection with their own father. Many men say they want to be a better father to their own kids than their father was to them. But lacking a good model, they don't exactly know what that means. They suffer from an unrequited yearning for father-son closeness, which may have been passed down for generations in a kind of "father hunger."

If you, as the father of a boy, experience these feelings, try the following exercise to help you identify what you feel you lacked from your father in your own boyhood.

Remembering What Didn't Happen

AN EXERCISE FOR FATHERS

I wish my father could have done this with me sometimes:

_____

_____

I wish my father had said something like this to me sometimes:

_____

_____

My father never seemed to

_____

_____

When I think about how my father felt about me in my boyhood, I wonder

_____

_____

Now that I'm a father, I think that my father

_____

_____

IF YOUR FATHER WASN'T THERE FOR YOU

If you lacked a model of caring fatherhood when you were growing up, you may be at a loss for how to be the kind of dad you want your boy to have. Try any of these ideas to help you get started and break the cycle of father hunger.

➤ Spend time with male friends or neighbors and their families, and observe what goes well for them.

➤ Join a fathers' group at a school, church or temple, or community center.

➤ Take an educational workshop for fathers.

➤ Share your stories and concerns with other fathers you know.

➤ Watch how your boy's mother interacts with him in different situations. You can take your cue from her, and soon you'll be developing your own versions of her techniques.

THE "NEST-FEATHERING" SYNDROME

If a father isn't sure how to support his family emotionally, he sometimes compensates for this by spending all his time and energy working to support them financially. Wanting to show his love through being a good provider, he'll work extra-long hours, forgoing vacations but "feathering the nest" with material comforts in abundance. Sadly, many fathers in this situation end up feeling deprived of contact with their sons. "I stood there in the store, wanting to buy my eight-year-old the perfect Christmas present," said one successful stockbroker. "I realized I had no idea what he would really like—I hadn't spent an evening playing with him for months."

Working fathers may also fear reprisal on the job if they take time for their families. They know they won't get that promotion without showing total commitment to their careers. It's unfortunate that today's workplace puts such unreasonable demands on parents. But a father who wants more time with his family may have to delay some of his career ambitions to get that time, just as many women do.

When both parents talk openly with each other about their values, a father can figure out the balance of work and family that suits his situation best. This could mean that he stays home while she goes to work, or that each parent works a limited number of hours, or that they forgo a new car in favor of a family vacation.

The following exercise will help you sort out and prioritize your own choices so that you don't fall into the nest-feathering trap.

Do We Need That?

AN EXERCISE FOR PARENTS

Order the following from 1 to 10, with 1 being the most important to your family's happiness and 10 the least.

___ Owning a house

___ Parents being home on weekends

___ Taking a family vacation

___ Visiting extended family

___ Sending children to private schools

___ Sending children to college

___ Attending events the children are part of

___ Private time together for parents

___ Special time for child alone with parent

___ "Extras" like additional cars, vacation homes, expensive clothes, and toys

This list can serve as a starting point for a conversation with your co-parent about what's most important to you and your boy, and what you might want to change in your current life to better reflect your values.

THE MOTHER-FATHER PARENTING TEAM

Even though mothers and fathers may have different roles to play in a boy's life, they each gain from having the other as part of the parenting team. (The same is true in nontraditional parenting teams such as grandparents or same-sex couples.) And their boy benefits from it, too. When a mother and father share things like cooking, kissing scraped knees, and telling bedtime stories, their boy learns not to associate tenderness and nurturing with women only. And when mothers share in letting their children know that some behaviors are unacceptable, neither parent is cast in the role of the sole authority or tough taskmaster.

This kind of cooperation also can lend vital support—both to the parents and to their boy—when conflicts arise. "I'm a yeller, and so is my son, Anthony," confided Francesca. "When we get in an argument it sometimes turns into a real shouting match. My husband, Tom, can save my life at a time like that. He's got this nice way of stepping in and separating us, maybe by asking Anthony to come do something with him for a bit. Somehow that gives us the time we both need to get our cool back."

TEAM TIPS FOR PARENTS OF BOYS

➤ Think of yourselves as partners, even if both parents don't live together. Communicate and compromise about things that affect your son.

➤ Watch each other's back. If you see that the other parent needs help with your boy, be there as backup, or to take over if necessary.

➤ Help the other parent learn unfamiliar skills, whether it's diaper-changing or talking about sex with your son.

➤ Accept the other parent's help, even if you wish you didn't need it.

➤ Agree on family policies and rules, so that your boy gets a consistent message of what you both expect.

➤ Keep each other informed of developments in your boy's life, from his report card to his important friendships.

What's My Co-parenting Quotient?

Reflect on your own family's situation, and write some of your thoughts in the spaces below.

My particular strengths as a parent of our boy include

_____

_____

_____

My co-parent's strengths include

_____

_____

_____

I think the two of us need to talk more about what to do when

_____

_____

_____

I know I need help learning how to

_____

_____

I think I could help my co-parent learn how to

_____

_____

One time I felt proud of the way we cooperated as parents was when

_____

_____

_____

4

BOYS' EMOTIONS

BOYS EXPRESSING THEMSELVES • FACING EARLY FEARS • SHAKING THE SHAME CYCLE • SADNESS AND DISAPPOINTMENT • SENSITIVE BOYS • LONELINESS • HOW BOYS SHOW THEIR LOVE

The first time seven-year-old Luke slept over at his friend Jared's house, his mother, Ellen, got a phone call at 11:30 P.M. from Jared's mother. "Maybe you'd better come pick Luke up," she said. "He's been crying ever since Jared fell asleep. I don't think he's sick, but he won't say what's wrong." Ellen agreed to come right over and fetch her son.

The next week, Ellen ran into Jared's father as they picked the boys up at Scouts. "Is Luke feeling better this week?" he asked as the boys ran ahead to the cars. "Oh, he wasn't sick," said Ellen. "He was just a little freaked out by the dog snoring right next to his bed. He's not really used to animals." Jared's father guffawed. "You'd better get that boy a dog before he turns into a scaredy-cat!" he said. As he passed Luke, he gave him a thump on the shoulder. "You weren't really scared by old Admiral, were you?" he teased. Luke threw his mother a mortified glance. "No way," he replied. "I just forgot something I needed at home."

Ellen understood her son's fear of sleeping in a strange situation. She gave Luke the support he needed by bringing him home. But seeing nothing shameful about a seven-year-old's anxieties, she forgot how vulnerable boys are to outside judgments of their courage and manliness. Though Jared's father meant no harm, his gentle teasing felt like public humiliation to Luke. It reinforced society's message that boys shouldn't feel fear—or show any emotion that isn't strong and brave. At seven, Luke must already don his mask of bravado, laughing off his true feelings and burying them from sight.

WHAT'S AT STAKE?

➤ Research has shown that male infants actually start out life as emotionally expressive as female babies, or even more so. But by the time boys start school they've learned to hide anything that might show weakness, vulnerability, fear, or despair.

➤ Society's "gender straitjacket" requires boys to live with only half a self— their tough, "heroic" half, action-oriented and physically dominant. Expressing anger and rage fits fine with this half of a boy's self. Being sensitive, vulnerable, subtle, or "different" doesn't fit—so boys learn not to let those qualities show.

➤ Like Luke, boys work hard on the stance of bravado that will protect them from anyone seeing that they have feelings (other than the only "okay" male emotion, anger). Eventually, they forget those feelings, lose touch with them, and forget they have a sensitive side altogether.

➤ This fact contains the secret to most of the anger and aggression boys act out. Recognizing that, we can encourage them to take off their masks and experience the full range of their feelings. If we show them that it's safe to cry tears, they won't need to cry bullets instead.

The kid who always gets picked on, the youngster who fails every math test, the teenager whose sorrow is an angry wound ready to erupt—all these boys have an overwhelming need to feel, recognize, and express what's really going on inside them. In this chapter, we'll explore ways to set up situations in which boys feel most safe opening up and sharing their real feelings— shame-free zones.

BOYS EXPRESSING THEMSELVES

If you are a man, you already know the following list of "sissy stuff" by heart. If you are a woman, you may be familiar with it from your relationships with men in your life.

THE BOY CODE FOR EMOTIONAL EXPRESSION

➤ Do not cry. (No "sissy stuff.")

➤ Do not cower, tremble, or shrink from danger.

➤ Do not ask for help when you are unsure of yourself. (Observe the code of silence.)

➤ Do not reach for comfort or reassurance.

➤ Do not sing or cry for joy.

➤ Do not hug your dearest friends.

➤ Do not use words to show tenderness and love.

But little boys aren't born knowing the code: They learn it through painful experience. We'll learn in later chapters how we can break the Boy Code and help boys shape new habits. But for now, it's important for us to recognize the few ways that boys are allowed to express their emotions—through action, withdrawal, bravado, and sometimes aggression.

What options for expression does a boy have, under the rigid strictures of the Boy Code we outlined above? In the following exercise, you'll put yourself in his shoes and try to walk the path society dictates.

Playing by the Rules

AN EXERCISE FOR PARENTS, TEACHERS, AND YOUTH WORKERS

Imagine that you must follow all the rules in the Boy Code box above. In each of the following situations, how would you actually feel? Given the restrictions, how might you react?

1. **Somebody shoves you in a public place, and you fall down and badly hurt your knee.**

How do I feel? (Check all that apply.)

___ I'm in physical pain.

___ I'm humiliated/embarrassed.

___ I'm angry.

___ I'm scared.

___ Other_____

How do I react?

_____

_____

_____

2. **Your best friend is leaving for a year away.**

How do I feel? (Check all that apply.)

___ I'm sad.

___ I know I'm going to be lonely.

___ I'm filled with love for my friend.

___ I'm afraid we'll lose touch.

___ Other_____

How do I react?

_____

_____

_____

3. **You think you're in love.**

How do I feel? (Check all that apply.)

___ I'm nervous.

___ I'm excited and happy.

___ I want to tell everyone.

___ I want to show my beloved how wonderful I think he or she is.

___ Other_____

How do I react?

_____

_____

_____

4. You're lost in an unfamiliar place.

How do I feel? (Check all that apply.)

____ I'm scared.

____ I'm upset.

____ I'm embarrassed.

____ I want help.

____ Other_____

How do I react?

_____

_____

_____

As you worked through this exercise, how did it make you feel to have to stay within the code? Check all that apply, or write your own thoughts.

____ I felt frustrated in not being able to express all my feelings.

____ I felt angry.

____ I felt isolated.

____ I felt like I couldn't be myself.

Other thoughts:

_____

_____

_____

Completing this exercise gave you a taste of what it's like to be a boy in our culture. But even the Boy Code can't keep a boy's emotions completely under wraps. While he may not speak openly about his love, or cry at a sad movie, he'll use his creativity and intelligence to come up with safe ways to let out his feelings. For example:

- Playing musical instruments
- Listening to music that has meaning to him and singing along
- Drawing pictures or cartoons and giving them to people
- Writing in a private journal
- Taking part in exuberant physical activities like jumping on a trampoline
- Struggling for fairness and justice in society

Encourage your boy to express himself like this. If he draws on the walls, praise his talent and get him sidewalk chalk or a whiteboard. When he plays loud rap or heavy-metal music, understand that this may be helping him release angry or alienated feelings in a nonviolent way. (We talk more about how boys relate to this kind of music in chapter 13, "Boys and the Media.")

EMOTIONAL SUBSTITUTES

Sometimes, in the process of circumventing the Boy Code, a boy falls into patterns of substituting one emotional reaction for another. For example, a boy who's humiliated may sometimes lash out in anger, or a boy who's lonely may become sexually aggressive. Some other common male "substitution behaviors" may include:

- *Picking fights* instead of *expressing sadness*
- *Withdrawing into solitude* instead of *expressing shame or humiliation*
- *Eating* instead of *reaching for comfort*

By picking up on some of these substitutions, adults might read a boy's emotions through his actions and understand better what's going on with him. "Johnny hardly ever cries anymore," said one mother of an eleven-year-old. "But I can tell when he's sad because he slams doors. That's my signal to make a little special time for us."

(*continued*)

In the classroom, teachers often use the same kind of cues to translate the causes of disruptive behavior. "We have to take state tests every spring, and if the kids do badly they have to go to summer school," a fourth-grade teacher said. "They don't talk about it directly, but for days beforehand the boys, especially, are bouncing off the walls. I finally realized what was going on, and we sat down and talked about how they were feeling. They suggested we spend part of every day practicing on old tests, so now they're not so worried."

FACING EARLY FEARS

Can you remember ever being afraid of any of the following things? Check off all that apply.

___ Loud noises	___ Clowns	___ Monsters
___ Thunderstorms	___ Santa Claus	___ Doctors and dentists
___ Fireworks	___ Teachers	___ Bigger children
___ Dogs	___ Strange people	___ Going on the
___ Horses	___ The dark	school bus

It's natural for children to have fears like these, but little boys—like Luke in the story at the beginning of this chapter—often feel ashamed that they're not brave enough. On television and in toy stores, the images they see are of brave heroes who aren't afraid to single-handedly fight off terrifying threats. Worse, they hear and see what happens to boys who do show their fear: At best, their fears are dismissed; at worst, they're teased, taunted, and bullied.

"Last year when Ben was five I had to spend a night in the hospital to have some minor surgery," said Arthur, a single father whose wife had died of cancer two years before. "Ben stayed with his grandparents for the night, but I guess he barely slept, and cried a lot." Arthur returned home to his wan-looking child, who clung to him and asked to sleep in his bed that night. "I set up a sleeping bag for him in my room, and we watched a video together and then talked," he said. "Ben finally asked if I was going to die

like his mom had. I explained the operation I had just had, and reassured him that I was definitely going to get better from it in a few days. But I also told him that if anything ever happened to me, we had a plan for him to live with his favorite aunt, Mary, and her children. He was glad to hear that, but he told me I better not die anyway. I promised him I would take good care of myself."

Of course, Arthur would never have teased his son for this fear, but it would have been easy to dismiss Ben's anxiety with a "Don't worry, I'm fine." Instead, Arthur had a serious conversation with his son about what would happen if he died. That conversation, combined with the reassurance of camping out in his father's bedroom and learning more about the operation, helped Ben bear his fear without shame.

"Everybody thought Lamar was probably old enough to come see Star Wars *with the rest of the family," said Latisha, mother of three boys under nine. "He's only four, but he'd been pestering us to go along. But as soon as he saw Darth Vader, he started to whimper and try to climb up on me. He was starting to get pretty upset and I finally decided to just take him out and wait in the lobby for the others." While they sat eating popcorn together, Latisha and Lamar talked about the difference between movies and what's real. "We actually had a pretty good time—I told him I didn't like scary movies much myself, and neither did his dad. Of course, by the time the movie was over, he wanted to go back and try again. We told him we'd rent the video instead."*

Latisha stayed alert to the possibility that her little boy would be overwhelmed at the movies. Without making a fuss about it, she took him out of the scary situation and helped him talk about his feelings. She also let him know that even big, strong people, like his mother and father, got scared sometimes at movies. And by promising him he could watch the video at home, she minimized his feelings of humiliation at not being one of the big boys, while making sure the same thing wouldn't happen again.

SHAKING THE SHAME CYCLE

Six-year-old Scott has fallen off his new two-wheeler at least ten times already, while his father, Roger, puffs alongside to steady him in the hot sun of the empty school parking lot. But finally the child, his lower lip trembling, refuses to get back on. "Come on, Scott!" Roger urges. "You're gonna be the only kid in first grade who can't ride a bike!" The boy doesn't answer. Instead, he kicks the bike where it lies on the pavement, hangs his head, and won't look at his father, who stands sweating and exasperated.

To his dad, Scott looks like a balking child who gave up too easily. But in fact, the boy is silenced by an overwhelming sense of shame—the intense feeling that he is unlovable and "no good." Shame is not the same emotion as embarrassment (which a child might feel, for example, at being the focus of attention). And it is less specific than guilt—the conscience's way of scolding us for some specific failure that invites correction.

Shame is different because it encompasses the whole self—connecting more to what a boy *is* than what he *does*. The feeling is overwhelming—it makes boys want to hide, disappear, or even die. If you've ever wanted to sink into the ground after a humiliating episode, you understand what a boy feels whenever he transgresses the Boy Code.

WHY ARE BOYS SO SENSITIVE TO SHAME?

While all children—and adults—know what it means to feel ashamed, boys are exquisitely sensitive to the emotion. They are so shame-phobic that they will do virtually anything to avoid it. In doing so, they can often develop lasting behavioral problems, from timidity to perfectionism or aggression.

A boy's shame has its root in our confusion about masculinity. He's terrified of shame because he knows that our culture fundamentally does not accept his deep qualities of vulnerability and fragility. We identify emotionality, openness, and vulnerability as feminine qualities, and sadly, "feminine" still carries a hidden meaning of "inferior."

A girl can act "boyish" and be considered cute; there are countless such characters on television, in books, and in movies. But it's still a boy's worst nightmare to be called a "girl."

Some things a boy might feel shame about:
➤ Showing emotions in public
➤ Not liking sports
➤ Appearing foolish
➤ Being shy
➤ Sexual feelings for people he sees as "off limits"
➤ Feeling pain
➤ Being defeated or overpowered

➤ Feeling smaller or weaker than other boys

➤ Feeling stupid in school

➤ Having an ongoing health problem

➤ Being a member of a minority group

➤ Having less money than other boys

HOW A SHAMED BOY ACTS

A boy learns to draw on a repertory of behaviors to use as protection from shame:

➤ **He acts tough and independent.** Wearing a mask of indifference, a boy might slouch down halls and sidewalks in the posture that brands him as invulnerable to insult. When someone pushes him, he knows just how to return the gesture or let it slide off.

➤ **He withdraws.** Hanging his head or refusing to answer, he literally collapses beneath his shame. He caves in, doesn't move, doesn't talk—as if he has been hit or stunned—before the shame dissipates.

➤ **He becomes mean, angry, and violent.** With his fragile identity and self-respect threatened, he lashes out to assert his worth. A boy who is humiliated because of his race or social class sometimes resorts to violence—joining a street gang or carrying a gun—just to keep from disappearing entirely. Many boys may become bullies, and many bullies are quite depressed.

WHAT ADULTS CAN DO TO HELP: SOME GUIDELINES

How can adults set appropriate behavior standards without destroying a boy's self-esteem when he fails to meet them? Responding to boys' behavior in routine interactions, we can help by paying attention to both *what* we take issue with and *how* we do it.

➤ When you must take issue with what a boy does, use feedback that is *as specific as possible.* For example, Scott's dad might have focused on some specific *technique* that was going awry. ("You're falling off when you look at your hands instead of looking out in front.")

➤ Separate *who the boy is* from *what the boy does*. The success or failure of his actions does not define his worth as a person.

➤ Be aware of your *facial expressions*. Critical messages come across vividly in expressions adults may not even be aware of making, but that speak louder than any words. Research has shown that adults commonly—and unconsciously—employ a specific and recognizable "disgust face" at behavior they dislike: nose raised, nostrils flared, and with the tongue extended as if to reject a bad taste.

➤ Because wholesale praise as well as wholesale criticism can end up causing a boy to feel shame, *rely on "I messages" in praise*. When your boy does well in the big game, say, "I was really proud of how you passed to your teammates," not "You're a real athlete!" That way, you're actually naming *your* experience and the evidence that supports it, not placing a label on the child that he might secretly disagree with. If children know that they can trust your praise, they are more likely to trust your criticism, too.

In the following exercise, you'll practice choosing responses that avoid shaming, working toward building a boy's self-confidence.

How Should I Say It?

AN EXERCISE FOR PARENTS, TEACHERS, AND YOUTH WORKERS

For each of the following situations, choose the response that you think is least likely to make a boy feel shame, based on the guidelines outlined above.

1. Your little boy behaves very well at a company dinner, following your family's expectations for good manners and playing quietly after he leaves the table. Afterward, you say:

___ "All the guests were impressed with what a good boy you are."

___ "Thank you so much for being good."

___ "I was so proud of the way you remembered to say 'Excuse me' when you needed to ask me something!"

2. *A boy wants to take his comfort blanket on the bus the first week of kindergarten. You say:*
___ "Don't you think a big boy like you should leave his blankie at home?"
___ "I'll pack it right here in your backpack so you can touch it when you need to."
___ "I'll pack it right here in your backpack so the other kids won't see it."

3. *Your boy brings home a rather misshapen clay pot he's made at camp. You say:*
___ "Wow! You're quite an artist, aren't you!"
___ "Hey, neat! I love the color you chose—this will be perfect for keeping all those paper clips in."
___ "Is this all you made in arts and crafts? You must have other things to show me, too."

4. *Your boy brings home a 70 on the algebra test. You say:*
___ "This looks like a hard test! Which problems gave you the most trouble?"
___ "This doesn't look that hard—must have been an off day for you, right?"
___ "Well, you're no math whiz. I was never any good at algebra, either."

5. *A boy, at twelve, is somewhat overweight. You say:*
___ "Don't worry about your weight, son—lots of boys outgrow their baby fat as soon as they hit puberty."
___ "You're going to make quite a linebacker, at the rate you're going!"
___ Nothing, but make sure to have plenty of healthy food available.

While the answers may have seemed obvious to you, it's easy to slip into shaming boys without realizing it. For example, subtle cues like tone of voice or facial expression can give the lie to even the most positive-sounding statement. No one adult can completely eliminate shame from a boy's life, but remembering his exquisite sensitivity (even when it seems like he doesn't care) can help a parent or teacher talk to a boy in the most supportive way possible.

TIPS TO REMEMBER

➤ **Watch your face and voice tones** when you speak to a boy.

➤ **Whether in praise or in criticism, focus on a boy's *actions*,** not solely on his inherent qualities.

➤ **Keep the total amount of complaint down.** The more you criticize, the more a boy will conclude that the whole self is no good. Even if your complaints are very specific, self-esteem will erode under constant wear and tear. Decide carefully whether any particular criticism is worth making given the larger picture.

➤ **Pay attention to the intensity of your response.** No matter how concrete your message, if you rebuke a boy in anger he will focus on your emotion, not the content of what you say. Wait to speak until you have more perspective.

➤ **Make time each day for "guy talk,"** when the boys in your care can share how they are doing and what they are feeling.

SADNESS AND DISAPPOINTMENT

Joel's best friend had been accepted Early Decision to a prestigious East Coast college, and Joel had his heart set on joining him there. He waited for the April decision anxiously, but when he finally got his letters from the admissions office, he hadn't made the cut. Only one college accepted him, and it was far from his first choice.

"His father and I don't know what to do for him," said his mother, Helene. "We've tried to talk with him because we need to send a deposit, but he seems to be avoiding us—he says he's 'busy' and then we don't see him for whole days. We called his college adviser, but she said Joel hasn't talked to her either. We sympathize with his disappointment, but he needs to move on and deal with the situation, doesn't he?"

Joel has an even bigger priority right now than sending in his deposit and getting on with his life. His disappointment and sadness are overwhelming him, and he needs time to deal with those emotions first.

Although both boys and girls feel the sting of rejection and other disappointments, a boy experiences a special hardship. The Boy Code forbids him from acknowledging failure or weakness—he's supposed to be "just fine" no matter what happens. Forced to hide and deny his sadness, a boy may become mired in it, unable to move forward.

Helene and her husband have the right instincts in trying to talk to their son. He needs their empathy and support as he comes to terms with his bitter disappointment. But if they push him into action too soon, they could be adding even more pressure to the pressure he already feels from his bottled-up emotions.

What can Joel's parents do to help?

➤ They can set aside their own anxieties about Joel's college plans for the time being.

> *Instead of saying:*
> "Now what are we going to do?"
> *They could say:*
> "Let's just take our time and let Joel consider all his options."

➤ They can trust that Joel wants to resolve the situation, and will do so in time and with their help.

> *Instead of saying:*
> "You've got to make a plan—time's running out!"
> *They could say:*
> "You've got time to think about what you want—let us know if you want to talk about it."

➤ They can understand and acknowledge that Joel is under terrible pressure from the Boy Code that tells him to pretend everything's okay.

> *Instead of saying:*
> "Don't worry—I'm sure you'll be very happy at that school."
> *They could say:*
> "It must be hard for you right now to be around kids who are really happy with where they got in."

> They can directly address his sadness without adding their own worries to the conversation.

> *Instead of starting conversations with Joel like this:*

> "So, what do you want to do about this deposit? It's due on the first of the month!"

> *They could try this:*

> "You must feel pretty awful about not being able to go to school with Charlie."

Once Joel sees that his parents accept his true feelings and still believe in him even though he feels he's "failed," he'll feel strong enough to face the tough decisions he has to make. Their expressions of love and support at this point will help him far more than any logistical actions they might take to "solve" his problem.

AGGRESSION CAN HIDE SADNESS: IS HE "BAD" OR "SAD"?

Older boys such as Joel tend to hide their sadness and disappointment behind a mask of stoicism or withdrawal. Younger boys may act out in aggressive ways, disguising what they feel are "weak" emotions. Parents and teachers should stay alert to the possibility that a boy who acts angry or aggressive may actually be feeling sad.

"Around the holidays last year, Bokani started to get really hostile toward me," said Peter, a sixth-grade teacher at a city school. "He was always making sarcastic remarks and trying to provoke me with disrespectful personal questions. Finally I had to talk to him privately after school." After some gentle prodding, Bokani's lip started to tremble as he said to Peter, "Why should I care about school anyway, we have to move next month and I can't go here anymore." Realizing the pain behind the boy's behavior, Peter decided to have his class make a special poster for Bokani with pictures and good-bye notes from them all. By the time he left, Bokani was back to his old self, lively and funny. "We still hear from him from time to time," said Peter.

Elsewhere in this book, we go further into ways to help boys whose behavior is angry or aggressive (chapters 5 and 6), boys who have suffered loss through death or divorce (chapter 7), and boys who may be depressed (chapter 8).

SENSITIVE BOYS

Rosalie fell in love with her husband, Ben, when she was still in law school and he was designing computer software for a startup Internet firm. When their first child, Tomas, arrived, she was thrilled that he seemed to reflect his father's intellectual bent. "He always seemed to understand everything that was happening around him," Rosalie said, "even before he learned to talk. Later, people always commented on how mature he was—he could hold his own at a company dinner by the time he was six."

Both parents began to worry, though, when Tomas reached elementary school. His teachers reported that, though precocious in reading and math, he shrank from social interactions with other boys and frequently endured their teasing with tears in his eyes. He did have one close friend from the neighborhood, but the boy went to another school, so they saw each other only on weekends, when they would spend hours together, poring over science and nature books.

For Tomas's tenth birthday, Rosalie and Ben wanted to invite ten children for a special outing to the city's Natural History Museum. But when his mother broached the subject, Tomas begged her not to go ahead with it. "He said the kids would only make fun of him," she said. "Ben and I don't know what to do—we think he needs to learn to relax and hang out in a group his own age. Even if he is a genius, he should still have a happy childhood!"

Why are Tomas's parents worried?

➤ His classmates tease him for being shy.

➤ He seems too sensitive, crying when he is teased.

➤ He has only one good friend.

➤ He seems afraid to have a party with a large group of other children.

Based on these observations of his behavior, Rosalie and Ben fear that their son is, or will be, unhappy. They say they want him to "learn to relax and hang out" with other children. Before they put pressure on Tomas to change, however, they might reconsider their data about his behavior.

Is there anything wrong with Tomas?

➤ He prefers the company of one close friend who shares his interests.

➤ He communicates with adults in an easy, mature way.

➤ He enjoys the world of ideas.

➤ He talks to his mother about his fears and insecurities.

Nothing about these traits indicates that Tomas will not develop into a balanced and happy person, whether or not he is a genius. In fact, the main problem here may not be Tomas's discomfort or unhappiness at all, but instead his parents' nagging feeling that society may not see their son as a normal boy. They love their son dearly and delight in his special gifts, but the Boy Code has created an underlying worry that he falls short of what a boy should be, and that somehow he will suffer for it.

What About Tomas's Birthday Party?

Given that Rosalie and Ben want Tomas to enjoy his birthday celebration, they shouldn't force him to have a party where he feels uncomfortable. There's nothing wrong with inviting just one good friend to the museum, for instance—that way, in fact, Tomas and his friend might have an experience tailored even more to their own interests. Or perhaps Tomas has another suggestion for his party.

The best present Tomas's parents can give him for his tenth birthday is simply to accept their son the way he is. This may involve simply changing their own perspective on his behavior, recognizing his strengths, and putting aside the expectations of the Boy Code.

If you have a sensitive boy, the following exercise will help you assess his situation clearly, observing his strengths and deciding whether he needs adult intervention to help him.

Is My Sensitive Boy All Right?

AN EXERCISE FOR PARENTS

Circle "yes" or "no" to answer the following questions about your sensitive boy:

Yes	No	Does he have at least one good friend?
Yes	No	Does he have any activity or interest that he really cares about?
Yes	No	Does he talk with adults?
Yes	No	Does he communicate his worries and bad feelings?
Yes	No	Is he doing well in his schoolwork?
Yes	No	Has he shown his sensitive nature from an early age?

Yes   No   Does he ever seem happy—smiling, talking animatedly, making jokes or laughing at them?

Yes   No   Does he get recognition from you or from others for his strengths or accomplishments?

Did you answer any of the questions with "no"? If so, reflect here on your answer. Has the situation always been as it is now? If not, what has changed and when did that change happen?

_____

_____

_____

_____

Did any of the questions make you think of something about your boy that you hadn't thought of before? If so, describe it here:

_____

_____

_____

Check all the adjectives below that you feel apply to your boy. Add your own at the end of the list.

___ Funny	___ Sweet	___ Smart
___ Demonstrative	___ Loving	___ Helpful
___ Talkative	___ Trusting	___ Quiet
___ Reflective	___ Curious	___ Perceptive
___ Spirited	___ Vulnerable	___ Independent
___ Intense	___ Dependent	___ Tenderhearted
___ Picky	___ Emotional	

Your own adjectives here:

_____

_____

Do you think you or the boy's other parent share any of your boy's qualities that you just listed? Which ones?

_____

_____

_____

Do you have worries about how your boy's qualities will affect his happiness? Why or why not?

_____

_____

_____

WHEN TO WORRY

➤ If a boy shows a sudden, drastic change in behavior—for example, if a rambunctious boy suddenly becomes quiet and weepy

➤ If a boy flinches or cowers with all adults, avoiding contact

➤ If a boy's schoolwork shows a sudden, drastic change—for example, a usually conscientious boy stops doing homework or fails several tests

These signs may indicate a serious problem, like abuse or depression. Talk to the other adults in the boy's life to decide what steps to take. (See chapters 8 and 9 for more on this.)

HOW ADULTS CAN HELP A SENSITIVE BOY

For a sensitive boy, adults can supply a haven of support and understanding. While other children may tease him for being different, your acceptance will counteract the shame he may feel, reassuring him that he is still a good and lovable person.

Some ways a parent, teacher, or other adult can help a sensitive boy:

- **Stay connected.** Make extra efforts to share activities with your boy that you know he enjoys, giving him the chance to open up and talk to you when he needs to.

- **Respect his voice.** If he is part of adult conversations, give him the same attention you'd give a friend. This may be a rare chance for him to speak openly.

- **Support what he likes to do.** Make sure he has opportunities to pursue the things that interest him. Get involved, where possible—even if it just means going to the library together to pick out books. Don't worry if his interests seem esoteric or age-inappropriate (either too old or too young).

- **Teach him skills to avert bullying.** The victim of malicious teasing can learn to respond in ways that protect him and de-escalate the situation. Help him see that a bully's behavior is not his fault, and teach him what to do about it. (See chapter 6, "Bullies and Troublemakers.")

- **Change the scene.** If a sensitive boy has a very hard time in school, sometimes a change of scene—camp, summer school, a visit to grandparents, or an after-school program—can give him a fresh start and a new focus. Let him help brainstorm possibilities, and then follow them up.

- **Don't compare siblings.** The family should be a place of indisputable acceptance, no matter what the differences among its members. Siblings can be an important source of support for a sensitive boy, as long as he doesn't feel pitted against them.

- **Create a "buddy group"** where the boy can connect with peers who share his interests.

- **Work with the teacher and the school.** With other parents who may have similar concerns, approach the school and help teachers consider other ways to respond to these normal behaviors.

LONELINESS

The news of Randy's suicide came as a terrible shock to his community. A junior at the local high school, he had been an honor student with many friends. But the note he left told a different story. "No one knows how alone I feel," it read. "I can't keep pretending to be what everyone wants me to be. I'm sorry, Mom and Dad."

Randy's sad story repeats itself too often to be a fluke. Suicide is now the third leading cause of death among young adults between fifteen and twenty-four, behind only accidents and homicide. And while more girls attempt suicide, at least four times as many boys as girls actually succeed in killing themselves. This epidemic of suicide among boys is a symptom of the terrible inner sense of loneliness that so many boys experience—even the ones who seem to be doing fine.

Boys are especially susceptible to loneliness. While girls learn from an early age to turn to others with their hurts and worries, the Boy Code tells boys to act strong and deal with their problems by themselves. As they struggle with that lonely dilemma, their pain increases. Trapped inside the vicious circle of loneliness, they may spiral toward the breaking point, disconnected from adults when they need them most.

THE CIRCLE OF LONELINESS

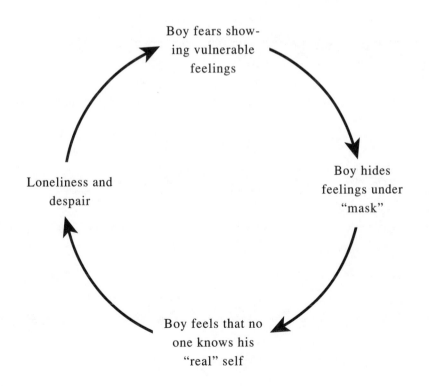

Boy fears show-
ing vulnerable
feelings

Boy hides
feelings under
"mask"

Boy feels that no
one knows his
"real" self

Loneliness and
despair

How to Tell When a Boy Is Lonely

Write your responses to the following questions about the boy you have in mind:

What kinds of social situations does he put himself in? If he is a member of any clubs or other specialized groups, do they encourage interpersonal connections (camping trips, retreats, shared service or adventure, or role-playing games)?

_____

_____

_____

Does he have friends whom he's known a long time? Have they been loyal, accepting him as he's changed through the years (dressing or looking different, choosing different activities)?

_____

_____

_____

Whom does he spend time with outside of school? Are there people he talks to about what's important to him? (Special teachers, best friends, favorite relatives, or serious romantic attachments?)

_____

_____

_____

Does he have chances to express his feelings through visual art, writing, or the performing arts?

_____

_____

_____

If you could answer even one of the above questions with a "yes," there's probably less cause to worry. The most danger comes when a boy feels totally isolated—when he thinks that no one knows his real personality and feelings.

WHAT HELPS A LONELY BOY CONNECT?

➤ *Feeling needed.* Tutoring younger or handicapped children, volunteering at a nursing home, helping out at Habitat for Humanity building sites, or any number of service opportunities work against loneliness by building strong connections.

➤ *Friendships with girls.* Sometimes talking to a girl—whether it's his sister, cousin, neighbor, classmate, or girlfriend—helps a boy feel more understood and accepted. Encourage opposite-sex friendships, and don't tease a boy for hanging out or talking on the phone with girls.

➤ *Other friendships.* As they start feeling more connected, we can help boys find buddies who share similar feelings, which will help them feel more positively about themselves.

➤ *Caring for animals.* Caring for farm animals or riding horses provides the chance for unspoken communication and warmth. And of course, household pets like dogs, cats, or even birds can give a boy a close relationship with a creature that depends on him. You don't need to live in the country or have a pet yourself to let a boy experience this—every animal shelter needs volunteers.

➤ *The arts.* For many lonely boys, the arts provide both emotional release and connection. Encourage your boy to take up an instrument, work with clay or paint, take photographs, or make movies with a video camera. Make the arts a normal household activity, from the time a boy can first cut out pictures from a magazine to paste together a collage. Attend his concerts, plays, or other performances.

HOW BOYS SHOW THEIR LOVE

Our culture has made a cliché of the belief that men don't like to say those three little words, "I love you." Of course, many boys and men don't have any trouble at all speaking their love in words. But even those who do are "speaking" their love all the time, in ways that many of us just don't recognize. While boys may feel awkward about expressing their tender feelings outright to the ones they love, they'll show their love through deeds. When we recognize their generous acts for what they are—"action love"—and speak our appreciation openly, we strengthen the connections that will sustain them.

When Rico's little sister, Alexia, made the junior high school swim team, their parents groaned at the prospect of driving her to six A.M. practices three days a week. An emotional argument at the dinner table ended abruptly when seventeen-year-old Rico spoke up. "I'll drive you," he said. "It's only ten minutes, and I should get up earlier anyway."

Mr. Spiegel, the school music teacher, is eight-year-old Eddie's favorite because of his humorous teaching style and obvious enjoyment of Eddie's exuberance in class. About once a week, Mr. Spiegel finds comic strips Eddie has cut out from the morning paper and left on his desk for him to chuckle over.

Mrs. O'Grady, the elderly widow in the apartment next door to eleven-year-old Doug, fell and broke her hip. Remembering the afternoons he'd spent in her kitchen over the years, eating cookies and playing with her little terrier, Doug showed up at her door when he heard the news. "Don't worry about Rusty," he said. "I'll walk him for as long as you need me to."

Rico, Eddie, and Doug are directly showing their affection in these cases, but not by using words. Instead, they rely on action to express what they feel. When they see things like this taking place, the adults in a boy's life can respond just as if he had bestowed a hug or a kiss— with genuine pleasure and feeling. "Isn't it just like you to offer!" Mrs. O'Grady told Doug. "I don't know what Rusty and I would do without your company."

5

ANGER AND AGGRESSION IN BOYS

GETTING THROUGH THE MASK • HANDLING A CRISIS: TIMED SILENCE • THE SIBLING WARS: WHEN IS IT TOO MUCH? • LISTENING TO AN ANGRY BOY • EMPATHIZING WITH ANGER

Harry and Gwen split up a year ago when their son, Jack, was ten, and Harry moved to a city a few hours' drive away. Though Jack will visit his dad for a month this summer, their contact is sporadic, and now Gwen is worried about the boy's behavior.

"He's been in several fights at school this spring," she said. "He's in and out of the principal's office practically every week. Last night his baseball coach called me up to say that Jack had punched out a couple of kids on the other team after the game. If he gets into one more incident, he's going to be off the team."

Gwen has tried everything, she said—she's had a conference with Jack's teacher, taken away privileges, asked his father to speak to him over the phone. But the boy seems sullen and defiant, spending most of his time in his room alone. He won't even make eye contact with her when she tries to find out what's wrong. "I can't help thinking that if his dad were around, Jack wouldn't be acting up like this," she worried. "How can I get him to shape up?"

WHAT'S AT STAKE?

Why might Jack be acting out? To what societal messages are he, his coach, and his mother responding? Before we try to come up with solutions for Gwen's problem, try this short exercise.

How might you feel if you lost a family member you deeply depended on? Circle all that apply:

afraid   sad   guilty   lonely   angry   needy   vulnerable   hurt   uncertain

other feelings: _____

How might a person express each of the feelings above? When you have felt these emotions, what did you feel like doing, even if it wasn't "allowed"? Write some expressions of the feeling next to it in the space below. (For example: "sadness—crying" or "anger—yelling, hitting.")

Try not to worry about how a person "should" respond; just write the simplest physical reaction you can.

Fear _____   Sadness _____
Guilt _____   Loneliness _____
Anger _____   Neediness _____
Vulnerability _____   Hurt _____
Uncertainty _____   Other feelings _____

Which of the behaviors you listed above—the expressions *of the feelings— do you associate with boys and men?*

_____

_____

_____

Imagine a grown man behaving in some of the ways listed above that you do not *normally associate with men. If you are a man, imagine doing these things yourself. If you are a woman, imagine a man you are close to (husband, brother, father, colleague) doing those things. How does it make you feel to think about it?*

_____

_____

_____

Let's go back to Jack's story. At an intensely vulnerable moment in his life, Jack has put on a mask of masculine bravado that hides his deep feelings of uncertainty and need, loss and loneliness. He knows that society thinks these feelings are unacceptable in men and boys—guys aren't supposed to be weak, or to ask for help or comfort. Fighting offers Jack the one outlet the Boy Code allows him in order to express his pain—anger.

Jack's anger is legitimate, of course, along with his feelings of sadness, vulnerability, and powerlessness after the loss of his father's daily presence in his life. His parents, teachers, and coach need to help him find safe ways to recognize, bear, and express the full range of those difficult feelings—not to funnel them into aggressive acts.

But when a boy undergoes a profound separation and loss, he may not feel safe expressing his genuine hurt and anger about it directly to a parent who has deep negative feelings of her own to deal with. A parent such as Gwen, in turn, may be too immersed in her own pain to listen to her son's feelings in a supportive way.

Still, it's crucial for Jack—as well as for his mother—to be able to express these real feelings in a safe place. The more that adults can imagine themselves in their children's shoes, the more empathically—and less punitively—they will respond.

However they manage it—even if it means seeing an outside counselor—this must be a priority if Jack's aggressive behavior is to stop.

GETTING THROUGH THE MASK

The Boy Code demands that boys hide their true feelings behind a protective mask of stoicism and bravado. The only emotion that they can legitimately let show is anger. In fact, society doesn't even like them to express anger in direct, verbal ways; and so, like Jack, they may strike out in physical ways instead.

If you are a parent, teacher, or coach dealing with an angry and aggressive boy, it may be hard to imagine how to break through the mask that he wears most of the time. Indeed, many an adult has been taken aback by how quickly a boy's anger can flare up, and over what seemingly small matters. But most of these boys, surprisingly, will open up in time, if we remember the keys to unlocking that mask: *connecting, listening* (sometimes through action), and *empathizing.*

But before you can even connect with a very angry boy, he needs time to cool off.

HANDLING A CRISIS: TIMED SILENCE

ONE SUCCESS STORY

Eleven-year-old Owen had been practicing hard for the big soccer league game. When the big day came, his parents drove him an hour to the town where the match took place. But as the crowd cheered, Owen found himself parked on the sidelines while the coach put in all the other players but him. As his family walked him to the car afterward, Owen didn't say a word. His friend Bobby ran past and gave him a slap on the shoulder, calling out, "Good game!"

"I couldn't believe how Owen reacted," his mother, Amy, said later. "He turned on Bobby and attacked him like an animal. Owen's always been a bit of a roughhouser, but this was totally different. I pulled them apart, but then I didn't know what to say—he was obviously feeling so hurt and humiliated." When the family got home, Amy asked Owen if he wanted to talk about it. "I just want to be left alone," he told her, and went up to his room with the dog.

That evening, as Amy was making dinner, Owen came down and sat at the counter, making patterns with a box of toothpicks. "Tough day," Amy said gently, as she layered the lasagna noodles and tomato sauce. Owen gave a shaky sigh. "Yeah," he said. "I guess I shouldn't have hit Bobby like that. But it just wasn't fair—how come the coach played everyone else but me?" His mother put down her spatula and sat down at the counter across from him. "I don't know," she said. "It didn't make sense to me either."

They talked for a while—about the team, about the coach, and finally about how Owen could have handled his anger without hurting another person along the way. "Why don't you give Bobby a call?" Amy said finally. "He's probably feeling bad, too." Owen got up, looking relieved at the suggestion. "Thanks, Mom," he said as he left the kitchen.

What did Amy do right?

Amy called on the Timed Silence strategy (introduced in chapter 1 of this workbook and explained in detail in *Real Boys* and *Real Boys' Voices*) to turn what could have been a confrontation into an opportunity for connecting with her boy.

➤ She stopped the fight, but she didn't assign blame or punishment before Owen had a chance to think and talk.

➤ She didn't push Owen to talk about his feelings right away—either directly after the fight or when the family got home.

➤ She gave Owen time to himself.

➤ She stayed alert, waiting for a signal that he was ready to talk.

➤ She trusted her instinct that sitting down at the counter and playing with the toothpicks was that signal.

➤ She stopped what she was doing to talk with him, even though making dinner was important.

➤ She showed Owen that she shared some of his feelings and that she was on his side.

➤ She helped him take responsibility for his aggressive behavior and see its consequences.

➤ She helped him find a way to make amends.

DOS AND DON'TS IN A CRISIS

Don't rush to discipline or punish. Talk with the boy and search for the pain behind his actions.

Do hold off setting consequences until you really understand what he's feeling.

Don't push a boy with concerned questions right away.

Do acknowledge what happened, but give him time to cool off in a private, shame-free space before you talk.

Don't assume that what he's acting angry about is what he's really angry about—or that he's really angry at all.

(continued)

Do listen actively to what he says (see pages 27–28), combining talk with doing something with him when possible. He may tell you something you don't know.

Don't withdraw your love and affection just because he messed up—even if you feel very angry yourself.

Do let him know that you're on his side, and will help him even if he's done something wrong.

Don't use physical punishment to discipline an angry boy. That just models the behavior you're trying to discourage, as well as humiliating the boy and increasing his anger. You may, however, find that you need to use firm but gentle physical restraint—holding him, for example—in order to keep a very angry boy from hurting himself or others.

Do give hugs, not punishment. Protect him and provide safety. Let older boys know you respect and love them. An arm around the shoulder might be all it takes to get him to open up; and even an older boy will sometimes tolerate a hug.

For more on the Timed Silence strategy, see chapter 1, pages 12–13.

THE SIBLING WARS: WHEN IS IT TOO MUCH?

"My house is like a battleground, my boys fight so much with each other," complained Iris. Even though she runs a "strict household," she said, eight-year-old Nestor and his brother, Wilkie, ten, are constantly at each other's throats. "Wilkie makes fun of his little brother in ways that are just plain mean," she said. "He picks at him all the time about every little thing." And Nestor reacts with fury, hitting and even biting his big brother to get back at him. "Wilkie always ends up winning," Iris said, "and that just makes everything worse. Nestor told me last night he hated his brother more than anyone in the world."*

Fighting between siblings often gives parents their first real taste of how boys act out the aggression and anger they feel. But how are the boys themselves experiencing this conflict? In their own words:

Wilkie: I like my little brother fine—everyone likes him. He's real friendly and happy and he's always saying hi, even to strangers. My mom says she loves us both the same, but she's always comparing us, because I kind of keep to myself and I'm not as popular as he is. Sometimes I just feel like taking Nestor down from how great he always thinks he is.

Nestor: Why does Wilkie always have to act like he's so right and I'm so stupid? I know he's really the smart one, like he always reads books and he tries to talk to the grown-ups. I wish he would still play with me like when we were little. We used to play in this fort we made under the table. He never wants to do that anymore—he says it's a stupid baby game.

If we listen to what the boys are saying, their conflicts may not seem so barbaric. In fact, these brothers seem to love each other a lot, beneath the tension both of them feel. But Wilkie is upset because he's not as popular as Nestor—he even feels as if his mother likes his brother better. And Nestor is too young to understand where the hostility is coming from.

The time for Iris to start may not be when the boys get to fighting. In fact, trying to identify who started the fight may backfire, as each child comes up with increasingly subtle ways to pin the blame on the other. Instead, she should look for other moments, when she can have "alone time" with each of them separately. Once she hears what her boys are really feeling, she'll be able to reassure them about their secret fears and worries.

If your children are in conflict:

➤ Stop fights when they happen, but don't take sides or punish the one who "started it."

➤ Make special time with each child alone.

➤ Don't be afraid to tell each child that some things about him make him extra special in your eyes. Let him know what those things are, without comparing between siblings.

Do say: "I love talking to you about your ideas. You're such a good thinker, and that makes you good at solving problems."

Don't say: "You're the smart one, and so you need to set an example for your brother."

Often, sibling rivalries stem from the older sibling's fear that he will be replaced in his parents' hearts by the younger one, who so often seems to get more positive attention. Take special care not to play favorites, and to occasionally re-create the days when the older child was your baby.

Some amount of physical struggle between children is normal, of course. What's hard is to tell where they cross the line into unacceptable behavior. "They were like puppies, rolling around on the floor and sitting on each other," said one mother of two older boys. "They would yell bloody murder—I just didn't know how much of it was drama for my benefit and when I really needed to intervene." In her family's case, younger brother Joseph took up wrestling in high school in order to gain the edge on Sam, his older brother. "But even now that they're eighteen and twenty-one, Sam still has the psychological edge," she says. "Joey lets Sam win because he'd feel terrible beating his big brother."

In fact, rough-and-tumble physical play can be a way for brothers to express their love for each other. At twenty-four and twenty-two, Andy and Paul still pounce on each other when they go home for Thanksgiving. "There's no one I can play with that way anymore," said Andy. "I hope Paul and I never stop wrestling."

WAR PLAY: GOOD OR BAD?

While many parents and teachers feel strongly against boys playing with toy guns, swords, and other mock instruments of death and destruction, forbidding battle games and toys presents its own dilemmas. For one thing, banning such activities sometimes just makes them more attractive to boys; and of course, adults

(continued)

---

don't supervise every moment of a child's play. Furthermore, boys who want to play with guns and swords will fashion their weapons out of anything at hand, from sticks and soda bottles to food. Don't try to stop aggression in boys by being aggressive yourself about their play.

The fact is, children of both sexes use aggressive play and battle games to work through their own feelings about violence. Make sure games are adventuresome, not hostile. Help boys make the distinction between fantasy play and real hurtfulness.

If a boy is engaged in violent war play, ask yourself:

➤ Are all the children involved in the play safe from physical harm?

➤ Even if it involves battle, does the game call on your boy's imagination and creativity (rather than straight play-acting imitations of TV shows or movies)?

➤ Is your boy using toys with "open-ended" possibilities, where he can decide what to do with them? (*Example:* With a stick he can play at being a knight, a soldier, or a space alien and share his feelings; with toy ninja throwing-stars, he must act as a character would in the ninja TV series.)

➤ Do you know firsthand what images your boy is seeing in the media?

➤ Do you limit the amount of violent action your boy sees in the media?

➤ Do you talk to your boy about violence and its consequences—reality versus fantasy?

If you answered "no" to any of these questions, you may want to reconsider your approach to dealing with violent war play. If you answered "yes" to them all, you're probably doing everything you can do. Don't worry—a boy's love of battle games and action doesn't mean that he's going to grow up into a violent man.

LISTENING TO AN ANGRY BOY

So you've managed to find time to connect with your boy. Maybe you've found a way to do something with him that opens you both up to talking together. Now it's time to really listen to him. But how do you get him to share his feelings? How do you know when he's ready to talk?

When a boy is angry and aggressive, it can be especially hard to listen well to him. Many adults—parents and teachers both—feel threatened by a boy's anger. Rage is a powerful emotion, and society sends us a strong message that masculine rage, especially, is something to be feared and controlled.

But if we want to reconnect with our angry boys, we're going to have to accept their rage. And no matter how scary a boy's anger seems, as long as he is talking about it and expressing it directly without physically hurting you, you are perfectly safe. Only when a boy has to bottle up his anger does the pressure build to the breaking point.

How can we lovingly listen to and accept a boy's anger? The following exercise will help you think of good ways to respond by imagining yourself in your boy's position.

Listen to Me—I'm Angry!

AN EXERCISE FOR PARENTS AND TEACHERS

Imagine yourself in conversation with another adult who is important and close to you—a spouse, significant other, sibling, or parent.

1. You say:
- "I hate my job. I wish I never had to go back."

When the listener says:
- Nothing, but keeps friendly eye contact.

  You feel:
  ___ Like talking more   ___ Like shutting down   ___ I'm not sure

- Nothing, and turns away.

  You feel:
  ___ Like talking more   ___ Like shutting down   ___ I'm not sure

- "You sound like you feel pretty angry."

  You feel:

  ___ Like talking more   ___ Like shutting down   ___ I'm not sure

- "Everybody I know hates their job."

  You feel:

  ___ Like talking more   ___ Like shutting down   ___ I'm not sure

- "Why don't you just quit?"

  You feel:

  ___ Like talking more   ___ Like shutting down   ___ I'm not sure

Which of the above responses would you most like to hear? Put a star next to it. Use this space to explain why.

_____

_____

_____

Which of the responses makes you feel the worst? Put an X next to it. Use this space to explain why.

_____

_____

_____

Did you mark "I'm not sure" for any of the responses? Why?

_____

_____

_____

Can you think of any other responses that would help you feel like talking more?

_____

_____

_____

2. You say:

- "I feel like I have to do everything around here."

When the listener says:

- "That's not true—I don't think you're being fair."

  You feel:

  ___ Like talking more   ___ Like shutting down   ___ I'm not sure

- "Did something happen recently that made you feel that way?"

  You feel:

  ___ Like talking more   ___ Like shutting down   ___ I'm not sure

- "I feel that way, too—it drives me nuts."

  You feel:

  ___ Like talking more   ___ Like shutting down   ___ I'm not sure

- "Nobody's forcing you."

  You feel:

  ___ Like talking more   ___ Like shutting down   ___ I'm not sure

- "That must be really frustrating."

  You feel:

  ___ Like talking more   ___ Like shutting down   ___ I'm not sure

Which of the above responses would you most like to hear? Put a star next to it. Use this space to explain why.

_____

_____

_____

Which of the responses makes you feel the worst? Put an X next to it. Use this space to explain why.

_____

_____

_____

Did you mark "I'm not sure" for any of the responses? Why?

_____

_____

_____

Can you think of any other responses that would help you feel like talking more?

_____

_____

_____

3. **You say:**

- "I hate it when you look at me that way."

When the listener says:

- "What way?"

   You feel:

   ___ Like talking more   ___ Like shutting down   ___ I'm not sure

- "Well, excuse me for living!"

   You feel:

   ___ Like talking more   ___ Like shutting down   ___ I'm not sure

- "You seem pretty upset. Want to go for a walk together?"

   You feel:

   ___ Like talking more   ___ Like shutting down   ___ I'm not sure

- "I won't bother you anymore—I'm going for a walk."

You feel:

___ Like talking more   ___ Like shutting down   ___ I'm not sure

• "I didn't mean to."

You feel:

___ Like talking more   ___ Like shutting down   ___ I'm not sure

Which of the above responses would you most like to hear? Put a star next to it. Use this space to explain why.

_____

_____

_____

Which of the responses makes you feel the worst? Put an X next to it. Use this space to explain why.

_____

_____

_____

Did you mark "I'm not sure" for any of the responses? Why?

_____

_____

_____

Can you think of any other responses that would help you feel like talking more?

_____

_____

_____

Just as some things made you feel more like talking and some less, a boy who is angry will have different responses depending on how you listen and react to him. Remembering the way you feel in similar situations can help.

But even equipped with all these techniques, it can be difficult for parents, teachers, and other adults to listen well when a boy is expressing angry feelings. It's tempting to defend yourself or push away a boy's feelings, but try to stay present and not to shut down—children sense when you're not genuinely listening to them. The following hints may help.

When a boy is very angry at you:

➤ Keep in mind that he wouldn't be so angry if he didn't really care about you and want your love and approval.

➤ Try to stay calm. By listening calmly and openly to his anger, you are forging a path to a closer, more loving relationship.

➤ Try to put aside feelings of guilt and shame, at least for the moment. Remember, you are not a "bad parent" just because you've made him angry or hurt his feelings.

➤ Tell him you're proud of him. It takes a lot of courage for a boy to confront a parent with his anger.

➤ If you feel overwhelmed and need a break, tell him. It's hard work listening to someone's anger. Make clear this "time-out" is for yourself, not him. Set a time to continue the talk later, and then do it.

MAKING IT SAFE

In some cases, especially when there is past history of violent or sexual abuse in the household, very angry boys may not feel safe talking alone with a parent. In these situations it is better to talk in the presence of a neutral third person: a therapist, guidance counselor, member of the clergy, or other trusted adult.

EMPATHIZING WITH ANGER

Suppose you've succeeded in opening up connections with a boy, and even listening well to him. But when he expresses rage—perhaps at you, or perhaps at something over which you have little or no control—what do you do?

Empathy can really be the key to making a boy feel that you're on his side. But when you're faced with an angry boy, adults often feel scared and threatened. In addition, sometimes it's hard to put aside your own feelings of anger, frustration, or guilt so that you can understand what an angry boy may be experiencing, and why.

You don't have to be a trained therapist to break down the wall between you and the boy. It's a matter of showing him that you understand his situation, and that you, too, have experienced the feelings that he is suffering through.

Parents and teachers can invite such exchanges by sharing with the boy various situations that prompted strong feelings, either in themselves or in other people. This works even if the circumstances are quite different, as long as the feelings compare.

"I remember when my older brother left home after he graduated," one mother told her son, watching a TV commercial that showed a happy graduation scene. "I was so mad—it seemed like he was getting everything he wanted while I had to be trapped at home for three more years."

The next exercise will help you explore your own experiences that evoked feelings comparable to those your boy is telling you about. Sharing these stories helps him feel like his own experiences are normal, not shameful. It also provides a powerful model of communicating about sore subjects rather than hiding behind a mask of invulnerability.

I Remember the Time . . .

AN EXERCISE FOR PARENTS AND TEACHERS

This exercise asks you to look back over your younger years and adult life and remember a few times when you, too, felt angry, alone, and scared enough to want to strike out. Don't worry—you don't have to share with your boy every story you remember. But stories like these can help you understand how a wave of powerful feelings could be affecting him.

One time I got in trouble for

_____

I remember feeling

_____

_____

Here's how I acted:

_____

_____

One time when I was really angry in my childhood, I

_____

_____

I was angry because

_____

_____

Here's what an adult did that I liked:

_____

_____

Here's what I hated:

_____

_____

One time I really hurt somebody by

_____

_____

Afterward I felt

_____

_____

One time I felt that nobody was on my side was when

_____

_____

All I could do was

_____

_____

I wished that

_____

_____

Remembering these things may make you feel terrible. And the boy is probably feeling just as bad, which may be why his behavior seems so negative. But if you respond to him not with blame or shame, but by connecting, listening, and empathizing, he'll be able to bear the bad feelings without having to hurt others to ease his own pain.

ONCE YOU'VE BROKEN THROUGH THE MASK

When boys sense that you're "on their side," they often feel an enormous sense of relief. Finally, they can share their feelings without having to feel ashamed. But for some boys, just talking isn't enough. They may need to yell, scream, and hit to rid themselves of built-up tension. Luckily, there are many safe and controlled ways in which boys can use that pent-up energy. Without making a big deal of why, give the boy you care about the chance to do one of them.

How can a boy "blow off steam" in ways that don't hurt anyone?

➤ Have a pillow fight
➤ Go to a sports game and yell for his team
➤ Work out with a punching bag at a gym
➤ Jump on a trampoline
➤ Hit a ball with a bat

- ➤ Go running
- ➤ Chop wood
- ➤ Sing in a gospel choir
- ➤ Go to a rock concert
- ➤ Play drums or electric guitar (something loud)
- ➤ Write in a journal or a letter

Add your ideas here, based on what you know the boy enjoys:

_____

_____

_____

_____

REMINDERS FOR ADULTS ON HANDLING ANGER AND AGGRESSION

A boy can only take so much stress and sadness without having it spill over into anger.

Younger boys often show this by erupting into a "tantrum"—which is actually simply a carrier for other emotions like hurt and frustration. The reason kids have an emotional outburst may seem trivial—they can't watch one more TV show, can't have the toy they see in the store, don't want to finish their peas. But behind it is a flood of overwhelming emotions, genuine and deep, which burst out when we haven't permitted their expression in any other way.

Older boys may lash out at peers with little provocation in the moment. Here again, the boy's aggression is a way of releasing strong pent-up feelings about something deeper that's troubling him. As long as he has no safe setting in which to express those feelings, they will plague him like a physical force he can't control.

"I worry that he's so extreme," one parent said. "It's draining; he wants things to be resolved immediately, and he expresses his feelings so intensely and impulsively." Another said, "Any kind of punishment just escalates the situation."

To punish such behavior only adds to the flood of emotions and intensifies the reaction. Instead, adults can work on enhancing a child's self-esteem and sense of security. This makes him less vulnerable to the feelings of frustration and indignity that made him act aggressively.

"When my boys used to fight with each other for no reason, I used to say, 'You need a spanking,' " one father told us. "They turned out to respond much better when I tried saying in a very serious tone of voice, 'Come here—I'm going to give you a *hug*.' "

We should try whatever works to help the boy release his sad, frustrated, or vulnerable feelings before they build up to the breaking point, when all his body's messages are telling him to strike out in an angry burst.

If we can help our boys identify, recognize, and express those negative feelings, the emotions won't come out so often as anger. They can actually learn to read their own body signals and deal with what's really going on before it spills over into aggression.

When something happens that actually *should* cause anger—for example, a boy's father or mother has left the household—we need to help him learn to express that anger directly in ways that don't get violent. He can learn to use words that connect his feelings with the things that are causing them. And he can also turn to other actions that release physical energy, from hitting a tennis ball or baseball to boxing with a punching bag.

Forming this habit in boyhood will serve him well all his life, as he avoids acts that are impulsively destructive. Adults can help by accepting the anger itself but asking a boy what else he can do to express it, rather than hurting other people.

It's possible, also, that a boy who strikes out is actually depressed, which is quite common in children as well as adults. (At least 5 percent of children under age nineteen in the United States, or about 3.5 million, are clinically depressed, and new research is starting to show those numbers may be much higher.) We think of depression as being a more passive, withdrawn state because that's how it often shows up in girls. But in boys, it's often expressed as anger or irritability. Whether or not you know what's triggering it, it's a good idea to get a psychologist's opinion.

What can a parent do to help a child overwhelmed by strong and difficult feelings? *The single most important thing:* Keep the lines of communication and connection open.

Every family's situation is different, but your boy needs to know that he and his feelings remain important. Understand, empathize, listen.

HANDLING A BOY'S AGGRESSIVE BEHAVIOR: WHAT TO AVOID

Don't unintentionally support a boy's aggressive behavior by identifying it with "masculinity" or saying, "Boys will be boys." If a child acts aggressively in order to obtain some goal—like grabbing another kid's bicycle—and he achieves that goal, it's more likely he will use that strategy again. Delinquent adolescent boys, one study found, had parents who encouraged aggression toward peers even though they discouraged it at home.

Don't model aggressive behavior to your boys. Physically punishing boys for aggressive acts actually reinforces their behavior, exactly the opposite of what you intend. In fact, a history of physical punishment is one predictor of aggression in preadolescents and adolescents. Common sense tells us that it also makes them angrier, perhaps increasing the aggression.

While staying away from physical punishment, don't permit aggressive behavior to continue. Be loving and understanding, but also very clear about what behavior you will and won't accept. Then be lovingly consistent about those expectations as you monitor and supervise the boy's activities.

While making it clear that violent behavior is not acceptable, stay away from shaming a boy if you sense that sadness, hurt, or loss is causing him to lash out. A hug is sometimes more effective than a scolding—it gives him the security, acceptance, and affection he really craves. Remember, it's not the boy who's unacceptable, but the behavior. The boy is still lovable, and in great need.

Boys may hide their feelings of vulnerability and pain behind a stoical mask. But just as with girls, the adults in their lives must take for granted that boys do in fact have those feelings—and remember that they will express them differently at first, often through negative activities.

They may not be talking as easily as girls would, but don't assume that boys can only "blow off steam" by hitting out. Like girls, they need to identify and struggle through their feelings. When eventually they come to say what's really bothering them, they need our acceptance, empathy, and support.

"Three of my son's buddies were in a car accident on Labor Day, and one of them was killed," said Larry, the parent of a seventeen-year-old boy. "He had spent the day with them, and would have been with them if he hadn't changed his plans at the last minute. It helped him that I was there for him through that night and the next day, being available to talk when he felt like it, sometimes just holding him and sharing our sadness. In the months after that, we came back to the subject often. For example, I brought it up when his school reports showed that he wasn't making progress in some subjects. It seemed to me that it might be connected to his grief."

Reading out loud together often evokes shared emotions of sadness or loss. "A particularly moving moment in *The Call of the Wild* had us both hanging on each word," another parent wrote. "Afterward we talked about our feelings and painful things in our lives that the episode brought up."

With younger children, too, deep feelings of fear and sadness about separation from parents may emerge in behavior that looks more like anger. "My seven-year-old son experiences fears that the world will end or other bad things will happen when he goes to sleep," another parent wrote. "He wants to sleep next to our bed in a sleeping bag, and I've decided to let him as long as he needs to. He is so grateful it breaks my heart; I chose to take the softer approach, and it's good."

TIPS FOR TEACHERS: HELPING BOYS MANAGE ANGER

➤ Provide safe settings for boys to vent any negative feelings without shame or fear of humiliation, so these feelings don't build into unmanageable anger.

➤ Establish student-teacher advisory groups that come together for regular support and activities. In facilitating these groups, use action as a way to get boys to reflect on managing anger—for example, by enlisting their help in projects that work against bullying or violence.

(continued)

> ➤ Suggest that your guidance department create an anger-management program based on the ideas in this workbook, to help boys learn to redirect their feelings in safer, more positive ways. Don't treat it as a punishment but as a learning opportunity for all students.
>
> ➤ Teachers and other school people often encounter boys whose expressions of anger are so persistent, defiant, or even explosive that the techniques we have described in these pages do not have enough effect. Sometimes these boys come from homes in which extreme expressions of anger are routine, or where no expression of anger is tolerated at all. In cases like this, professional intervention is often the only helpful course to take.

6

BULLIES AND TROUBLEMAKERS:

AGGRESSIVE BEHAVIOR AT SCHOOL

**TAKING ACTION TO STOP BULLYING • HELPING VICTIMS
TAKE CONTROL • HELPING BULLIES CHANGE
• SCHOOL TROUBLEMAKERS: MEDIATING CONFLICT**

The first year after Tom's divorce and his subsequent move to Houston, his eight-year-old son, Kenny, arrived to spend July with him, and Tom signed him up for lessons at the local swimming pool. "When I went to pick him up on the second day," he said, "Kenny told me he didn't want to go back." At first Tom thought his son was just shy in the strange situation; he urged Kenny to stick it out, and the boy reluctantly complied. "Then he started getting these splitting headaches," Tom said. "The doctor said it was stress, and that made sense—he's away from his mom, and he hasn't made friends yet here."

It wasn't until the next Monday that Tom guessed Kenny's real problem. He arrived at the swimming lesson a few minutes before it ended, hoping to ask the teacher how Kenny was faring. At first he didn't see his son—the teacher was coaching kids on the diving board—but then he noticed a group of boys clustered in a corner of the pool area, laughing. "One of them was pointing at Kenny, who was huddled in a towel," he said. "It was like they were after him somehow."

*In the car going home, Tom asked Kenny about what had been hap-
pening. "It's just this one kid, Travis," Kenny mumbled, obviously uncomfortable. "He goes around pushing kids in when they're not looking." It had
started on the first day, he reluctantly told his father, but the teacher didn't
seem to pay much attention.*

*"I don't know what to do," Tom told his brother on the phone that
night. "Should I tell him to stand up to the bully? Should I interfere with the
situation myself? I remember how scared we used to be of bullies—but I'm
not sure we would have wanted Dad to get involved."*

*"Why don't you tell him to just laugh it off?" his brother suggested.
"He's got to learn to take a joke." But the more Tom thought about it, the
less he wanted to shrug off Kenny's troubles as a normal part of growing up.*

We've talked about angry boys who strike out in aggressive ways. But what
about boys who appear to act "just plain mean," consistently picking on
those who are smaller, weaker, or different in some way? What can a parent,
teacher, or youth worker do to deal with a bully?

We know that teasing and bullying behavior can take place in the
school yard or the backyard, on the streets or on the school bus. It can include physical threats or verbal taunts; it can happen in secret or out in the
open. Experts currently estimate that up to 75 percent of students in our na-
tion's schools are bullied.

The boy who bullies asserts his power by putting down others in every
way he can. He can make his victims' lives into a waking nightmare. The effects can last a lifetime—or even take away a boy's life.

Yet it is astonishing how little we talk about or hear about bullying,
and also that we don't know how to stop it. Many children and adults seem
reluctant to report or even talk about the problem. In fact, the power of the
bully seems to arise partly because so many people fear him—even adults
such as his teachers, parents, and coaches. School people often have no idea
what to do about a bully, whose problems they perceive as being outside
their domain. To make things worse, some adults even model bully behavior by ridiculing or shaming young people in the family, in the classroom, or
on the playing field.

Sometimes bullying behavior takes the form of sexual harassment, and when a boy hears the common put-down "gay" or "fag" in such banter, the hold of the gender straitjacket on his behavior grows painfully tighter. Whether bullying has this sexual element or not, often the line between play and unacceptable behavior becomes blurred. A victim of real bullying is almost always too ashamed to say anything about it to anyone. If the "victim" is laughing and talking about what happened, either in the moment or later, there may be nothing to worry about. Or he may be protecting against the shame of the bullying that occurred.

IS A BOY BEING BULLIED OR TEASED? SOME WARNING SIGNS

A boy who is being bullied or teased may:
- ➤ Show signs of depression (see page 168).
- ➤ Stop talking about school or about a particular class or activity at school.
- ➤ Try to go to school late every day, take alternate walking routes or transportation, miss classes, or miss school entirely (perhaps by getting "sick").
- ➤ Make sudden or radical changes in his group of friends.
- ➤ Appear to have few friends or no friends at all.
- ➤ Become moody or act irritable, aggravated, or frustrated.
- ➤ Act tired, withdrawn, or sullen.
- ➤ Become aggressive with peers, friends, or family.
- ➤ Begin to act like a bully himself, teasing or taunting younger siblings or children.

TAKING ACTION TO STOP BULLYING

Many kids are neither victims nor bullies. When kids are secure enough to stick together and stand up for victims of bullying, they can have an enormous effect on improving the climate of a group. But they need the encouragement and support of adults to break through their fears and do so.

Especially at school, adults can provide this by speaking openly about what they expect if bullying takes place. Make the topic public, not shameful. Play role-taking games, or have older students put on skits for younger ones. Use comic strips about kids, like *Calvin and Hobbes* or *Peanuts,* to initiate discussions about bullying. Let kids know you're aware of the problem and that you support them.

Schools are often most effective in addressing bullying when they openly regard it as a form of harassment and a violation of human rights. By creating a culture that sees it as courageous and even heroic to report or stand up to a bully, they make it safe for youngsters who fear breaking the Boy Code's stricture against "ratting" on another boy.

When a boy is being teased or bullied, his self-esteem will plummet. He may begin to believe that he is "bad," unlikable, or friendless. You can help in several ways:

➤ ***Remind him of what you like about him.*** Praise his strengths, and show him that you love him and want to spend time with him.

➤ ***Stay connected.*** Build an alliance with the boy to resolve the problem, rather than rushing to stop it on your own. Let him know that this is a widespread national problem and that you will work with him to keep him safe and solve the problem together.

➤ ***Help him develop a group of allies.*** Make sure adults at school are aware of the problem and have a plan to step in without shaming the victim or spurring on the bully to more aggressive acts. Help him identify and approach peers who can act as "buddies" to stand with him against the bully.

➤ ***Be cautious about contacting the bully's parents.*** Though it's natural to want to bring them in, it's difficult to predict how the parents of a bully may respond. The best approach is to build a group of allies first. If someone in the group has a relationship with the bully's parents and judges this to be a wise approach, that person might then contact them and ask their help in changing the bully's behavior.

HAVE A PLAN EVERYONE KNOWS

Once bullying is identified, adults need to have a plan that everybody knows about. Make an urgent case in your school and community for a clear, fair, and sensitive antibullying program. When everyone is armed with good strategies for dealing with bullies, kids won't be afraid to stick up for themselves or their friends—even if the bully is a feared adult.

Establishing norms in your school for how to act when bullying takes place is the single most important step to addressing the problem. Create an environment of connection so that every child can talk to at least one adult without fear. Let children know that talking is an act of courage, not cowardice or weakness.

➤ Refuse to stand by without intervening. Interrupt what's going on.
➤ Report the behavior. Rather than a "zero tolerance" policy, make the environment comfortable and safe for kids to report bullying as a violation of their human rights. Respect the anonymity of the victim and the reporter, if they want it.
➤ Distract either the bully or the victim. Reframe the situation so they have something more positive in which to invest themselves.

Write your ideas for how to initiate discussions with kids about bullying:

_____

_____

_____

Are We Doing Everything We Can?

AN ANTIBULLYING CHECKLIST FOR PARENTS AND SCHOOLS

Since bullying pervades a culture both in and out of school, it's important to work on several fronts at once to stop it. Use the following list of questions as a starting point for discussion among parents and school people who want to see positive change take place.

➤ Have we educated ourselves and our community about the reality of bullying here?
➤ Do we talk openly, at home and school, about the ways that the Boy Code harms boys and encourages a climate in which bullying is tolerated?
➤ In the classroom and at home, can we recognize the warning signs that a boy is being teased or bullied?
➤ Do we create safe and shame-free ways for boys to talk when we think they are being teased or bullied?
➤ Do we encourage groups of youngsters and adults to act as allies for a boy who is teased or bullied?
➤ Do our school and community structures encourage mediation in a bullying situation, rather than punitive or "zero tolerance" policies that may inadvertently escalate the behavior?

HELPING VICTIMS TAKE CONTROL

In the case of Kenny at the swimming pool, Tom decided to speak first to the instructor and alert her to the problem. Then he coached his son in possible responses to the swimming-pool bully. Knowing that the situation was upsetting but not physically dangerous, Tom suggested some ways that the boy could respond:

TIPS FOR BOYS WHEN A BULLY PICKS ON YOU

➤ *Recruit other kids to your side.* Create a team of other people who want to stop the bully. Make a deal that if they see him going after someone, they'll act as a group.

➤ *Resist the bully's action when he's picking on someone else.* Say, "Stop it!" in the loudest voice you can. (Tom and Kenny practiced this, with Tom pretending to be Travis. Kenny laughed with embarrassment at first, but by the end of the session he was using his biggest voice to say, "Stop it, Travis!")

➤ *When it happens to you, walk away and do something else.* Go join another group of kids in another area or activity. Don't worry about standing up for yourself. The bully just wants you to look like you're bothered—so don't give him that satisfaction.

➤ *Get a group of kids to report the bully together.* That way no one person looks like a tattletale—you're just breaking the power the bully has over the group.

Tom also talked with Kenny about his own childhood experiences. "I told him how much I wished that another kid would step in and say something," he said. "But I also told him how scared I used to be, and how hard it was for me to stand up to mean kids." It wasn't Kenny's job to act tough in this situation, his father reassured him. "Let's just try to get through it the best we can," he told him.

Tom's instinct to practice these techniques with Kenny was just right. Even if it seems silly, acting out how they'll respond to such situations helps kids more than anything to prepare for the bully's strikes. If possible, get other people involved, too—friends, siblings, and other family members could all take roles and help think of good responses. Aim to take away the shame from being the victim of a bully.

It sometimes helps to have the victim role-play the aggressor's actions. After Kenny played the bathing-suit bully's part, Tom noticed that his son seemed much more confident of his own power to resist.

HELPING BULLIES CHANGE

What makes a boy act like a bully? Like most aggressive boys, he is probably fighting his own strong feelings of sadness, inferiority, or inadequacy. Many bullies are just lonely and desperate for connection. What looks like violent and aggressive behavior can be a masked form of making contact, especially with other children who project the weakness or neediness that the bully himself secretly feels. In fact, recent research shows that many bullies are some of the most sad and depressed boys in the group.

Bullies must be stopped, and told in the clearest terms that their behavior is unacceptable. But in addition, and depending on the hurt or damage inflicted in any particular situation, adults should be asking themselves what *pain* lies behind the bully's action.

Perhaps the most effective intervention, many schools have found, is redirecting the bully's time, energy, and need to feel powerful into a positive setting with a strong connection to at least one adult. Finding a place where a boy is really needed can turn around even the most aggressive bullying behavior. For example, try telling the boy that somebody has been picking on the younger children, and ask him to protect them. With coaching and support from an adult who cares, a boy's role can reverse from aggressor to guardian.

Think of a boy you know who is engaged in bullying behavior. Try to understand the need and pain that might lie behind it. Can you think of a place in your environment where his presence could be genuinely needed or useful? Here are a few suggestions:

➤ Tutoring younger children
➤ Training in water safety or emergency medical techniques
➤ Helping coach a sport or lead an adventure
➤ Peer mediation
➤ Serving the homeless or disabled
➤ Assisting sports coaches
➤ Working with animals

Write any other ideas here:

_____

_____

_____

_____

A boy with a history of bullying needs supervision, but he also needs to know that you trust him to act in a responsible way. Expect the best from him, praise his positive acts whenever they occur, and you may be surprised how quickly he lives up to your higher expectations.

If a bully persists in his behavior after he has been given empathetic help in appropriate ways, he may ultimately need to be moved out of the setting in which he is bullying and into another setting where he can receive support and close supervision. But he should never be abandoned to play out his pain and shame alone. "Zero tolerance" policies too often focus on rejecting the boy himself, not his violent or aggressive behavior.

ASKING THE BULLY FOR HELP: A TEACHER'S STRATEGY

Eleven-year-old Ricky had been a problem on the playground all year. His teacher, Lana, had tried parent conferences, the principal's office, and detention, but nothing seemed to stop his habit of picking on the younger children, dumping them off their swings, and grabbing their hats off their heads.

One day on the playground Lana saw another boy turning over the trash can, and had an inspiration. "Ricky," she called, "I need your help." When the boy came over reluctantly, she said, "I wonder if you can help me out with Alex over there. He'll listen to you—can you get him to stop doing that with the trash and make him pick it up?" Amazed, she watched as Ricky, obviously enjoying his new responsibility, set the situation straight without any bullying in a matter of minutes.

"Since then I've made him my playground monitor," Lana said. "I never would have thought I'd see Ricky watching over the girls' jump-rope games!" Since she started using a more positive approach, she added proudly, Ricky's classroom behavior also improved. "No one ever wanted to work in a group with Ricky before," she said. "Now he's doing fine with the

*other kids—he's even made friends with a girl! And his work is getting bet-
ter, too."*

SCHOOL TROUBLEMAKERS: MEDIATING CONFLICT

If you are a teacher or other adult working with angry or aggressive boys,
you may not always have the opportunity to work through the process of
connecting, listening, and empathizing in as individual a fashion as parents
do. But some schools and youth groups have found that choices they
make—about how to structure their activities, respond to troubling behavior, and support adults in their learning—achieve dramatically more effective results. Ask yourself these questions about your everyday practices:

*Do you know your students well enough to be able to guess when something
else is behind their aggressive behavior? What steps might your school take
to create a more personal context for teachers and students?*

_____

_____

_____

*Does your classroom or group have a regular means to get students to ex-
press and connect with their experiences and feelings in a supportive context? What ideas do you have to begin such a practice?*

_____

_____

_____

*How could you help students learn the skills of conflict resolution as a reg-
ular part of their school day? Some current methods of conflict resolution
work better with boys because they use more active methods, rather than the
largely verbal methods of relating that many girls prefer.*

_____

_____

_____

Do you have a professional context in which you can develop and share new techniques for dealing with aggressive or difficult students?

_____

_____

_____

Is anything about your response to a student's aggression different when it's a boy, not a girl, who's involved?

_____

_____

MEDIATING CONFLICT

Many successful schools routinely address behavior issues using mediation techniques, in which two people work out their interpersonal problem with the help of a neutral third party—a counselor, another teacher, or even a student trained in facilitation techniques. Both parties are asked a series of questions, and then they move to negotiating a solution that both can live with.

Mediation works only if it becomes genuinely integrated into the culture of the school. As an "add-on" to a school's routine punitive routines, it will soon lose power and authenticity. Only when it empowers both students and adults to routinely initiate procedures that solve problems—among students, adults, or students and adults—will it establish a norm of genuine respect that can change the climate of a community.

He's Driving Me Crazy!

AN EXERCISE FOR TEACHERS AND YOUTH WORKERS

Once you learn the technique of mediation, you can apply it to any number of problems that come up among students and adults at school. Try this simple exercise to explore how the technique might play out in a situation you face.

Think of the most disruptive boy in the group you work with. What does he do that creates problems for you?

_____

_____

_____

Now try writing down two or three things you like or appreciate about that student. They don't have to relate to his disruptive behavior; perhaps you appreciate that he struggles with a learning disability, or you like the fact that he sticks up for his friends.

_____

_____

_____

Next, write down two or three things the student does that bother you.

_____

_____

_____

If you were in mediation with this boy, he would also be expressing things he likes and appreciates about you, and the thing you do that is creating or feeding the conflict. Then you each would come up with one thing the other could do that would improve the situation from your perspective. Each of you would be invited to say whether that thing might be possible for you to do, opening up a dialogue on further possibilities.

Do you think this would work? If not, write down three reasons why not.

1. _____

2. _____

3. _____

For each reason, think of a way you could get past that problem to a possible solution.

1. _____

2. _____

3. _____

TIPS FOR ADULTS WHO WORK WITH BOYS

➤ Outside adults can't take the place of caring parents, but a teacher or coach can be there for a boy in crucial ways. Research shows conclusively that if even one person at school knows him well enough to connect in a caring way, his violent behavior will improve observably.

➤ Again, *connecting* makes more sense than striving for tighter *controls* in a situation like this. Schools that create small advisory groups, in which students meet regularly with the same teacher to talk through both academic and nonacademic issues, have found that incidences of conflict decrease across the school.

➤ Though factors outside of school are also behind a boy's aggressive behavior, boys typically take out their sense of confusion and powerlessness by being defiant and difficult at school. The way schools respond to a boy may either help or heighten the problem. All too many schools continually tell boys what to do, how to do it, and how well or badly they've done it, rather than understand, coach, and guide them.

➤ Find ways to work with difficult boys without shaming them. Some schools have found effective ways of mediating boys' conflicts that take advantage of their preference for action over talk. Others bring the family in for a three-way conference, resulting in a contract in which everyone claims ownership to the boy's problem and agrees to specific tasks that will improve things. Restitution can also help boys act responsibly and feel better about themselves after they have hurt others.

(continued)

➤ Adolescents best learn to interact in peaceable ways when they can practice those skills in group activities designed to foster self-confidence, accept differences among people, and resolve conflicts without aggression.
School clubs, church youth groups, Scout groups, and Outward Bound
programs all provide good places to develop such skills.

➤ Children of all ages learn to respect law by helping to make the rules in
their own classrooms, groups, and families, and by helping resolve the
conflicts that come up. Boys have a particular penchant for fairness and
justice. It's well worth creating multiple opportunities to do this in and out
of school. The more they feel that they have a meaningful part in a demo-
cratic school structure, the less time adults will have to spend telling them
what to do.

7

LOSS: HELPING BOYS WITH DEATH
OR DIVORCE

**THE MYTH OF THE STIFF UPPER LIP • HELPING BOYS WHEN
SOMEONE DIES • THE TRAUMA OF DIVORCE**

*Eight-year-old Tyler had spent weekday afternoons with his grandmother
Pearl ever since the age of three, when his single mother returned to work.
When Pearl suffered a massive stroke one afternoon, Tyler called 911 and
rode in the ambulance with her to the hospital. Though Tyler's mother,
Martha, was at her side in the days that followed, Pearl was unable to com-
municate. A week after her stroke, she died.*

*"At first I thought the worst part for Tyler was that he didn't get to say
good-bye," Martha said. "He was always very close with my mother, and
liked to tell me the little ways that he helped her out around her apartment. I
was surprised when he didn't seem to cry much at the funeral, but I thought
maybe he was just too young to understand." A few days later, Martha took
Tyler with her to help sort through her mother's belongings. Halfway through
the morning, she found him huddled up in the bedroom closet, crying.*

*"I should have called the ambulance faster," Tyler sobbed. "I was sup-
posed to be taking care of Grandma!"*

Like girls, boys suffer through all the normal stages of grieving when
they lose someone close to them. But boys may shoulder an additional bur-

den placed on them by the Boy Code. Tyler, for example, felt responsible even at eight years old for being the "man of the house" for his mother and grandmother. Afraid to show his terrible feelings of guilt, shame, fear, and grief, Tyler hid them in his grandmother's closet.

THE MYTH OF THE STIFF UPPER LIP

The Boy Code doesn't let boys express their grief in public, even in the most traumatic of circumstances. The stoic face of Prince Harry after his mother, Princess Diana, died, and three-year-old John F. Kennedy, Jr.'s poignant salute before his father's coffin, were applauded by the press and public as signs of these young boys' strength, and even heroism. But the traditional "stiff upper lip" of manhood keeps boys from dealing with their grief in the natural ways that will eventually heal their pain.

This holds true even more in the case of divorce, where a boy's community may be far less sympathetic to his family's plight. Whereas a boy whose grandmother dies may be excused from school, or given hugs and sympathy from teachers and friends, the boy of divorce often suffers his painful feelings in isolation and silence.

Prevented by the Boy Code from expressing grief naturally and openly, a boy who suffers a loss may act out in any of the following ways:

➤ Instead of crying at a funeral, a young boy may throw a "tantrum" about wearing his suit.
➤ Instead of telling his parents how sad their arguing makes him, he may get into fights at school.
➤ Instead of sharing his fear that his parents' breakup is his fault, he may act hostile toward both parents.
➤ Instead of grieving his mother's death from cancer, he may focus on being unhealthily "perfect" at home or school.
➤ Instead of sharing his grief over his dog's death with his friends, he may avoid his friends altogether.

Has a boy you care about experienced a significant loss in his life? Check all the losses that might apply.

____ Death of a close relative

____ Death of a friend

____ Death of a pet

____ Loss of friends or relatives through moving away

____ Separation of parents

____ Loss of important caregiver (baby-sitter or relative)

____ Loss of a favorite teacher

____ Loss of his familiar home

____ Other (*describe here*)

_____

_____

_____

Did his behavior change after the loss? Check any ways that apply.

____ Increased aggressive behavior

____ Despondent or depressed behavior

____ Increased concern about doing well in school

____ Decreased interest in schoolwork

____ Spending more time with friends

____ Spending more time alone

____ Unpredictable or volatile emotional swings

____ Increased neediness or clinging behavior

____ Other (*describe here*)

_____

_____

_____

Look at your responses to the two lists above. Were any of the losses that you checked off things you hadn't previously considered as issues in his life? Were any of the behaviors you checked off things you hadn't previously linked to a loss in the boy's life? If so, write your thoughts and observations here:

_____

_____

_____

_____

_____

_____

HELPING BOYS WHEN SOMEONE DIES

In the story at the beginning of this chapter, Martha has just realized the many ways in which Tyler needs help working through his emotions about his grandmother's death. Many adults don't know what a boy needs when someone close to him dies—and, of course, every situation is different. However, there are some concrete steps adults can take to ensure that boys get a chance to come to terms with death. By keeping the lines of communication open, adults can stay with their boys throughout the grieving process—and in doing so, strengthen their connections with their boys.

STEP ONE: UNDERSTANDING WHAT HAPPENED

Miles was five when Flip, the family's old collie, got hit by a car. Miles's parents explained to him that Flip was so badly hurt that the veterinarian had to put him to sleep, and that he would never wake up again. The family buried Flip's ashes in the backyard, and Miles, although grief-stricken, seemed to accept the finality of his pet's loss.

"The next week, though," remembered Miles's mother, "we had a terrible time keeping his one-year-old sister down for her afternoon nap. Miles kept coming downstairs with her, saying Molly had 'waked up.' We finally realized that Miles was waking her up himself, because he was worried that 'putting Molly to sleep' meant that she would never wake up—like Flip!"

Whatever a family's beliefs about what happens after someone dies, boys need to understand what death means in a physical sense. Young boys won't understand what adults mean if they say, "Grandpa went away," or "The angels took your baby brother up to heaven." They will understand a clear, concrete description of what happens to a person's body at death.

Instead of saying:

"The vet had to put Flip to sleep."

Try explaining:

"Flip was hurt so badly that his body couldn't work the right way anymore. The vet gave Flip some medicine to make his heart stop, so that Flip would die and not hurt anymore. When your heart stops, your body stops, too—like pulling out the plug on the light. We can remember Flip, but his body is dead now. We're going to bury Flip's ashes in our backyard, so we can keep remembering him."

Although this kind of explicit talk about dying may seem too scary for a young boy, it's actually less frightening than what he can come up with in his imagination. One boy, for example, locked his windows every night and quaked in his bed, terrified that the angels would come for him the way his mother had said they came for his grandfather.

With an older boy, understanding what happened includes knowing medical details about the circumstances surrounding a death. Even a consultation with a doctor is not going too far.

Sometimes this scientific approach can help a boy not only answer his questions, but also approach his emotions:

"Russell had known about his older sister's cystic fibrosis for years," said his ninth-grade biology teacher, Mr. Dempsey. "A few months after the girl died, Russell came to me and said he wanted to do his final project about the disease. I've never seen a student work as hard on anything as he did on that paper. He understood every detail of what had taken his sister's life. After he handed in the paper, I scheduled a special conference about it with him. We started by having a long talk about genetics, but we ended by sitting quietly together and looking at some pictures of his sister."

As an outside adult, Mr. Dempsey played an important role in helping Russell through his grief, in a way that might have been too painful for Russell's parents to handle alone. Friends and teachers can help by offering a boy opportunities to talk about what happened in quiet and safe surroundings.

STEP TWO: EXPERIENCING THE PAIN

Once a boy understands what has happened, he needs support as he goes through what can feel like unendurable pain. Boys may not feel comfortable expressing directly the grief they feel, and instead hide their pain behind aggressive, hostile, or withdrawn behavior. Or they may delay experiencing their feelings altogether, only to have them crop up later when new events echo the old loss.

If boys are to heal the wounds that loss inflicts, they need to have safe places where they can identify and show their feelings. But many boys, even in the safest of places and with the most understanding of listeners, have a very hard time breaking down their internal barriers and letting the tears out.

Sometimes very direct approaches help a boy to cross that line:

➤ *Say good-bye.* The actual word "good-bye," familiar since babyhood, has enormous power to unlock emotions accompanying loss. Have a ritual—a private gathering of family or friends—where everyone, in turn, says, "Good-bye," and then the name of the person who died. Give each person plenty of time to cry, repeat their good-byes, or add other words.

➤ *Laugh together.* Recalling funny things about the person who died can break down emotional tension with laughter, which often leads naturally to tears. Sometimes there's little difference between tears and laughter, and they can combine to yield emotional release.

➤ *Look at pictures.* Sitting quietly with a boy and looking at pictures of the person who died may stir up buried feelings and let them spill forth.

➤ *Link other strong emotions explicitly with his grief.* If he lashes out in anger, say, "I know how hard it's been for you since Dad died." Don't worry if this provokes even more anger. If you stick with your boy through his anger, he'll find the way to his grief.

Do any of the suggestions above seem like things that could work in your boy's situation? Write down your thoughts and ideas here:

_____

_____

_____

_____

GRIEVING TAKES TIME

Remember, no boy can go through all his grief at once. In fact, children especially need to space out their bouts of grief, because they can't tolerate too much at once. Give your boy plenty of chances to cry about his loss:

➤ Stay alert to anniversaries (a week later, a month later, six months or a year later) and mark them with special rituals.

➤ Talk about important "firsts" as they happen: the first trip to the beach without the loved one, or the first day of school.

➤ At family rituals that used to include the loved one, make time for grieving (bedtime, birthdays, churchgoing, or weekly outings of any kind).

When a boy knows he has regular opportunities to express his grief and that it will be accepted without shame, some of the pressure comes off him and he may feel more comfortable opening up.

STEP THREE: THE RITUALS OF REMEMBERING

When a boy faces an important loss, he needs a structure to help him get through what can feel like a chaotic time. Adults can help by creating rituals of remembering, which provide the boy a chance to express his feelings through positive action.

Every month, Gregory and his father stop at the place on the nearby state highway where Gregory's best friend, Andy, died in an accident caused by a drunk driver. The boy's friends and family have put up a marker at the site, and Gregory and his father leave some flowers and sit for a while in their car, remembering Andy and talking about what he would be doing if he had lived.

Terrence's family had to move abruptly after a fire destroyed the apartment house where they had lived for his whole life. A new building is going up in its place, and every Friday after school Terrence and his mother go by the construction site, watching the cranes and cement trucks do their work. They talk about the treasured items they lost in the fire, and compare the new building's design with that of their previous home.

Do any of the following rituals seem like possible ways to help your boy remember and commemorate what he has lost? Check any that you'd like to try, adding your ideas after each that fits your own situation.

___ Make a special box in which the boy can keep objects that remind him of the lost person.

Example: *Terrence could put a small piece from the burned building into his remembrance box.*

How this might work for my boy:

_____

_____

___ Regularly visit a place that your boy associates with the lost person.

Example: *A boy who lost his grandmother could take cookies to her friend in the nursing home where she lived.*

How this might work for my boy:

_____

_____

___ Volunteer for an organization associated with the cause of the loss.

Example: *A boy whose mother died of cancer could participate in a yearly fund-raising walk to support cancer research.*

How this might work for my boy:

_____

_____

Add your own ideas here:

_____

_____

_____

_____

The last step in helping your boy through his loss is to attempt to return his life to normal. This process is much the same whether his loss involves death or his parents' divorce, so we will address it at the end of this chapter, in the section called "Going On with Life After a Divorce or Death."

THE TRAUMA OF DIVORCE

Delia was thirteen and Wilson was nine when their parents' constant fighting finally escalated to a divorce. As their parents spent their savings on battling out the details of the settlement in court, they had little energy and money left for the children's needs. "They seemed to be handling it okay, so I was shocked when I got a phone call from the police," said Annie, the children's mother. "Wilson got caught in a vacant lot on our block setting a fire in a trash can. I guess I'd been relying on Delia too much to keep an eye on Wilson after school—I was just so busy with everything."

Wilson is giving his parents a clear signal that he's in emotional pain. By setting a fire, he's alerting them that they need to pay more attention to his needs, even in the midst of their own turmoil.

Studies have shown that girls tend to suffer in silence through divorce, only to have their painful feelings resurface many years later. Boys, on the other hand, tend to act out either before or during a divorce, making their angry feelings very plain through aggressive and hostile behavior. But such behavior masks a boy's painful feelings of loss and loneliness, and too often leads to punishment. Without an adult's understanding, respect, and help, he may never express his genuine sense of loss.

What can parents and other adults do to help a boy through his parents' divorce? How can parents set aside their own messy feelings in order to attend to those of their boys? How can we read boys' signals well, and take the action they need from us, whether at home or in school?

YOUR FEELINGS ARE NOT HIS FEELINGS

When a loved one dies, everyone in the family experiences similar feelings of grief. The family has many chances to work through their feelings together, and the community supports their efforts by bringing food, expressing sympathy, and joining the family at a funeral.

But in a divorce, the people involved typically experience no such unity. As the parents' marriage breaks up, the whole family feels the shock of fragmentation. A boy whose parents are divorcing feels alone and isolated. Pulled by conflicting loyalties, he needs his parents to stand by him just when they are least able to do it.

The first step to supporting your boy through a divorce is to see how your feelings may be affecting him. The following exercise will help you identify your own feelings about the divorce, and put them in a new perspective.

How I Feel About Divorcing

AN EXERCISE FOR PARENTS

1. Which of the following statements best describes how you feel about getting divorced? (Check all that apply.)

___ I'm relieved not to have to live with my spouse anymore.

___ I'm ashamed that I couldn't make my marriage work.

___ I'm afraid of what people will think of me.

___ I think it's mostly my fault that we're divorcing.

___ I think it's mostly my spouse's fault that we're divorcing.

___ I don't understand why we have to get divorced.

Write some thoughts here about the statements you checked:

_____

_____

_____

If you were thinking about your own parents divorcing instead of yourself, would your answers be different? Explain why or why not.

_____

_____

_____

_____

2. *Which of the following statements best describe how you feel about your own future? (Check all that apply.)*

___ I'm glad to have a chance to start fresh.

___ I feel overwhelmed at having to do everything in the household myself.

___ I'm afraid I'll never have a romantic life again.

___ I'm worried about being able to make enough money on my own.

Write some thoughts here about the statements you checked:

_____

_____

_____

If you were thinking about your own parents divorcing instead of yourself, would your answers be different? Explain why or why not.

_____

_____

_____

_____

3. Which of the following statements best describe how you feel about your ex-spouse? (Check all that apply.)

___ I feel generally amicable and hope we can be friends again when this is over.

___ I feel angry and betrayed.

___ I feel sad and wish we were still together.

___ I'm disappointed that we couldn't work things out after so much effort.

___ I've lost respect for him/her—I can't believe I ever married that person.

Write some thoughts here about the statements you checked:

_____

_____

_____

If you were thinking about your own parents divorcing instead of yourself, would your answers be different? Explain why or why not.

_____

_____

_____

_____

Working through this exercise, you probably noticed significant differences between the way you experience your own divorce and the way you might experience that of your parents.

Think about the feelings you would have experienced, or did experience, as a child, watching your parents get divorced. Which of the following feelings and concerns would you have?

___ Financial worries

___ Shame and anxiety about what other people think of you

___ Guilt that you may have contributed to the breakup

___ Fears about household arrangements changing

___ Grief at losing a parent's presence

___ Disbelief

___ Disappointment

___ Anger at one or both parents

___ Fear for your own future happiness

___ Hope that parents will reunite

What are your thoughts about the differences between a child's and a parent's perspective during a divorce?

_____

_____

_____

_____

What Are the Agendas?

Children and parents often have very different agendas during a divorce. The following table outlines some of the ways that they often differ.

A BOY'S AGENDA	A PARENT'S AGENDA
Preserving home as a safe and warm emotional space	Escaping from a relationship that doesn't work
Keeping the love of both parents	Wanting children to be happy
Keeping parents from fighting with each other	Meeting own emotional needs
Wanting parents to be happy	Meeting family's financial needs
Wanting to maintain familiar economic status	Starting fresh with new and better life

If you are ending a marriage, what is your agenda? Write your thoughts here:

_____

_____

_____

_____

How do you think your boy's agenda might differ from yours?

_____

_____

_____

_____

What do you think your own agenda and your boy's agenda might have in common?

_____

_____

_____

_____

MAKE THE DIFFERENCE CLEAR TO HIM

➤ ***Make sure he knows that the divorce is about the two parents, not about him.*** A boy who senses one parent's anger and resentment toward the other may worry that those feelings will be directed at him, too. Try not to let anger at your ex-spouse "spill over" into your interactions with your boy—and if it does, apologize and explain.

➤ ***Be honest about your feelings, within reasonable limits.*** If you're feeling too sad one day to joke around at dinner like you usually do, don't pretend. Explain that you're feeling blue without going into great detail, and make a plan to spend time with your boy later.

➤ ***Don't ask him to take sides.*** It's normal for the two parents to have very different feelings and agendas. Try not to discuss these issues with your son. Even what seems like harmless complaining about the other parent can feel devastating to him. If he complains about the other parent to you, listen without agreeing or disagreeing.

Jasper was twelve when his parents, Mort and Gerri, told him they'd decided to get a divorce. "I guess I was pretty freaked out," he said, at sixteen. "They always used to fight about whether I could watch TV and stuff—my mom is one of those no-watching-commercials types. So I kind of thought it might have been my fault that they couldn't get along. And in a way it's true—they still can't agree on how I'm doing in school."

Jasper's parents also disagreed over his custody. "That part was awful," he continued. "I mean, I just wanted us all to live together—I didn't want to have to choose. But they kept trying to persuade me how much better it was at each of their places by making these remarks about the other one. In the end they just sent me off to boarding school anyway, so it didn't even matter. Now school is my home, I guess. I don't talk about my family to anyone there, and I try to go away in the summers, too. It's just easier that way."

Reading between the lines of Jasper's account, it's easy to see his conflicting feelings:

➤ He feels guilt, afraid that it was conflict about him that broke up his parents' marriage.
➤ He feels torn by his love for both parents.
➤ He feels angry at both parents for involving him in their disputes.
➤ He feels resentful that they sent him away to school as a way of solving their problems.
➤ He feels vulnerable without a place that feels like home.
➤ He feels anxiety about going to either parent's home, and stirring up more conflict.
➤ He feels shame about his family's situation.
➤ He feels disconnected from his family and from his school community.

Mort and Gerri both care deeply for their son, and desperately want to remain connected to him. That's why they fought about custody. And realizing that the constant disagreement was hard on Jasper, they finally agreed that the best solution would be to remove him from the bitter scene altogether. They thought this would make him happier in the long run, by keeping things more peaceful. But sadly, their strategy backfired and contributed to Jasper's emotional isolation, as well as his physical removal from the scene.

Many boys of divorce share Jasper's feelings in some form or other, though their circumstances may differ. And like Jasper, they often retreat into seeming indifference, burying their pain underneath a stoic exterior.

THE COMMUNITY DOESN'T HELP

When a parent dies, the community may reach out to console a bereaved boy. But divorce usually brings no such comfort; in fact, a boy may sense disapproval and disappointment from his extended family, neighbors, or friends. Ashamed, he avoids talking about his situation, and retreats behind his mask.

"I don't want to tell my friends about how my parents fight," said twelve-year-old Ezra. "They would just think I was being a crybaby, and they wouldn't understand."

A boy of divorce often feels lonely and isolated. Like Ezra, he finds himself caught in a vicious circle: he tells no one about his feelings, afraid they won't understand—but then no one knows how bad he feels, and he feels even more alone.

HOW TO HELP A BOY THROUGH HIS FEELINGS WITHOUT HIS MASK

Every family's case is different, but your boy needs to know that he and his feelings remain important. As in so many other situations, adults can help by staying connected to a boy, listening well for his feelings, and empathizing with his responses. Make safe spaces and special times with your boy, when you have the time and attention to really focus on him. (For more on this, see the sections on listening and talking with boys in the first two chapters of this book.)

This can be very hard in the case of divorce, when parents are often overwhelmed with their own emotions. If you're feeling scared, threatened, or guilty when you hear what your boy says, it's hard to let down your own guard enough to listen and empathize. You may feel the urge to defend yourself or shut down.

Using the following worksheet will help you avoid distancing yourself from your son, as you both work through the problems of co-parenting that your divorce presents.

Working Through the Important Questions

A WORKSHEET FOR DIVORCING PARENTS

Check the questions you want to ask your boy:

___ What do you think happens when two people get divorced?

___ Why do you think your mother/father and I have to get divorced?

___ What have you heard happens to kids when their parents get divorced?

___ Do you know other kids whose parents are divorced?

___ Have you been able to talk with anybody about what's going on?

___ Are there any rules you'd like me and your mother/father to follow as we're getting this divorce?

___ What would be the worst thing for you that might happen because of our divorce?

Add your own questions here:

_____

_____

_____

After you've asked your boy any of these questions, use the following space to make notes on his answers:

_____

_____

_____

_____

_____

_____

Which questions were the hardest for you to ask? Write your thoughts here:

_____

_____

_____

Which answers were the hardest for you to hear? Write your thoughts here:

_____

_____

_____

WATCH FOR TROUBLE

In the turmoil of a divorce, it's sometimes easy for a parent to miss a boy's signs of acute distress, as the following stories illustrate:

Nina was glad that her teenage son, Dominic, had a group of friends to support him emotionally as she and her husband divorced. "He spent pretty much every day after school with his pals, and I was just happy he wasn't home alone," she said. "But then I got a call from the principal. Dominic and his friends had been caught throwing their empty beer cans at passing cars on the road behind the school. It turned out most of their time together was spent drinking and smoking pot. I can't believe I was so blind to it."

Thirteen-year-old Sam routinely responded "I'm fine" when either of his divorcing parents asked how he was doing. "We were so relieved that he seemed all right, we didn't really probe for trouble," said his father, Vincent. "Then his birthday came around, and I offered to take him and his friends to the water-slide park, where I knew they all loved to go. He didn't want to go, and he didn't want to say why. That's when I realized how depressed he was—but it had taken me months to see it."

> *Reassure, but don't deceive.* Give him honest facts about what's going on, and make clear what hasn't been decided yet. Reassure him that both parents still love him and will listen to what he needs.

> *Co-parent consistently.* Reach agreements with your ex-spouse on rules and policies affecting your boy.

> *Try to tolerate and harness his rage.* He needs to be able to express his anger and pain in safe ways. (More on this appears in chapter 5, "Anger and Aggression in Boys.")

> *Hang in there with patience and love when he withdraws.* Don't push him to talk before he's ready, but don't give up on him, either.

> *Lean on other adult loved ones for help.* This not only supports you, but it models for your boy that it's okay to depend on other people.

> *Stress that it's okay to be afraid.* Your boy may feel ashamed of his fear, thinking that it's a sign of weakness. Share some of your fears, where appropriate, and give him openings to communicate his own.

> *If it is possible, maintain the boy's ties with the noncustodial parent.* Keep open the possibility of the boy at some point living with the other parent.

> *If you are a single mother of a boy, don't treat him like "the man of the house."* He needs to know that his place in the family has not changed, and that he doesn't bear responsibility for filling his father's shoes.

> *Teach connection.* Throughout the divorce process, remember to give your boy lots of love and affirmation, even when it seems the hardest.

> *Focus on your shared future.* As his familiar world is falling apart, he needs to know that it won't always be this chaotic. Talk together about your plans and hopes.

Parents need to stay alert to trouble by watching for changes in a boy's behavior. Make sure you know who his friends are, and if possible, what they're up to. Keep in touch with other parents and with his teachers.

And even if he assures you that he's doing fine, don't be too quick to believe him. He may desperately want to talk, but not want to burden you with his problems when he sees how upset you are. Or he might be ashamed to show how vulnerable he feels.

TIPS FOR TEACHERS: EXTRA SUPPORT FOR BOYS OF DIVORCE

➤ Be aware of changes in children of divorce, without expecting that they will exhibit problems.

➤ Stay sensitive to school situations that may particularly affect children of divorce, such as discussions about families or Father's Day card-making. Avoid comments that might make children of divorce feel ashamed or stigmatized, and address any insensitive comments that other students make.

➤ Don't take a boy's hostile outbursts personally. Remember, boys often react at school to situations at home.

➤ Stay in touch with a boy's parents, and talk with them about how the divorce might be affecting the boy's behavior in school.

➤ Find out about the boy's custodial arrangements and the role of the non-custodial parent.

➤ Understand that boys living in single-parent homes may have more trouble affording special activities like class trips and tutoring.

➤ Create a support group through the guidance office for children whose parents are divorced or who come from single-parent families.

GOING ON WITH LIFE AFTER A DIVORCE OR DEATH

It's important for a boy to feel that though his life has changed, it will go on and he can be happy again. Of course this takes time, but adults can help by restoring his routines to normal in many little ways.

After an important loss, one of a boy's most pressing questions is "What's going to happen to me?" Sometimes he won't express this directly, but don't forget that he is worrying about it. Answering this question as directly and promptly as possible will reassure him that the immediate chaos of his loss will not go on forever.

8

RECOGNIZING DEPRESSION

WHY BOYS GET DEPRESSED • SADNESS OR DEPRESSION?
• THE KEY SYMPTOMS • BOYS AND SUICIDE
• TREATING DEPRESSION

"Joey has always been the kid we could count on to be fine," said Miriam, the mother of a sixteen-year-old boy and of a daughter a year younger. "We've taken his sister, Ariel, to a therapist for years now—she started dieting obsessively when she entered high school, and this past year she got into trouble for shoplifting." But Joey did well in school, his mother said. He played on the basketball team, went out with friends, showed a normal interest in girls.

"It was only this past spring when I began picking up signals that made me worry," Miriam said. "He'll never talk about his day anymore when the family has dinner together, and he seems tense and somehow not his old self. I tried to talk to him to find out what's wrong, but he always just says, 'I'm fine,' and his teachers don't seem to have any problems with his schoolwork. One night last week, though, I found him at the kitchen table in the middle of the night. He said he couldn't sleep—but I'm wondering if he could be depressed. I know this might be just an adolescent stage that will just blow over, but how can I tell?"

Miriam is right to wonder if Joey might be depressed. He may appear to be functioning as usual—doing his homework, keeping out of trouble, coming to dinner. But his stoic exterior may conceal emotional pain and even despair that the Boy Code has taught him not to express.

Girls and women may often show their depression by becoming weepy; openly expressing hopelessness, helplessness, and despair; showing dependence on others; or seeking out and then rejecting help from others. But boys and men frequently see behavior like this as an expression of weakness. They hide their depression behind a mask, and find ways to divert their real feelings into other channels.

Conventional diagnoses of depression, unfortunately, rely more on typical female symptoms than they do on the subtle signs of male depression. It is easy to miss depression in a boy—but Miriam has picked up the cues.

WHY BOYS GET DEPRESSED

Boys may be especially susceptible to depression because they have spent so much of their lives hardening themselves against the shame of feeling vulnerable, afraid, or other "unmanly" emotions. Eventually, however, those emotions will force themselves to the surface. Since they must deny their need for help, boys may erupt in anger or aggression. Or, just as likely, they might show up as withdrawal or tiredness, obsessive or risk-taking behavior, moodiness or impulsiveness, academic difficulties or low self-esteem—all of which could be signs of depression in boys.

THE PATH TO DEPRESSION: ONE BOY'S STORY

As they repress their sadness and shame, boys may slip into depression without an outsider even noticing. The following example shows how adults close to a boy recognized the signs in time:

A senior in high school, Ira had been going out with Samantha for almost a year when she blew him off for a popular, more athletic boy. "At first it seemed as if he didn't care that much," his parents told me. "But in the next few months we noticed that he was staying out much later than he used to, and we began to have a feeling that the weekend parties he went to involved drinking or drugs. He would get calls from girls at all hours, and yet it seemed like he wasn't seeing anyone in particular. When we asked him, he would just blow up at us." Despite Ira's resistance, his parents called a school guidance counselor whom they knew he liked, and asked her to explore with Ira whether something was wrong. "She said he was showing symptoms of a serious depression," they said. "Through our health plan, we arranged for six to eight weeks of counseling, and now he seems to be beginning to work it through."

Ira had alert adults in his life who noticed the small signals he gave that all was not well. Without making a big deal of it, these adults provided a safe place for Ira to express the full range of his feelings, not just those that fit the stereotype of strength and success.

Some things that could trigger depression in boys:
- ➤ A romantic breakup
- ➤ Failures in school
- ➤ High pressure or unrealistic expectations from adults (getting into the right college, making perfect grades, excelling in sports)
- ➤ Loss of important friendships
- ➤ Being the victim of ongoing teasing or bullying
- ➤ Trouble at home (divorce, abuse, money problems)

Add your own ideas to the list above:

_____

_____

_____

SADNESS OR DEPRESSION?

It's difficult to tell the difference between sadness and depression in boys. Because society trains boys to hide sadness, it can be very difficult to know when your boy is not doing well. In fact, boys and men can get so good at minimizing or denying their pain and sadness that they often don't even know themselves when they're depressed. They tend to mask their feelings behind an array of behaviors that make depression much harder to recognize than it might be in a girl.

How Boys Cope with Sadness

"I was watching for signs that Leo might not be handling it well in the few months after his dog, Zorro, died," said Maria about her eleven-year-old son. *"But he didn't seem depressed to me—if anything, he was more hyper than usual. He would go out and play pickup basketball on the corner court for hours and hours. When he got home, he was too tired even to eat—he would go into his room and be asleep by nine o'clock. Still, I had to wake him up to get to school on time. And he won't say a word about what's going on with him."* One day, Leo came home with a skinny puppy trailing him at the end of a makeshift leash. *"He's been hanging around the park for two days, starving to death,"* he told his mother. *"I think Zorro would want me to take care of him. Please, Mom, can I keep him?"*

Leo is going through a typical sequence of a boy experiencing sadness:

➤ Ashamed by his "weak" emotions, he won't let himself dwell on or ruminate on his sadness.
➤ He tries to "let go" of his emotions or forget about them, put them aside or eliminate them.
➤ He retreats into privacy to feel his emotions, but won't acknowledge them openly.
➤ He comes up with some action strategy to relieve or resolve his feelings.
➤ He distracts himself with actions, like his basketball marathons, that require full concentration and help discharge his turbulent feelings.

It's easy to understand why boys distract themselves, act hostile, or withdraw when they're feeling sad. Much of this is to protect against the shame they would experience in a society that doesn't let boys show their vulnerable emotions.

Even those of us who don't feel inhibited about crying can't always just let go and cry when we're sad. Instead, we use coping strategies to postpone the full release of our emotions. The following exercise will help you identify the ways you do this. Although it's designed for parents and teachers, older boys may also enjoy completing it.

How Do I Cope with Sadness?

AN EXERCISE FOR PARENTS AND TEACHERS

When I'm overwhelmed with sadness, and I don't want to cry, I sometimes:
(Check all that apply.)
___ Clean the house
___ Get mad and snap at family members
___ Go shopping
___ Cook or bake
___ Eat
___ Drink or use substances (including nicotine)
___ Exercise
___ Watch TV
___ Read
___ Withdraw or "zone out"
___ Take a nap
___ Take a bath or shower
___ Engage in sexual activity
___ Work very intensely
___ Other(s)_____

What do you like about the activities you checked off on the list?

_____

_____

_____

Which of the activities you checked do you wish you didn't do? Why?

_____

_____

_____

Pick the strategy you use most often. How well does it work for you?
____ It makes me feel better while I'm doing it, but later I feel sad again.
____ It takes away my sadness, and I forget about it later.
____ It doesn't really help at all—it just makes me feel worse.

Other thoughts:

_____

_____

There's nothing wrong with having a coping strategy or two, as long as they don't hurt anyone and we acknowledge the real sadness that prompts them. The key is to postpone, not ignore.

One new, nondestructive way I'd like to try postponing my sadness is:

_____

_____

Sadness has to come out somehow, whether it's through simple crying or other expressive activities like talking, singing, writing, making art or music, dancing, or just laughing.

Is there anything that seems to take away your sad feelings altogether? Describe it here:

_____

_____

_____

If you're not sure whether a particular activity is a coping strategy or a genuine release, check any of the following statements that are true for you about the activity:

After I do this activity:
___ I feel lighthearted and energized.
___ I feel as if a burden has been lifted from my shoulders.
___ If other people are involved in the activity, I feel close to those people.
___ My sad feelings are less overwhelming.
___ I feel more "clear" and like I understand things better.
___ I feel relieved and calm.

If you could check any of the statements above, then the activity is probably a good way for you to release your sad feelings. If you couldn't, the activity probably is just postponing the feelings, and you'll need to release them another way.

One way I would like to try releasing sadness that I've never tried before is:

_____

_____

TALK TO YOUR BOY ABOUT COPING WITH SADNESS

You can talk with your boy about the ways you tend to postpone and then release your sadness. You could start by sharing with him some of your answers to this exercise. Did anything surprise you? Did you have any new thoughts about your patterns of dealing with sadness? Talking together about these things might give your boy the opening he needs to acknowledge his own sadness.

WHEN NORMAL SADNESS TURNS INTO DEPRESSION

Though sadness and depression often overlap, there are ways to distinguish between them. The trick is to determine the degree of the symptoms—how *often* the behavior occurs, how *intense* it is, and how *long* it lasts.

He's probably experiencing sadness if he:

    Doesn't want to go to the semiformal after a breakup with a girl

    Won't come to the family gathering after his grandfather's funeral

    Wants to stay home from school for a day after a hard week

He may be depressed if he:

    Loses all interest in social events that he used to enjoy

    Hides alcohol in his room and drinks heavily at every opportunity

    Says he hates school and never wants to go back

As long as you stay connected to your boy, you'll probably be aware of what's going on with him, and whether he's coping well with his feelings. When a boy does need extra attention, remember to:

➤ Create a safe space.

➤ Listen carefully.

➤ Be especially careful not to shame your boy.

    If a depressed boy does not have the sympathetic presence of a caring adult, his normal, action-type coping strategies may become overwhelmed.

Things may be getting worse if he:

    Seems especially restless, impulsive, or unable to focus

    Can't behave appropriately

    Acts irritable or hostile

    Attempts to hurt others

    Takes dangerous risks

    Complains often of headaches, stomachaches, or other ailments

    Withdraws, or becomes sullen or estranged from those close to him

THE KEY SYMPTOMS

Depression is a syndrome with a wide range of behavior and symptoms, on a continuum from mild to extreme. It can appear many different ways in boys—a depressed boy may act sad, anxious, numb, sullen, withdrawn, agitated, aggressive, or full of rage. He may misbehave in school, abuse alcohol or drugs, or just seem glum or in a bad mood. There are also differences between the ways younger and older boys show their depression.

Because a boy's depression can show up in so many different ways, the traditional textbook checklist by which psychiatrists typically diagnose depression does not always prove helpful. The chart in the next exercise, with symptoms based on long clinical experience with boys and men, may be useful for both parents and professionals as they seek to identify the risk of depression in a boy. (Of course, it cannot substitute for the diagnosis of a qualified mental health professional and should not be used in this way.)

Remember, very rarely will a depressed boy exhibit all the symptoms in the following chart. Likewise, he will rarely display just one. More likely, if your boy is depressed you will notice several of these symptoms, and they may range from mild to severe. But as soon as any symptoms show up, it's wise to take steps to help him.

Is My Boy Depressed?

SYMPTOM	FREQUENCY 1—NOT FREQUENT; 2—FAIRLY OFTEN; 3—USUALLY	INTENSITY 1—MILD; 2—QUITE NOTICEABLE; 3—SEVERE	DURATION 1—DAYS; 2—WEEKS; 3—MONTHS
Seems impulsive, unpredictable, or irrational			
Seems "depleted," tired, dispassionate, bored, or sluggish			
Withdraws from relationships and has problems in his friendships			
Seems anxious, fearful, nervous, worried, or tense			
Seems more irritable or has more intense angry outbursts			
Takes dangerous risks or acts with unusual bravado			
Shows new or renewed interest in alcohol or drugs			
Talks about death, dying, or suicide, even in casual or joking references			
Behaves with increased aggression			
Can't concentrate and has sleep problems (either too much or too little)			
Shows physical symptoms such as sudden weight gain or loss, stomach-aches, loss of appetite, or headaches			
Seems excessively critical of himself or perfectionistic			
Experiences academic difficulties			
Becomes obsessed with academic work or sports			
Denies experiencing pain (physical or emotional)			
Avoids the help of others			
Seems unable to cry, even if injured or in middle of emotional trauma			
Interest in sex shows pronounced increase or decrease			
Acts unusually silly or becomes brunt of others' jokes			
Demands autonomy ("Leave me alone") and resists adult authority			

Once you've completed the previous chart, it's time for a little analysis. The following questions will help you understand what the chart is telling you about your boy and where you should go from here.

Count up how many 1s, 2s, and 3s you marked down. Record the number here:

1s:_____   2s:_____   3s:_____

Pick the one symptom you considered to be the most severe, and answer the following questions about it:

When did you first notice this symptom in your boy?

_____

_____

Can you think of any reasons other than depression *that your boy might be acting this way?*

_____

_____

Has anyone else besides you noticed this symptom and spoken with you about it?

_____

_____

Now look back at your count of how many 1s, 2s, and 3s you marked. There's no "cutoff number" that means your boy is depressed. But if you marked several 2s and even one 3 anywhere in the chart, you might want to consider talking with a counselor about the possibility that your boy is suffering from depression.

If you do talk to a professional, the chart and your answers to the above questions will be invaluable information for him or her to see.

BOYS AND SUICIDE

"I was reading through the journals I ask students to write in response to their reading assignments," said Ms. Hancock, a ninth-grade English teacher, *"and something one boy wrote caught my eye. One of the characters in the book had committed suicide, and Will's journal entry focused on that as what he called 'the right choice.' He said how in some situations, life wasn't worth living—that it was better to be dead than to be in really intense pain all the time."* The next morning before class, Ms. Hancock showed the journal entry to the school guidance counselor. *"Do you think we need to call his parents?"* she said. *"I haven't noticed anything else wrong with Will, but I see a hundred and fifty students a day and I might have missed something."*

Ms. Hancock is right to be concerned. The signals that a boy is considering suicide may be very small or subtle, and we should take each one seriously, even if everything turns out to be fine with him. And a boy may be at risk for suicide without anyone having noticed his distress. Gay teenage boys, for example, commit suicide at a disproportionate rate, yet often their struggle with sexual identity is virtually invisible to others.

KNOW THE FACTS

Though girls attempt suicide more than boys, boys are four times more likely to *die* from suicide.

WARNING SIGNS TO WATCH FOR

Does he:

➤ Give away his possessions?

➤ Talk or joke about death, dying, or suicide?

➤ Seem fascinated with morbid subjects?

➤ In letters or school assignments, describe people who commit suicide?

- ➤ Make arrangements for the care or distribution of things he cares about "if anything happens to me"?
- ➤ Start saying good-bye to people as if he might not see them again?
- ➤ Seem either very shaken up by a recent loss of someone important to him, or not appropriately affected by it?
- ➤ Have a close relationship or involvement with someone who has recently attempted or committed suicide?
- ➤ Display any of the warning signs of depression in the chart above in a more extreme form?

If you know a boy who does or says any of these things, or displays any of these signs, don't hesitate to immediately contact anyone who might help— his parents, his teachers, his guidance counselor, his friends, or others who know him. Talk to him, too, and tell him what you have noticed, letting him know specific places he can turn to for confidential help. Don't worry that you will seem interfering, overanxious, or intrusive. You may have saved his life by noticing his distress before it is too late.

WHERE A BOY CAN GET HELP

Most communities have the following resources, or others, to help teenagers in crisis. Fill in the numbers of those you would feel most comfortable working with, and keep them in case of a crisis:

National hotlines: _____

Local crisis centers: _____

Mental health community agencies: _____

Emergency rooms: _____

Church counseling: _____

Twelve-step programs, such as Alateen: _____

TREATING DEPRESSION

Though Henry was diagnosed with a learning disability when he was nine, his school kept him in the mainstream classes, pulling him out for extra help in the resource room each day. But as the district's high-stakes tests approached, his teacher noticed that Henry began to withdraw from classroom activities. "One day I kept him in at recess to finish his homework," she said, "and he put his head down in his arms and wouldn't look up. 'What difference does it make?' I heard him mumble. 'I'm never going to be smart enough.' I can tell he's depressed, but I'm not sure what I can do to help."

Henry's teacher has already helped by staying alert to his feelings and actions. Now is the time for early intervention, to keep Henry from spiraling down into a cycle of depression.

WHAT CAN HENRY'S TEACHER DO TO HELP?

➤ She can reassure Henry, through words and daily actions, that she will help him do well in school.

➤ She can call in his parents and the resource room counselor for a joint conference.

> She or his parents can request that Henry be exempted from these high-stakes tests. (Some districts and states will allow this; others will not.)

> She can set up a session for Henry with a school counselor.

Parents, too, have many questions about what to do once they suspect a boy is suffering from depression. The section that follows addresses some of the most commonly asked questions about depression and its treatment.

QUESTIONS AND ANSWERS ABOUT TREATING DEPRESSION

When should we consult with a therapist?

It's never a bad time to ask for a therapist's help. In today's society, it's more and more common for people to seek guidance on mental health issues, just as they do for other health problems. Though you may choose to keep the treatment a private matter, seeking help for depression does not reflect badly on either you or your boy.

Many health plans pay for a short series of consultations with a mental health professional. Community agencies may also provide intervention and counseling free of charge. If the situation demands long-term treatment, a counselor can help you figure out where to go and how to pay for it. It is important, however, that you seek out a well-trained, appropriately licensed clinician, preferably one who is familiar with the particular symptoms and problems that boys show when they are depressed.

What about medication?

Medications can be a huge benefit to a boy who is mired in the depths of clinical depression. But medicating a boy is rarely enough. A depressed boy also needs therapy with someone who appreciates boys' needs and is sensitive to the shaming culture that boys grow up in.

If your boy is diagnosed with a chemical imbalance that affects his emotional well-being, a combination of therapy and medication may be able to correct it. Other factors may also come into play, such as diet, exercise, stress levels, and family interactions.

If your doctor recommends putting your boy on medication for depression, don't hesitate to get a second opinion. The doctor prescribing the medication should be trained in the specialized field of child or adolescent psychiatry, and be very familiar with the effects of such drugs on younger patients, especially.

Why did this happen to my boy?

There are many factors that may cause or trigger depression. As with other health problems, depression seems to run in some families. But a vulnerability to it can be created at any point—through early deprivation, a lack of healthy, loving relationships, or repeated blows to self-esteem.

Anything from how he's treated at school to the quality of his friendships, his family life, or the emotional support he receives can affect a boy's susceptibility to serious sadness or depression—and his vulnerability to the effects of the Boy Code.

Can his depression be cured?

Adults can't guarantee that a boy will always be happy. But they can offer him strategies that will surely help him through some of his tough times. They can talk honestly with him about how tough and disappointing life sometimes can get. They can share their own emotions without embarrassment or shame. And they can acknowledge the ways in which boys face particular difficulties in today's gender-straitjacketed society.

A combination of loving connections with adults, professional treatment, and medication, if necessary, can help a boy learn to manage his depression even if it comes and goes throughout his life.

Do you have more questions about depression and treatment? Write them down here.

_____

_____

_____

_____

These questions can probably be answered by the school guidance counselor, your doctor, or a trained and licensed mental health professional. In the space below, write down the names and phone numbers of people you think could help you get information about how to help your boy if he suffers from depression.

Name _____   Phone _____

Name _____   Phone _____

Name _____   Phone _____

Name _____   Phone _____

Major national resources

American Psychological Association:
1-800-964-2000; *www.helping.apa.org*
American Psychiatric Association:
1-888-357-7924; *www.psych.org/public_info/*
National Association of Social Workers:
1-800-638-8799; *www.naswdc.org*
Yellow Ribbon Campaign:
1-800-784-2433; *www.yellowribbon.org*
National Suicide Hotline:
1-800-784-2433; *www.suicidehotlines.com*

9

BOYS AND DRUGS

• WHY BOYS USE DRUGS • PREVENTING DRUG ABUSE
• IF YOU FIND OUT YOUR BOY IS USING DRUGS
• WHEN BOYS BECOME ADDICTED

"I was collecting laundry from Trevor's room when I noticed joint-rolling papers on his bedside table," said Susanna, the mother of a sixteen-year-old boy in a suburb of St. Louis. "I didn't feel good about it, but I admit I went looking for more. In the back of his closet was a water pipe, a couple of ounces of pot, and an envelope filled with cash—all evidence that Trevor is not just smoking pot, but selling it to other kids. How could this have happened to a good kid like mine, a boy who's had nothing but the best upbringing from us?"

Susanna has just had her wake-up call: Boys are experimenting with drugs at increasingly younger ages. Parents who think their boy is too young, their neighborhood too safe, or their family too respectable for drugs are asking for trouble.

When it comes to youngsters using harmful substances, a parent's two biggest enemies are ignorance and denial. This chapter will explore the reasons boys turn to drugs and other substances, as well as providing information on the substances they might use. And if you discover your boy is using drugs, it will help you understand what led him to this point and address the situation without damaging your relationship.

You, Your Boy, and Drugs

Your approach to this issue may vary based on the boy's age and prior experience, your own attitudes and experience, or other factors. To get a sense of where you and the boy you care about stand, check the answers that apply on the following items:

As far as I know, the boy

___ Has not yet tried tobacco

___ Has tried tobacco but does not use it now

___ Uses tobacco regularly

As far as I know, the boy

___ Has not yet tried alcohol

___ Has tried alcohol but does not use it now

___ Uses alcohol occasionally in small amounts

___ Uses alcohol regularly or in large amounts

As far as I know, the boy

___ Has not yet tried marijuana

___ Has tried marijuana but does not use it now

___ Uses marijuana occasionally

___ Uses marijuana regularly

As far as I know, the boy

___ Has not yet tried other drugs

___ Has tried other drugs but does not use them now

___ Uses other drugs occasionally

___ Uses other drugs regularly

If the boy uses other drugs,

___ I think he uses_____

___ I don't know what he uses

In my view, tobacco use is acceptable

___ In middle school

___ In high school

___ In college

___ As soon as the law permits it

___ Never

In my view, alcohol use is acceptable

___ In middle school

___ In high school

___ In college

___ As soon as the law permits it

___ Never

In my view, marijuana use is acceptable

___ In middle school

___ In high school

___ In college

___ Never

How much exposure does this boy have in his school and social life to harmful or illegal substances? Write your opinions about this after each of the categories below:

Tobacco: _____

_____

Alcohol: _____

_____

Marijuana: _____

_____

Other drugs (say which, if you know):_____

_____

_____

WHY BOYS USE DRUGS

"My wife, Tory, and I have a cocktail or two after work most days," said Alan, an executive with a consulting firm. "We keep the liquor cabinet stocked, and I guess we didn't notice when our thirteen-year-old, Danny, started to dip into our supply. I'd been thinking he was pretty withdrawn lately, and I was about to say something about it, when we came home last week to find him passed out on the bed in his room. We took him to the emergency room with alcohol poisoning. I guess he had started drinking with another kid in the afternoons—he must have been feeling worse than we ever thought."

Increased involvement in alcohol or drugs is a classic sign of depression in boys, as in men. As a boy experiences the enormous hormonal changes of adolescence, he also feels growing pressure to fulfill the impossible expectations of the Boy Code. Unable to share his pain, he may turn to these substances to stave off overwhelming feelings of despair and inadequacy.

Using substances may feel to him like one way he can escape painful feelings of being different, awkward, or socially unacceptable. Or they can help him avoid conflict about situations he finds intolerable at home or in school. Finally, they can provide a mask of "coolness" to cover the loneliness and isolation he may be feeling.

Some reasons a boy might use harmful substances:

➤ To alter a mood (boredom, despair, etc.)
➤ To see what it's like
➤ To escape a condition such as conflict, stress, or physical pain
➤ To make social interactions more comfortable
➤ To supply sensory pleasure
➤ To show rebellion against authority or reject its values
➤ To imitate an important adult who uses or talks about using substances
➤ To feel accepted or part of a group
➤ To feel older or more mature

- ➤ To establish an identity
- ➤ To perform better in sports or in other performances or projects (amphetamines for studying; steroids for athletes)
- ➤ Out of habit or dependence

Add your own ideas to the list above:

_____

_____

_____

BOYS WATCH WHAT ADULTS DO, NOT WHAT THEY SAY

In the previous story, Danny saw that his parents drank regularly to unwind and feel better after a tough day. They obviously didn't think it was bad to use alcohol that way, and faced with the stress of his own life, he decided to try it, too.

As adults, we need to help our boys learn how to decide for themselves which substances to use and which to reject, and how to use what they use. And in doing so, we must face up to our role as models for the boys we care about.

"The principal called last week and said he was giving Brian in-school suspension for smoking in the rest room," said Tom, the father of a thirteen-year-old boy. "My first reaction was to call the kid on the carpet and yell at him—not just for breaking the school rules, but because smoking is a terrible addiction." But Tom, a smoker himself who has tried to quit half a dozen times, worried about looking hypocritical. "How can I expect him to listen to me?" he asked. "Tobacco's not the worst substance his mother and I have ever tried, either—and I'll bet Brian knows that, too."

As Tom thought over how to talk with his son, he came up with several ideas. For each idea, he worried about problems that might come up with it, and he tried to find ways of dealing with those problems. On the following list he made of his possibilities, fill in the blank spaces with your own ideas of how Tom might proceed, and how those ideas might play out:

1. *How Tom could respond:* He could talk to Brian about why he himself had started smoking in the first place (it looked cool, everyone else did it).

    The problem that could come up: It could reinforce what Brian already thinks about smoking.

    A way to counteract this problem: He could talk with Brian about how bad he feels about smoking and how hard it is to kick—even perhaps bringing Brian to a doctor's appointment to look together at an X ray of Tom's lungs.

2. *How Tom could respond:* Together, father and son could make a deal that Tom would quit smoking if Brian would stop, too.

    The problem that could come up: Tom might not be able to keep his part of the contract.

    A way to counteract this problem: They could agree on what to do if either one of them broke the contract (giving money to a cancer research group for any cigarette smoked, for example).

3. *How Tom could respond:* _____

    _____

    The problem that could come up: _____

    _____

    A way to counteract this problem: _____

    _____

It is virtually impossible to stop an adolescent boy from experimenting with drugs simply by force of adult authority. What he needs far more—just as when you give him guidance about sex—is your trust, support, and information. *If you respond to him not with blame or shame, but by connecting, listening, and empathizing, he'll be able to make it through this difficult period without relying on drugs.*

A boy will notice any hypocrisy or dishonesty in the stance you take. The following exercise will help clarify your own thinking on what substances you use, and how.

What Substances Do I Use?

Think about your own use, now and in the past, of substances that are harmful to health, habit-forming or addictive, or illegal. Use the following chart to make notes for yourself on that use and its frequency or intensity.

SUBSTANCE	HOW OLD I WAS WHEN I BEGAN USING IT	I DON'T USE IT ANYMORE	I STILL USE IT	I HAVE TRIED UNSUCCESSFULLY TO STOP USING IT
Caffeine				
Alcohol				
Nicotine				
Marijuana				
Other _____ _____ _____				

After looking over the chart of your own substance use, write your responses below to these questions:

Do you use any substances that you would not want boys to use? If so, which ones?

_____

_____

_____

Why would you want boys to stay away from them?

_____

_____

_____

How did you feel about talking with your parents or other people in authority about that use?

_____

_____

_____

Would anything have made it easier to talk with them?

_____

_____

_____

Now that you've thought about your own experience, what might you want to say to a boy about his use of harmful or illegal substances?

_____

_____

_____

HOW DRUGS HARM BOYS

The specific effects of particular substances on the brain vary widely, so it is hard to generalize about their dangers. Many substances pose deadly risks when used in combination—cocaine and nicotine, for example, or alcohol and sedatives. And new forms of drugs come along regularly. For example, the new smokable form of methamphetamines (known as "ice" or "glass") is extremely dangerous. "Club drugs" are also increasingly popular among young people. These include ecstasy (or MDMA); "liquid E" (gamma-hydroxybutyrate or GHB); LSD; and "roofies" (Rohypnol), which makes unsuspecting users vulnerable to rape.

In addition to threatening his health, of course, drugs can also pose grave risks to a boy's safety. For example:

- If he gets arrested for possession of drugs, the penalties could devastate his life and leave a permanent blot on his record.
- Buying drugs illegally on the street can put him in settings where he is at risk for other crimes as well.
- Drug dependence is expensive, causing serious money issues in the short and long term.
- Drug use may induce or exacerbate an inclination toward depression or suicide.

ABUSING RITALIN

"My friend Rob's little brother takes Ritalin for ADD," said James, a high-school senior. "One night we had to read this humongous assignment for English class, and Rob had the idea to steal some Ritalin to help us concentrate. It worked, too—it even turned out to be really fun. We ended up reading the whole thing out loud all night, and then talking till seven the next morning. Now we sometimes take some for parties, just for fun."

Many high-school students think Ritalin is harmless because it's prescribed so commonly to little kids. But in fact, this amphetamine can be deadly in combination with alcohol or other drugs and can cause heart damage. If Ritalin is available in your home, treat it with the same caution that you would use with any dangerous substance, and make sure it is dispensed by an adult.

PREVENTING DRUG ABUSE

Prevention is always easier than treatment. These three guidelines will help parents keep their boys away from drug abuse:

Talk about it early. Parents of boys should talk to them about drugs as soon as they enter school. Even little boys can have conversations about how smoking makes people sick, or the danger of taking medicine without the doctor telling you to.

One way I can imagine doing this:

_____

_____

_____

Get others to help. From early adolescence on, teachers, older peers, and trusted adults other than parents can play a major positive role in counseling boys in this area. Identify people you and your boy both trust, and ask them to help.

Some people I might ask to help:

_____

_____

_____

Educate yourself. Your credibility will erode if you rely on all-purpose slogans like "Just Say No" or "Users Are Losers" without knowing exactly what you are talking about.

Some places I might go for information:

_____

_____

_____

WHAT YOU CAN DO WHEN YOUR BOY IS YOUNG

➤ Make sure he has supervised after-school activities, involving yourself whenever possible. Kids who are left unsupervised after school are roughly twice as likely to smoke, drink, or use marijuana, one report has shown.

(continued)

- ➤ Watch what you use. Parental substance abuse appears to have common origins with children's drug use.
- ➤ Stay at home in the evenings as much as possible, sharing activities when you can. When he goes out, make sure you know where he is and who he's with.
- ➤ Help him do well in school, and seek help when he needs it.
- ➤ Teach kids to manage stress in healthy ways, like exercise.
- ➤ Make sure your boy's school and community is equipped to advise students effectively on substance abuse, preferably in peer discussions and activity groups.
- ➤ Get to know the signs for boyhood depression, because depression often accompanies drug use.

THE OLDER BOY AND THE "NATURAL HIGH"

"Some of my friends use drugs, but I think it's kind of dumb," said Doug, outfitted in baggy pants and with three rings through one of his nostrils. "I mean, I feel great every time I spend an afternoon on my skateboard trying to land a new move."

With his baggy clothes and a punk haircut, Doug might look like the kind of boy who hangs out with the drug-using crowd. But his words show that not all kids who look like they're using drugs are choosing that method to make their statement against the establishment. And he makes it pretty clear that a boy can look cool and fit in without doing drugs.

It's a normal human impulse to vary conscious experience in pleasurable ways—to get "high." But to do so, it's not necessary to risk the difficulties, dangers, expense, or potential addiction of drug use. As the following exercise shows, many positive experiences can connect us with such a state:

Ways to Get "High" Without Drugs

Check on the following list any experiences that have made you feel unusually exhilarated, intensely connected with a sensory state, or otherwise "high":

___ Someone praised you or your work.

___ Someone gave you a warm hug.

___ An unexpected check arrived in the mail.

___ You won a sports contest or game.

___ You ran a long distance.

___ You played music alone or with others.

___ You created a piece of art.

___ You went downhill skiing.

___ You immersed yourself in a beautiful natural setting.

___ You won a card game.

___ You kissed someone.

___ You ate a great meal.

___ You meditated or chanted.

___ You did yoga.

___ You went hang gliding or bungee jumping.

Add any others from your own experience:

_____

_____

Based on what you enjoy doing, are there experiences you think might yield the same kind of "natural high" in your boy?

_____

_____

Can you think of ways to make them happen more regularly?

_____

_____

TIPS FOR TEACHERS

➤ In a conversation about substance abuse, the goal should not be to preach, but to correct misinformation.

➤ Encourage boys to question and reflect on what they're doing and connect the dry facts about harmful substances to their own life experiences.

➤ Talk about the latest brain research detailing the chemical changes in the brain when various substances enter the system.

IF YOU FIND OUT YOUR BOY IS USING DRUGS

If you think a boy is struggling with feelings of loneliness, insecurity, or depression, stay alert to signs that he is turning to substances for relief. This means much more than checking his room for cigarette papers or his eyes for dilated pupils. For example, ask yourself:

➤ Has he lost interest in activities he used to find engaging?_____

➤ Does he avoid family meals or outings?_____

➤ Does he come and go for unexplained reasons or at unusual hours?_____

➤ Is he associating with a different group of friends or other people?_____

➤ Has his overall health appeared to change (bloodshot eyes, loss of energy)? _____

➤ Does he seem to need money for unexplained reasons?_____

➤ Is he more aggressive, angry, or irritable than usual?_____

➤ Has he had trouble with the law (accidents, stealing, fights)?_____

If you answered yes to any of these questions, drugs may be part of his problem. But don't panic.

If a boy you care about is using harmful substances, you will want to sit down with him for a good talk. But it won't be easy. The very same things that led him to rebel in this way will also make him reluctant to share his feelings with you in this situation. The more you understand this, the more likely you are to overcome the barrier to communication and have a conversation that helps.

Some reasons that a boy might resent an adult's concern:

➤ He doesn't want you to control him and tell him what to do.
➤ He thinks you are criticizing and judging him as bad.
➤ You might not know all the facts but act as if you do.
➤ You might not be listening to what he has to say.
➤ You might treat him as if he can't be trusted or is less mature or capable than he actually is.

But if you prepare for the conversation thoughtfully, you have a good chance of success. The following steps may help:

Step one: Gather information.
The boy may be afraid to tell you the answers to your questions. Refer to your notes on pages 177 and 178, and then use common sense and observation to write down what you think the answers are to the following questions, and why:

What drug you think the boy is using, and why you think that:

_____

_____

How often you think he is using it, and why you think that:

_____

_____

In what context you think he is using it (at home, at school, at parties, at friends' houses), and why you think that:

_____

_____

What particular dangers this substance poses to the boy, given what you know about his personal goals (for example, alcohol use will interfere with his ability to drive):

_____

_____

Step two: Be open to conversation.

The tone you set in your talk with a boy could make the difference between a productive dialogue and a battle of wills. For example:

Don't start with accusations or criticisms.
Do tell him you are worried about him and why.

Don't assume you know what led him to use harmful substances.
Do share information about what harm the substances can do to him.

Don't assign blame or punishment before he has a chance to think and talk.
Do listen to what he has to say.

Don't withdraw your love and affection, just because he messed up—even if you feel very angry.
Do let him know that you're on his side, and will help him even if he's done something wrong.

Don't evade your own responsibility in modeling safe behavior.
Do help him take responsibility for his behavior and see its consequences.

Step three: Set clear guidelines.

What can you realistically do to promote the boy's good decisions on substance use and protect him from harmful situations? The best route is to come to a mutual agreement on the rules and structures you can both respect. For example:

➤ Keep illegal drugs out of your house.
➤ Don't drink and drive, ever.
➤ Don't attend parties or hang out at someone's house without a responsible adult present.

Consider including yourself in some of these restrictions. Are you willing to give up your own use of harmful substances, for example?

Step four: Provide alternatives.

If a boy is going to avoid using harmful substances, he needs to find acceptable, nonshaming ways to remove himself when the opportunity arises to use them. Some possibilities:

➤ Make yourself available for rides home from dangerous situations, no questions asked.
➤ Help him become involved with other intense experiences—a demanding sports activity, a challenging job, a volunteer activity.
➤ Stay home in the evenings and hang out as a family.
➤ Make other opportunities for relaxation available—playing pool, playing cards, making music.
➤ Help him find friends who don't engage in dangerous activities.

Opening up dialogue with a boy in this area may be very difficult. Use the following space to talk about your fear about the situation:

I'm afraid these steps won't work for our situation because:

_____

_____

I'm afraid this might be all my fault because:

_____

_____

Other fears:

_____

_____

It's not unusual to feel anxious about taking up such issues. But don't let it stop you. The stakes are too high.

WHEN BOYS BECOME ADDICTED

While you may not approve of any kind of drug use, it's important to make a distinction between a boy's *use* of a substance and his *dependency* on it or addiction to it. Some substances—tobacco, crack, or opiates, for instance—are almost impossible to use without getting addicted. Others may not be technically addictive, but a regular user can become dependent on them, organizing life around getting and using them.

Talking about the dangers and coming up with a negotiated approach may work if your boy's drug use is just at the occasional or experimental stage. But if he is truly dependent, a different kind of treatment will be necessary. How can you tell the difference?

Look back on your answers to the list of questions on page 188. As you can see, the signs of substance abuse include not only what you can directly see your boy using but also warning signals in social and emotional realms.

There is no way that a simple test can tell you for certain whether a boy is "just using" or has become dependent or addicted. The answer will vary depending on a range of complex factors, such as his biological predispositions or psychological vulnerabilities. But the following chart might serve as a beginning:

HE'S PROBABLY JUST USING IF HE . . .	HE'S PROBABLY DEPENDENT IF HE . . .
Has a couple of drinks at parties	Frequently drinks in binges or alone
Takes a hit off a joint of marijuana sometimes	Smokes pot every morning when he wakes up, or smokes alone
Experiments with a hallucinogenic drug as an older teenager	Uses LSD frequently or as his only way to have fun

If your boy becomes dependent on drugs:

➤ He needs to admit he has a problem with substance abuse.

➤ He needs to want to recover.

➤ He needs to be open to accepting outside support and help.

➤ He needs to know you love him.

Help is available for addicted boys, whether it is from a doctor, a counselor, a social worker, or a member of the clergy. Use the following space to fill in names and phone numbers for services that will help with any substance use problems your boy is having:

RESOURCES FOR HELPING YOU AND YOUR BOY

Local information:

Police: _____

Fire: _____

Ambulance: _____

Hospital emergency room: _____

Poison control center: _____

Boy-friendly school services:

Guidance counselor: _____

Drug and alcohol counselor: _____

Student assistance program: _____

School nurse: _____

Other: _____

Boy-friendly community services:

Al-Anon/Alateen: _____

Alcoholics Anonymous: _____

Alcohol detoxification center: _____

Drug detoxification center: _____

Counselors and therapists: _____

Treatment programs for drugs and alcohol: _____

Smoking cessation programs: _____

Drug or alcohol hotlines: _____

National hotlines and information centers:
    Al-Anon/Alateen family group headquarters:
    1-212-302-7240
    Mothers Against Drunk Driving (MADD) national office:
    1-214-744-6233
    National Cocaine Hotline:
    1-800-COCAINE (1-800-262-2463)
    National Federation of Parents for Drug-Free Youth:
    1-800-554-KIDS (1-800-554-5437)

National Institute on Drug Abuse:
1-301-443-2403
Parents' Resource Institute for Drug Education:
1-800-241-7946
Students Against Drunk Driving (SADD) national office:
1-508-481-3568

10

YOUNGER BOYS AND SCHOOL:

PRESCHOOL AND ELEMENTARY YEARS

IS YOUR BOY READY FOR SCHOOL? • YOUNGER BOYS IN THE CLASSROOM • THE QUESTION OF "ATTENTION DEFICITS" • HOW DO BOYS LEARN BEST? • READING AND WRITING

When six-year-old Eric brought home his first report card, his teacher had written on the bottom, "See me! Eric's behavior is disrupting the class." Eric was a cyclone of physical energy in class, the teacher said at the conference. He often knew the answers, but he spoke out loudly and interrupted other students; he hated to read, though he knew every computer-game scenario by heart.

Eric's parents knew that he was a bright and enthusiastic boy. But they worried that he wasn't adjusting well to the classroom environment. Did he need another year in kindergarten? Was he in the wrong school or with the wrong teacher? Did he have a learning disability or some psychological disorder?

Many parents have the same questions as their boys start school, and the same issues continue to show up right through high school. In this chapter and the next, we'll address the special challenges that boys face at school: first as younger boys, and then as adolescents.

Much attention has been focused on how schools don't serve girls. But the evidence suggests that our classrooms somehow fail most boys, pressing them into a mold that inhibits their engagement and motivation.

MANY CLASSROOMS DON'T GIVE BOYS WHAT THEY NEED

- ➤ They expect students to sit still and receive information passively, even if they would learn better if they could move around.
- ➤ They don't respect a boy's normal behavioral tempo and rambunctiousness.
- ➤ They rarely connect academic learning to things that matter to students in their own lives.
- ➤ They give teachers so many students that they rarely know their charges well and cannot make caring connections with them.
- ➤ They value a right answer more than the ability to take risks and learn from mistakes.
- ➤ They organize routines and structures to control and contain students, not to make use of their energies.

Although some boys nonetheless rise to the top, the conventions of schooling favor passivity and compliance, traits our culture encourages in females beginning at birth.

SOME WORRISOME FACTS ABOUT BOYS IN SCHOOL

- ➤ Although boys outnumber girls significantly in the top 2 percent of math and science performers, they also clump in disproportionate numbers at the *bottom* of the heap—especially in reading and language arts.
- ➤ Reading readiness and fine motor control for writing develop in boys nine months later, on average, than they do in girls; yet we teach reading and writing at the same age for both.
- ➤ Over two thirds of all special education students are boys.
- ➤ Sixty-seven percent of girls go on to college, while only 58 percent of boys do.
- ➤ Boys are at much higher risk of dropping out.
- ➤ Eighth-grade girls are twice as likely as boys to aspire to careers in management, the professions, or business, according to one study.

➤ While boys may receive more of the teacher's attention in the classroom, that attention often focuses either on keeping them quiet or on rewarding them for "dominant male" behavior as they compete to be noticed.

What can parents and teachers do, from the early years through high school, to counter these prevailing attitudes and trends? How can we make our classrooms and schools "boy-friendly," while also continuing to address the very real equity issues that have historically limited girls in their achievement? The *Real Boys* approach rests on the belief that an "either/or" attitude to gender equity serves no one well.

Instead, parents and teachers can take advantage of the wide spectrum of how children learn to vary the classroom environment and make learning more exciting and engaging for girls *and* boys.

IS YOUR BOY READY FOR SCHOOL?

When a boy has trouble with leaving his parents or caregiver and then acts up in the classroom, many parents wonder if he's "ready" to be in school at all. And in fact, more than a third of our children enter kindergarten not prepared to learn, according to a recent survey by the Carnegie Foundation for the Advancement of Teaching. Because research shows that kids who start school with strong learning skills enjoy greater success throughout their educational experience, what happens in the preschool years clearly makes a big difference to the rest of a child's life.

When parents train their attention on their children's preschool learning needs, however, that doesn't mean they should teach them academic skills. The things that help kids most in getting ready for school success, in fact, are so woven into the everyday life of the family—going to the post office, taking a bath, making a meal—that you may not even realize that you are teaching at all. For boys, it's also important not to push them away prematurely from the closeness of the family, as the Boy Code too often dictates.

But if the classic "three Rs" aren't what parents should be teaching their children, what *are* the basics of readiness? A review of the research reveals that what might be called the "five Cs"—connection, curiosity, creativity, communication, and cooperation—lay the best foundation for the thinking activities that spell success in school.

As long as you have encouraged your boy to express himself, to ask questions, to play imaginatively, to share and cooperate, and to not hit or bite—then he's probably ready to be in a school situation.

HELPING A YOUNG BOY IN SOCIAL SETTINGS

➤ *Introduce at an early age the concept of taking turns.* This will help later on when he enters school. Whenever you can, make it part of something fun—four-year-olds can play simple card games like Go Fish, for example. And model turn-taking in your adult interactions, too.

➤ *Praise him for cooperating.* When your boy helps you on a household task like putting away toys or sorting laundry, praise him specifically for his actions and fairness. ("We got finished a lot quicker because you were working with me!")

➤ *Let your boy choose between several acceptable options.* This is a good way to work on cooperation in areas like getting dressed or going where you need to go. (Does he want to wear the blue socks or the red ones? Should you take the teddy bear or the truck along in the car?)

➤ *Give your boy authoritative, firm guidance.* You can have a warm, supportive relationship without lapsing into "permissiveness." And you can create structure without being a dictator. Your willingness to share decision-making and allow disagreement, spontaneity, and privacy helps your boy build self-esteem and an experience of success.

➤ *Encourage him to think for himself.* Instead of directing your child's behavior ("Put this block here, then that one there"), try asking him to *plan* the task ("How do you want to sort the blocks?").

(continued)

> ➤ *Give direct feedback on his behavior.* When he's frustrated because he can't build the tower, let him know it's not okay to throw the blocks; when he wants someone else's toy, help him learn not to take it without asking. To do well in school, your child will need a grasp of rules and conventions, some ways to control his frustrations, and an ability to accept criticism when it comes his way.

IDENTIFYING THE CHILD-CENTERED, BOY-FRIENDLY SCHOOL

Many educators believe we're on the wrong track when we question a boy's "readiness" for school. That implies, they say, that a school's job is merely to offer a fixed academic curriculum to children whose job is to receive it passively and give it back in the form expected by the system.

We might do better to ask if the *school* is ready for the *boy*—ready to take his curious, active mind and encourage it to explore things further, take chances, test out his guesses, handle frustration, and keep trying.

Before you send your boy to kindergarten, pay a visit to the elementary school he'll be attending. If you can, talk to the principal, to classroom teachers, and to other parents who have children there. Decide for yourself whether this is a place that merely appreciates compliance and passivity or one that values and nurtures children in all their different and challenging styles.

Look in all the classrooms, not just the kindergarten. Do you see evidence of:

Young readers, writers, and mathematical reasoners at work?
___ Books arranged invitingly in the room, easy to take out and put away
___ A variety of books, including ones with action and quest that are not violent
___ Words at work (print on the walls of the room, labeling classroom objects)
___ Graphs, charts, and other math work displayed
___ Materials that children can use to help them understand math concepts

Themes that give depth and unity to classroom studies?

___ Books, charts, student work with a common focus

___ Art projects, cooking, and music related to this focus

___ Large-scale projects that look like they have been going on for days

___ Photographs, art, class books about trips in the neighborhood and city

Children working independently?

___ A place in the room for each child's individual storage

___ Areas where children can work on their own

___ A schedule for the day posted in the room so children know what to expect

___ Supplies stored so that children can get what they need to do their work

Children working cooperatively?

___ A place in the room where the whole class can sit together and talk

___ Tables arranged so groups of children can work together

___ A chart of class jobs

___ Older children helping younger children

___ Children helping each other solve problems

Children making choices?

___ A variety of activities going on at the same time

___ Materials (such as computers) that invite children to explore and find out more

Teachers supporting and extending children's efforts?

___ Children's work displayed attractively on the walls of the room

___ Small groups working with teachers on specific challenges

___ Recognition of boys' unique learning styles and behavioral tempos

___ Folders, notebooks, or other systems to individualize assignments

___ Teachers questioning, encouraging, and praising children

If you can check off most of these elements, you have found a school where your boy will probably thrive.

Parents often wonder whether their little boy has learned enough in kindergarten to move ahead to first grade. Either they think that kindergarten hasn't "taught them enough" to move on to an academic first grade, or they worry that their boy has not developed the social maturity to move into a more demanding classroom.

Don't worry. For the first several years of school, children develop at very different rates, and it makes little sense to keep strict tabs on what they "should know" by the time they finish kindergarten.

The question of social maturity is somewhat more complicated. Does the teacher mistake your boy's energy and exuberance for immaturity? Or does the child need more time in the kindergarten environment before he must begin to conform to the stricter expectations of first grade? Part of the answer depends on what kind of first grade he will be going on to. If the school embraces a more developmental approach to the early grades, he may do just fine even if he seems a little less mature as he ends kindergarten. If not, you might advocate for a more flexible and positive approach that works well for change—or if this is not possible, even consider looking for a school more suited to his needs.

HOW SHOULD WE TEACH KINDERGARTEN BOYS?

Expose them to a rich array of basic knowledge about the everyday world at their fingertips. By doing and observing, talking and listening, and recording what they see—whether it's a turtle in an aquarium or a castle built from blocks—children are actually acquiring the fundamental methods of gaining knowledge.

Let boys "mess around" and ask questions. Through skillfully joining with children in their interests and explorations, the teacher guides them through new challenges that next year will be called "math," "science," and "language arts," but for now are just "play."

YOUNGER BOYS IN THE CLASSROOM

If he is lucky, a boy's kindergarten experience will allow his whole self to shine out in whatever ways feel natural to him. But by the time they reach third or fourth grade, many boys end up being treated more like delinquents than learners with something important to offer in the classroom. They lose interest in their work, stop trying, and give the teacher nothing but trouble.

But the boys who display wild classroom behavior aren't "bad" or doomed to academic failure. They may simply have too much energy for the typical classroom protocols, which are often geared toward adult control, with an emphasis on maintaining silence and passivity among students. Energetic boys quickly grow to resent those protocols and the teacher who enforces them, sensing on some level that their natural qualities are not valued and respected. In addition, when a boy must focus his willpower on taming his natural energies, he has less room for concentrating on what's being taught.

To help you understand better what a very energetic boy may be feeling when he acts unruly and disruptive in class, try the following exercise.

My Body Won't Listen!

AN EXERCISE FOR PARENTS AND TEACHERS

Name some times when you have had to sit still and listen without getting up for at least half an hour. They may be special occasions (a wedding, a graduation ceremony) or more mundane, regular occurrences (a staff meeting, a church service).

_____

_____

Look at your list. Can you remember a time when you had to sit through such an event, even though your body felt extremely uncomfortable? (Terrible back pain? Itchy mosquito bites? Urgent need for the bathroom?

Headache?) Describe how your body felt in as vivid detail as you can re-
member. If it was a headache, which exact part of your head hurt? Where
was the maddening itch?

_____

_____

_____

_____

_____

Now think about what you were supposed to be paying attention to. De-
scribe in detail the content of the service, meeting, lecture, or ceremony—or
as much detail as you can recall.

_____

_____

_____

_____

_____

Looking at your two descriptions above, how much of your attention and
brainpower do you think was focused on your body on that occasion?

____ Less than 10 percent

____ About a third

____ About half

____ About two thirds

____ More than two thirds

Which of the following statements most accurately describes your feelings
about that occasion?

____ I could barely listen to what was being said; I was way too distracted by my
discomfort.

____ I listened to what was said, but I didn't really think much about it.

____ I listened and thought about what was said; it helped distract me from my discomfort.

Would you say that the feeling in your body prevented you from re-membering as much of the event as you otherwise might have? _____

Would you say that the feeling in your body prevented you from enjoy-ing the event as much as you might have? _____

Some very high-energy boys must move around in order to concentrate. If such a boy is forced to sit still, the discomfort he feels can be maddening. While he wants to be "good" to please the teacher, after a while what started out as excess energy can build to terrible frustration and anger. But before kicking a chair becomes overturning a desk, teachers can step in and help.

TIPS FOR TEACHERS

For boys who need to move around a lot, sitting quietly and completing a work-sheet can be torture. But teachers can make it easier if they:

➤ Give a restless boy a physical task or errand (fetch new chalk, pass out pa-pers, erase the blackboard).

➤ Punctuate periods of sitting with easy class stretching and moving exer-cises. (This can be a relief to you, too!)

➤ Have as many recesses as the class needs.

➤ Recognize and praise a restless boy who tries to sit still, even if he doesn't completely succeed.

➤ Model well-directed physical energy in the classroom. Have students help rearrange seats for different class activities. Sing songs as often as you can. Find ways to let students vocalize energetically together.

➤ Allow boys to intellectually "forage," roaming around the room to explore interesting books or activities, as long as they don't disrupt the learning of others.

THE QUESTION OF "ATTENTION DEFICITS"

Millions of children in the United States are classified as "learning disabled." Attention deficit and hyperactivity disorder (commonly known as ADHD or ADD) make up one of the fastest-growing categories of these disabilities. The number of children with this diagnosis doubled from 1990 to 1995, to include more than 2 million school-age youngsters—and four out of five of them are boys. Of the more than 1 million children taking Ritalin, a powerful stimulant medication for ADD, three quarters were boys. Despite these numbers, the medical community still does not agree on exactly how to diagnose and treat this condition—and this very confusion constitutes "a major public health problem," according to a November 1998 panel at the National Institutes of Health.

How many of these boys genuinely have this disorder? Parents and professionals often label very active boys as "hyperactive," for example. Misdiagnosis with ADHD is common; some boys labeled ADHD are actually depressed, while other children are correctly diagnosed but overmedicated. Finally, some boys who do suffer from ADHD never receive that diagnosis at all; instead, adults call them "troublemakers," and punish them instead of treating them.

Given how difficult even medical professionals find the diagnosis, how can a parent or teacher tell whether a boy is simply rambunctious or suffering from ADHD?

The *key difference* between kids with attention deficit disorders and kids who are simply very spirited lies in the fact that often ADD or ADHD kids can't focus even when they want to. The *Real Boys* approach holds that much of the behavior we typically label as "attention deficit disorder" or "hyperactivity" may actually be just the externalization, through action, of boyhood emotions. Some boys who act out and "can't pay attention" may need our empathy, love, and understanding more than they need diagnoses and medication.

If you think a boy might have ADD or ADHD, ask yourself:
Has the boy recently experienced a disruption in his family (a new baby, a death or divorce, a move to a new city or neighborhood, a sickness)?

_____

_____

Have you ever seen the boy focus on any task for at least ten minutes? (If so, note the activity, which may provide clues to his preferred learning style.)

_____

_____

Has the boy been tested for other physical problems (eyesight, hearing, dyslexia, or other learning disabilities)?

_____

_____

Does the boy's classroom provide adequate opportunities for him to move around and use his voice and body in energetic ways?

_____

_____

Bring your answers, and your own questions about your boy's behavior, to a reputable medical, psychological, or educational professional. If possible, find a clinician recommended by someone whose experience and judgment you trust. If your intuition tells you something's wrong with the diagnosis, get a second opinion. If possible, look for professionals with specialized training in this arena—behavioral pediatricians, pediatric neurologists, or child neuropsychologists—who have the expertise and special testing equipment to provide a more definitive diagnosis. Also, talk to other parents about their experiences; they may be able to refer professionals they have found helpful.

IF YOUR SON IS DIAGNOSED WITH ADD OR ADHD, YOU HAVE OPTIONS

Taking medications like Ritalin or antidepressants is not the only choice for children who have been found to have genuine attention deficit disorders. Some parents have found that diet management such as eliminating sugar and/or dairy products can help. Others have tried "psychoeducational" programs or behavior modification programs with success. Again, talking to other parents in similar situations, perhaps through a local or national support group, can be invaluable.

While medication can be a godsend for kids who need it, it can also have serious side effects, including weight loss, headaches, irritability, and changes in mood. Talk with your boy about this, and if you do decide to go with medication, keep a daily log of how he's feeling and responding.

HOW DO BOYS LEARN BEST?

Just like girls, boys do best when schoolwork connects to the things they care about. The best teachers for your boys will know this, and arrange their curricula to take advantage wherever possible of what they know about their students.

➤ Does your boy like to dig for fossils? It's a great entry point to learning about history.

➤ Does he like to build model planes? It can help him learn important principles of meteorology, physics, history, math.

➤ Any interest can be explored through reading. There's no reason kids should be reading *Dick and Jane* rather than delving into the story of how the *Titanic* sank. Many boys are particularly excited by reading books about action, quest, or adventure.

Children also succeed most often in school when the things they are asked to do fit well with their own styles and temperaments, whether those are sensitive and quiet or action-oriented and exploratory. Though generalizations about how boys or girls learn will always contain important flaws, many teachers and researchers notice patterns in what students of different genders prefer to do.

Boys often like playing a well-defined competitive game, with rules and teams. They may like playing math games in the classroom, or acting out the events of the Revolutionary War by taking characters and re-creating campaigns.

For boys who learn best through action, movement, games, or hands-on and sometimes messy or noisy experimentation, the conventions of many classrooms can feel like a prison. And they can stifle a boy's feeling of academic competence and success, leaving marks that endure into adulthood.

To get a sense of how this might feel, in the next exercise you will explore your own preferred ways of learning.

How Do I Like to Learn?

AN EXERCISE FOR PARENTS AND TEACHERS

When I want to tackle a big or difficult book, I like to:
___ Find a quiet place and curl up with the book
___ Listen to it on tape in the car
___ Read it together with a few other people
___ See the film first so I can "get into it" more easily

When my car needs an oil change, I like to:
___ Get out my car maintenance book and follow the directions
___ Fiddle around under the car until I figure it out
___ Take it to the local garage—I'm no mechanic
___ Get a friend to come over and show me how

If I have to make a presentation at work, I like to:
___ Write out a speech and memorize it
___ Write out key points on index cards and speak from them
___ Write out topics for discussion and initiate a dialogue with the audience
___ Create graphs on the computer and use slide projections

When I just have to remember something, I usually:

___ Write it down—otherwise I just forget

___ Picture it vividly in some setting I will remember

___ Use a "word trick" to remember it

___ Sing a little jingle about it to myself

When I need to find an unfamiliar place, I like to:

___ Write down exact directions in words

___ Look at a map and keep it "in my head" as I go

___ Get lost and ask directions from people along the way

___ Figure it out by myself—I don't usually need directions

Looking at the styles you marked, and drawing from any other experiences you may have had, write a brief description of yourself as a learner and thinker. Do you learn better visually or through listening? By yourself or with others? Through asking questions or through trial-and-error? Do you feel most comfortable expressing yourself through speaking, writing, or graphically?

_____

_____

_____

_____

_____

Can you think of one way of learning that you find particularly difficult? (Interpreting a graph? Learning a song? Memorizing a list?)

_____

_____

Have you ever been forced to learn something in that particularly difficult way? Briefly describe the experience.

_____

_____

_____

How did you feel afterward? (Humiliated at having failed? Proud at having "made a go of it"? Delighted at unexpected success?)

_____

_____

_____

How would you feel if you were always *forced to learn in a style that felt foreign or extremely difficult for you?*

_____

_____

_____

Much research has been done on different learning styles and how to teach best to each of them. The Internet abounds with exercises on how to categorize yourself as a learner. In fact, you may learn in many different styles, or change your learning style as you grow older. It's most important just to remember that these different ways of learning exist. Forcing a boy to learn in a style that feels terrible to him—for instance, sitting still and memorizing facts—creates a situation where the boy feels that his teacher is his enemy. This, in turn, may cause a boy to act out in the classroom.

WHAT CAN PARENTS DO TO HELP?

➤ Get to know your son's learning style through game-playing and activities. Does he prefer being read to or reading to himself? Drawing or singing? Building or making things?

➤ Talk to your son about his schoolwork. Ask him to explain things to you. Remind him of topics he's learning in school when they relate to something he's doing.

➤ Have a conference with your son's teacher and ask whether classroom activities are varied to suit different learning styles. Tell the teacher the kinds of activities your son enjoys at home.

(continued)

- ➤ Help your boy keep a journal about his experiences, thoughts, or interests as a way to both improve his learning and gain perspective.
- ➤ Volunteer in your son's school or start a once-a-week after-school workshop in your home for kids. What do you know how to do that boys might find fun and interesting? Short-wave radio broadcasting? Star-gazing? Videotaping and editing? One parent started a "History-Art Workshop" where kids practiced woodworking, painting, and sculpture while learning about different cultures and historical periods where those arts were prominent. Other parents act as coaches for the nationwide "Odyssey of the Mind" competitions.

How Can I Get Boys to Learn?

AN EXERCISE FOR TEACHERS

Many teachers learn in their training how to introduce concepts in their subject areas from several different angles, so that children with different learning styles can all understand them. This same approach can help them out as they work with groups in which some children—often the boys—seem to need a different kind of activity that involves more action, noise, or even competition. This exercise will help you brainstorm ways to take advantage of this predisposition:

Name three topics that you plan to teach in the next few months.

_____

_____

_____

Choose one of the three. What subject-area content do you want your students to have under their belts after you teach this topic? (Times table? Vowel sounds? Telling time? Fractions?)

_____

_____

What skills *do you want them to practice with this topic? (Reading and writing? Oral presentation? Artistic expression? Mathematical problem-solving?)*

_____

_____

Can you imagine a way to teach this topic in which:
Students get out of their seats and move around the room?

_____

_____

Students make something with their hands?

_____

_____

Students use loud voices?

_____

_____

Students play a game with rules?

_____

_____

Students leave the classroom building—even if it's only going to the school yard?

_____

_____

If you wish, repeat the exercise for the other two topics, using a separate sheet of paper.

READING AND WRITING

Because reading unlocks so many other areas of learning, it forms a crucial building block of every child's development. Whether a boy will grow up to be a firefighter or a physician, an architect or a teacher, his success will probably depend, more than any other factor, on his ability to communicate through written language. Even on standardized tests, this link shows up. Every hour of reading each week translates into a half-point increase in achievement test scores, while each hour of watching television decreases scores by a tenth of a point (on tests in which the mean score is 100), according to a recent study by the University of Michigan's Institute for Social Research.

Yet many boys display little interest in reading in their early years. They may be caught up in more active pursuits, or they may gravitate toward computer games, television, or other media. "My son won't read!" many parents worry, wondering how print can compete in a culture in which video images dominate.

Amazingly, the answer may lie not in their son's reading habits but in their *own*—one of the biggest factors that can affect children's success at reading and writing. When parents not only read to their children, but also read themselves, they model reading as an important and pleasurable part of daily life. The following exercise will help you analyze your own reading habits.

Do I Read?

AN EXERCISE FOR PARENTS

*Do you receive one or more daily newspapers?*_____
*Do you receive any periodical magazines?*_____

Does your morning routine include any kind of reading?_____ If so, what? (Cereal boxes count!)

_____

Do you have books in your house?_____ If so, where are they kept?

_____

Have you read them?
___ Only a few   ___ Some   ___ Most   ___ All

Do you read for pleasure in your free time?_____ If so, what? (Books or magazines/newspapers? Fiction or nonfiction?)

_____

_____

Name some "texts" that you must read in order to accomplish a practical task. (Recipes? VCR manuals? Directions to the party?)

_____

_____

When you read, do you usually read alone or with your family in the room?

_____

Do you have a library card?_____ If so, how often do you visit the library? Does your son ever go with you?

_____

_____

When do you read out loud to your boy?
___ Every day; it's part of our routine.
___ Whenever he asks me to.
___ Not often; he'd usually rather do something else.
___ Hardly ever.

Which of the following statements best describes how you feel about reading?

____ I love reading. It is extremely important to me.

____ I like reading, but it's not my favorite thing to do in my spare time.

____ I've never been a big reader—I'd rather do other things.

____ I only like to read about certain kinds of things I'm really interested in.

____ I dislike reading and only do it when I have to.

You don't have to be a voracious reader to model good reading behavior for your children. The key is to find the times when you *do* read, and try to do it in your son's presence. Read out loud every chance you get—and not just bedtime stories. When you're driving together, read out the road signs. When you're cooking, read the recipe. Read your horoscope in the morning paper. *If you make reading a normal part of your own day, your boy will see reading as an important, useful, and even fun activity.*

Remember: Any reading is good reading. It's okay if your son only wants to read comic books or trashy series. If your boy doesn't seem to like books, what about letting him subscribe to a kids' magazine? If he isn't into sitting and turning pages, what about letting him read on the computer? (Some boys find computers "cooler" than books.) You could even help him set up his own e-mail account so you could send each other messages. Or he can send his own stories to be published on one of the many websites for children's writing.

READING AND WRITING AS CONNECTION

The eleven boys and fourteen girls in Mrs. Olsen's first-grade class were all over the map in their abilities and attitudes toward reading. Four children were already reading on their own, and most of the others seemed to be making progress with the "phonemic awareness" system she had been taught to use. But two boys in particular seemed not to respond to any of her techniques. Kenny acted wild, and disrupted class whenever she tried to introduce a new phonetic combination. She knew he couldn't even say the alphabet yet. Tomas was hesitant about speaking English; he sat silently through the lessons, marking nothing on his papers.

"One day I had an inspiration," Mrs. Olsen says. "At the start of the day I handed out a special spiral notebook to every student." For the last ten minutes of every day, she had the children "write the teacher a letter"—in words or pictures—that described "How Today Went for Me." She collected the notebooks, and handed them back the next morning with a short reply in each—even something as simple as "Thank you, Kenny!" with a smiling face drawn next to it.

Mrs. Olsen reasoned that her children needed to start seeing writing and reading as a way to *connect* with other people, not just as a school subject they had to master. "I told them that even if all they wrote was a picture of an unhappy face, it was important to me to know how they felt," she said. "That's all Tomas did for the first week—but then he started putting a T underneath the face, and I would write back to him with 'Tomas' and a heart. I'll never forget the day I opened his notebook and saw a smile and a T-O-M on the page.

"I began to realize that both Tomas and Kenny had been feeling ashamed at what they couldn't yet do," she said. She responded to Kenny's initial angry scribbles encouragingly (one day she wrote, "Kenny was mad!" and a heart) and continued praising him verbally as she handed back the notebooks. ("I love reading your message every day," she would say.) Gradually, she noticed both boys begin to pore over her written responses each morning, and both started to show more interest in the reading lessons. By the end of the year, each boy was on target, reading and writing simple sentences.

Keeping a daily journal or log of things important to boys serves a double purpose—it gives them the message that their feelings matter, and it gives them a crucial tool for expressing them. This technique works equally well for teachers and parents. How can *you* use reading and writing to connect with your boys?

READING AS ADVENTURE

Once a boy reads fairly easily, books let him experience many of the same elements as having an active adventure would. He can explore fantasy worlds or parts of the world he's never been near; he can imagine himself as a sword-wielding hero battling the forces of evil, or a clever sleuth ferreting out a long-hidden secret. He can learn how to build a rocket ship or fly a jet plane. If your boy seems not to like reading, consider the possibility that he just hasn't found the books he likes.

Also, never underestimate the power of reading out loud to a boy. When adults read with boys, they can tackle books together that may seem daunting for a boy to try on his own. Reading out loud allows you to connect with a boy in a powerful way, and can serve as a springboard to talking about issues or feelings in the story that may connect to a boy's real emotional life.

Some great books for middle-school boys to read on their own:

➤ *Harry Potter and the Sorcerer's Stone* (Book 1); *Harry Potter and the Chamber of Secrets* (Book 2); *Harry Potter and the Prisoner of Azkaban* (Book 3); *Harry Potter and the Goblet of Fire* (Book 4). All by J. K. Rowling. Arthur A. Levine Books.

➤ The Earthsea Trilogy: *A Wizard of Earthsea; The Tombs of Atuan; The Farthest Shore.* All by Ursula K. Le Guin, Ruth Robbins (illustrator). Bantam Books.

➤ *Charlie and the Chocolate Factory; Charlie and the Great Glass Elevator; James and the Giant Peach.* All by Roald Dahl. Puffin Books.

➤ *The Dark Is Rising; Greenwitch; Silver on the Tree; The Grey King; Over Sea, Under Stone.* All by Susan Cooper. Aladdin Paperbacks.

➤ *Ender's Game,* by Orson Scott Card. Tor Books.

➤ Chronicles of Narnia: *The Lion, the Witch and the Wardrobe; Prince Caspian; The Voyage of the Dawn Treader; The Silver Chair; The Magician's Nephew; The Horse and His Boy; The Last Battle.* All by C. S. Lewis. HarperCollins.

➤ *Tales of a Fourth Grade Nothing; Superfudge; Fudge-A-Mania.* All by Judy Blume. Yearling Books.

➤ *Bunnicula: A Rabbit-Tale of Mystery,* by Deborah Howe, James Howe, Alan Daniel (illustrator). Aladdin Paperbacks.

➤ *The Adventures of Captain Underpants: An Epic Novel* (and three sequels in the Captain Underpants series), by Dav Pilkey. Scholastic Books.

Some great books to read aloud with a boy:

➤ *The Hobbit; The Lord of the Rings Trilogy.* All by J.R.R. Tolkien. Houghton Mifflin.

➤ *Where the Sidewalk Ends,* by Shel Silverstein. HarperCollins.

➤ *Tom Sawyer,* by Mark Twain. Viking Press.

➤ *The Call of the Wild,* by Jack London. Scribner Classics.

➤ *Bridge to Terabithia,* by Katherine Paterson. Turtleback Books.

- *Tuck Everlasting,* by Natalie Babbitt. Farrar, Straus & Giroux.
- *The Black Stallion,* by Walter Farley. Random House.
- *The Trumpet of the Swan,* by E. B. White. Harper Trophy.
- *Lad: A Dog,* by Albert Payson Terhune. Puffin Books.
- *Watership Down,* by Richard Adams. Avon Books.
- *The Iliad* and *The Odyssey,* in translations for young readers.

IF YOUR BOY DOESN'T READ BECAUSE OF A LEARNING DISABILITY

Three times as many boys as girls struggle with a neurological disorder called dyslexia, which makes it hard to recognize and process words on a page. We don't know what causes dyslexia, though recent research indicates that it could stem from anomalies in the respective functioning of the left and right hemispheres of the brain. We do know that it tends to run in families.

Dyslexia usually becomes apparent in the early school years, when for no apparent reason a child has unusual difficulty learning to read. Often he will read and write words and letters in reversed sequences, or reverse words and letters in his speech. His handwriting may be very hard to read. If your boy has been diagnosed as dyslexic, his school must by law offer him special reading and writing instruction geared toward this disability.

For a boy with dyslexia, the most important thing a parent and teacher can do is *counteract the feelings of shame* he may carry about his disability. He may be embarrassed to read out loud in class, or he may fear that other kids will think he's stupid because he needs special instruction apart from the group.

You can help by speaking about dyslexia openly and naturally with him and with other children, too. Let them know that dyslexia does not show anything about lack of intelligence. (In fact, on tests of nonverbal intelligence, people with dyslexia often perform higher than other people.) Remind them of famous and successful people who have overcome this challenge—Napoléon, Albert Einstein, and Pablo Picasso are just a few. Tell them about Internet sites like "Teens Helping Teens" (*www.ldteens.org*), written by and for kids with dyslexia.

Finally, keep in mind that with your help and a strong support system, the connecting power and adventure of books and written communication can remain open to the dyslexic boy.

HOW CAN I HELP MY DYSLEXIC BOY READ AND WRITE?

➤ Read aloud to him—either in person or via the wonderful array of books on tape available through any public library. Play books on tape when you take long car trips together. This can also provide an important way for him to share and connect with you.

➤ When he wants to write a letter or a story, cheerfully take down what he dictates to you, and read it back to him.

➤ Help him learn to use a computer for writing. He can routinely ask the machine to spell-check for the errors he cannot identify.

Though he may continue to read and spell poorly, the boy with dyslexia will probably be able to read at a functional level by adulthood. But more important, you will have helped him navigate the world of language and literature with joy and confidence—giving him a key to his future that cannot be overestimated.

11

ADOLESCENT BOYS AT SCHOOL

**CHANGES ON EVERY FRONT • BOYS WHO AREN'T DOING
WELL IN SCHOOL • THE BOY-FRIENDLY CLASSROOM
• THE SINGLE-SEX SCHOOLING ALTERNATIVE • HOMEWORK
• SCHOOL OVERLOAD • WHY BOYS DROP OUT**

Keith had always been a spirited child with an enthusiastic nature. But as he entered middle school, he began to be a fixture on the bench in the principal's office. His standardized test scores were as high as ever, but his grades were steadily going downhill, and he refused to do his homework, saying it was "stupid" if he already understood the material. In the eighth grade, his language arts teacher recommended that he be put in the remedial track, while his math teacher wanted him sent to a magnet high school for talented students. Bewildered, Keith's parents asked themselves what kind of schooling could reach the boy they knew had been bright and eager, but who now seemed impossible to motivate.

Keith was a bright and eager boy who seemed to lose all motivation and interest in school as he hit the middle-school years. Around the age of twelve or thirteen, indeed, this pattern begins to show up in a disproportionate number of boys. They stop doing their homework. They goof off in class. They test the limits with authority figures in any way they can. By high school, they may fall so far behind that they risk not being promoted, being slotted into low-level classes, or even dropping out of school altogether.

Alternatively, some older boys experience these years as a steady pressure to excel at everything. They cram their schedules with schoolwork, after-school sports and activities, and paying jobs, and may accumulate so much stress that they lose all sense of balance.

But older boys don't have to fall prey to these conditions. School can offer them a place where their connections become richer and stronger, their strengths are valued, and their voices are heard. The support they find there can bolster their emerging identities, both emotionally and intellectually, in ways that will pay off for years to come.

CHANGES ON EVERY FRONT

Most people experience a series of momentous changes in the years leading up to high school. Their bodies may change rapidly—or not rapidly enough. They may switch schools, leaving the more nurturing elementary school environment for a place of lockers and crowded hallways, more classes and less flexible schedules.

In addition, students must negotiate a daunting array of social changes. Popularity becomes of paramount concern; romance and sexuality enter the picture; and suddenly, looking "cool" is not just desirable, but essential for survival. And while girls may feel more comfortable discussing their problems with one another and with their parents, the Boy Code forces boys to remain silent behind a mask of invulnerability.

With all this to deal with, it's no wonder that boys often seem unmotivated and distracted as they move into middle and high school. To help you understand and relate to what your boy may be experiencing, try the following exercise.

Who Was I in Seventh Grade?

What did you look like in seventh grade? Be specific. How tall were you? What size clothing and shoes did you wear? How much did you weigh? At what stage of puberty were you? Did you wear glasses or braces? What were your skin and hair like?

_____

_____

_____

_____

_____

Name three teachers you had in seventh grade, and the subjects they taught.

_____

_____

_____

Describe one of these classes. Do you remember what material you covered? How a daily lesson went? What the homework was like?

_____

_____

_____

What important lesson did you learn in one of those classes that has stayed with you?

_____

_____

Did you ever really mess up in seventh grade on a test or in an academic class? If so, how did you feel about it?

_____

_____

What were the ramifications of your academic error? (Grounded by your parents? Had to stay after school for extra help?)

_____

_____

Now name three popular students in your seventh-grade class.

_____

_____

_____

Were you ever invited to a birthday (or other) party at one of their houses? If yes, what was it like? Did it have a theme? Were there boys and girls there? What food was served?

_____

_____

_____

What important lesson did you learn from the popular kids that has stuck with you?

_____

_____

Did you ever really mess up in a social situation in the seventh grade? If so, how did you feel about it?

_____

_____

What were the ramifications of your social error?

_____

_____

Whose approval do you think was most important to you in seventh grade?

____ Your teachers

____ Your parents

____ Other students

If you lacked the approval and support of one or more of these three groups, how did you cope?

_____

_____

_____

Rate the following things in terms of their importance to you in the seventh grade. (Put a "1" next to the most important, and so on.)

___ What you were learning in school

___ Your grades

___ Your physical appearance

___ Competitive sports

___ Other extracurricular activities

___ Your same-sex friendships and social interactions

___ The approval of peers of the opposite sex

Can you think of a person whose support helped you get through the seventh grade? (A special teacher or coach? A guidance counselor? A grandparent, parent, or sibling? An older student?) What was the nature of this person's support?

_____

_____

_____

_____

As this exercise probably reminded you, the turmoil of adolescence can be a major distraction from academics. At this time of life, students' attention focuses chiefly on their own developing bodies and identities. Academic learning will have a far better chance of making it onto their agenda if it does so in a way that directly connects with those primary concerns.

BOYS WHO AREN'T DOING WELL IN SCHOOL

Sometimes it's hard for parents to even know when their boy is having trouble in school. Interesting new research has shown that boys tend to exaggerate their successes, bragging even when they are really struggling. Ashamed to reveal any weakness because of the Boy Code, they hide from friends and parents behind a shield of bravado.

When the boy who told you he was doing just fine brings home a report card full of low marks, remember how fragile he may be feeling inside. The exercise that follows will help you explore the complex set of circumstances that accompanies the simple word "fail."

How Have I "Failed"?

Think about the work you do. Write a brief description of your responsibilities. What must you produce? What kinds of duties do you have from day to day? (Full-time parents should consider parenting their work.)

_____

_____

_____

_____

To whom are you accountable in your work? Who judges what you do?

_____

_____

Can you remember a time when you failed to fulfill your responsibilities? Describe the situation. What caused your lapse?

_____

_____

_____

_____

How did the people to whom you're accountable find out about your failure? Did you tell them or was it "discovered"?

_____

_____

What was their reaction? How did it make you feel?

_____

_____

_____

_____

What happened afterward? Were there long-term consequences? Did you get another chance?

_____

_____

_____

_____

Looking back, what do you think were the underlying factors that led you to fail that time?

_____

_____

_____

Now think about a boy you care about who's doing poorly or "failing" in some way at school, and ask yourself the following five questions.

1. *How do you know your boy is "failing" (progress reports, report cards, call from the teacher, boy tells you)?*

_____

_____

2. *Who else knows the boy is "failing"? How public is the knowledge?*

_____

_____

3. *What's at stake if he does poorly? (Promotion to next grade, college admission, tracking to more challenging classes, social labeling?)*

_____

_____

4. *Who cares about this boy's success or failure? How dependent is he on those people and their approval?*

_____

_____

5. Will this boy get another chance to succeed in this area?

_____

_____

Those five answers would make a good starting point for a three-way conference among parents, teachers, and the struggling student. When the conference takes place, keep in mind how much a boy's feeling of shame affects his ability to talk openly about these issues.

WHAT ELSE MIGHT BE MAKING HIM FAIL?

As you try to understand why a boy is doing poorly in school, don't jump to conclusions—either about the boy or the school. Ask yourself what else is going on in his life. His struggle may derive from a number of other sources:

➤ He may have emotional problems outside of school (trouble in the family, struggle with stereotypes about his racial/economic/ethnic/religious background, substance abuse, sexual identity).

➤ He may be under too much pressure in other areas (sports, job, girlfriend).

➤ He may be suffering from undue stresses in his school environment (his embarrassment at poor reading skills, worry about achievement, shame about not being smart enough, fear of asking for help).

➤ His learning style may not match up well with the instructional methods used in his classes.

➤ His pace of learning may go against the tempo of the curriculum (either faster or slower).

➤ His teachers may be conveying low expectations for his learning.

In a safe emotional setting, free of blame and judgment—a "shame-free zone"—some trusted adult should explore these possibilities with the boy. Any action aimed at improving the boy's success in school must take account of such circumstances if it is to work.

TIPS FOR TEACHERS WHEN A BOY IS DOING POORLY

➤ **Advisory groups can serve as an important support for academic growth.** At key transition points (the end of eighth grade, the beginning of high school, approaching graduation) they can provide a place to coach students on what lies ahead and how they need to prepare for it.

➤ **Have students show their abilities by collecting their work in portfolios.** Many students do better with this kind of assessment than on standard (or standardized) tests. Even if your school does not formally support portfolio assessment, a classroom teacher can ask students to put in one folder several samples of work showing their progress. They can reflect in writing on why one piece is a "personal best" and how they can do better on another. Finally, they can present the portfolios to their families in a conference.

➤ **Connect academic outcomes to a project in the community.** This kind of "action learning" often brings interest and motivation to students who turn off to traditional book learning and reconnects them to the educational task. Ask them to interview World War II veterans instead of testing them on battles and dates. Get them to make and distribute a brochure explaining sources of water pollution in their neighborhood. Pick projects that matter and make sure students get plenty of public credit for their work.

➤ **Institute a network of peer support that connects students and allows them to talk through personal problems.** Aside from "red flag" situations involving abuse, suicide, or the like, such information should be held in strict confidence; students should learn simply to listen supportively, to help others sort out issues and come to their own conclusions, and to refer their peers when necessary to the appropriate professional help. A side benefit is the opportunity for students to gain perspective on others' feelings, and for boys and girls to interact as friends.

➤ **Organize special events or a buddy system for students who are new to the school.** A buddy system pairing older and younger students can also help students who are struggling socially or academically.

(continued)

> ➤ **Invite guest speakers to talk about life issues that students face (substance abuse, sexual harassment, homophobia).** Follow any lecture with small discussion groups, separated by gender if appropriate.

THE BOY-FRIENDLY CLASSROOM

Teachers who are most successful with their boy students have often taken steps to "guy-ify" their classrooms, while making sure that the conditions that enhance girls' learning also remain present. They've turned away from the notion that good students are passive and compliant, and instead, they've turned the energy, drive, and high spirits of boys into learning opportunities for everyone.

The following exercise will help you analyze your boy's learning situation, and decide whether his school is boy-friendly enough for him.

Is School Giving My Boy What He Needs?

AN EXERCISE FOR PARENTS AND TEACHERS

Think back to a time you learned something that has really stuck with you (how to drive a stick shift, give a speech, identify a constellation). Who taught it to you, and where? Describe the situation and what you learned.

_____

_____

_____

_____

What made that learning experience positive? For each of the statements below, circle a T for true or an F for false.

T   F   I liked the person teaching me, and felt that he or she liked me.

T   F   I made mistakes before I got it right.

T F What I was learning mattered to me.

T F What I was learning mattered to the teacher.

T F What I was learning had importance to some audience outside school.

T F I got to move around if I wanted to while I was learning.

T F I got to talk a lot while I was learning.

T F I got to show off what I had learned in a way that was fun for me.

Is your boy having problems at school? If so, describe the problem or problems.

_____

_____

_____

_____

Do you think the statements in the True/False exercise above would apply to your boy's school experience? Why or why not?

_____

_____

_____

THE SINGLE-SEX SCHOOLING ALTERNATIVE

Much research in recent years has explored the question of whether girls do better in single-sex classrooms and schools. It has been widely reported that private girls' schools bolster girls' academic achievement, empowering them to feel more confident about who they are and what they're capable of.

But the question of whether boys, too, have greater success in single-sex environments provokes a flurry of controversy, sometimes even before their results can be examined. Because all-boy institutions educate the so-called dominant sex, people tend to think of them as dangerous, toxic breeding grounds of misogyny and aggression. And the federal courts have rejected some efforts to create all-boy academies for African-American students as unconstitutional "separate but equal" arrangements.

Private schools can make decisions about single-sex instruction based on educational philosophy. But most public-school teachers don't think they have the power to separate girls and boys without causing a major furor in the school community. Even instituting separate math classes for eighth-grade boys and girls would probably entail complicated schedule changes, and few school boards will support an action that might land them in court.

But these obstacles shouldn't stop you from trying in other ways to see if your students will learn better when separated by gender. Here are some ways you might go about it:

➤ Create separate in-class groups of boys and girls that meet in separate areas (the hallway, a "breakout room," even outside). Move between the groups and give them responsibility for monitoring themselves as well.

➤ Start a class taught by a team of one male and one female teacher. During the course, separate out students by gender and later bring them together again. Observe and document—using various assessment methods, including interviewing the students and teachers—any differences in learning style, emotional climate, and academic outcomes.

➤ Form a team with four or five teachers who see the same group of up to one hundred students in the course of a week. Work creatively to arrange flexible class groupings that can sometimes include single-sex groups.

➤ Start a single-sex academic support group after school. Even if it meets just once a week for half an hour, it can help you see if the boys do better on their own.

HOMEWORK

Perhaps no other school issue causes as much trouble in a boy's world as homework. He doesn't want to do it, or he has too much of it, or he doesn't understand it, or he doesn't have time for it. When homework doesn't get done, teachers blame parents, parents blame schools, and everybody blames the boy. No wonder so many boys approach their homework with at worst, dread, and at best, annoyance.

But homework doesn't have to be a source of continual strife. Homework can provide a window for parents into their boy's life at school, and a way for the teacher to get to know a boy's particular needs and strengths.

So what do you do when you find out your boy isn't doing his homework? Before you overreact, take the time to look at the situation carefully and analyze what's going on. The next exercise will help you do this.

My Boy Just Won't Do His Homework!

AN EXERCISE FOR PARENTS

What subjects does your boy have homework in?

_____

_____

Does he actually do his homework in any of these subjects? If so, which? If he does some, but not enough, of the homework in a subject, note that, too.

_____

_____

Are there subjects in which he hardly ever does any of the homework? What are they?

_____

_____

Describe a homework assignment that he hasn't done.

_____

_____

_____

_____

Can you tell what the purpose and meaning of this assignment is? Why do you think the teacher wants this assignment done?

_____

_____

Which of the following reasons does your boy give for not doing his homework? Check all that apply.

___ There's too much in each subject, so something has to go.

___ There's no time, given all the other commitments he has (sports, clubs, work, family responsibilities, lessons).

___ The teacher never checks the homework anyway.

___ Doing the homework isn't necessary for full participation in the class.

___ The homework is trivial and boring.

___ The homework is too hard, and he gives up.

___ He sits still and works all day in school; why should he have to do it at home, too?

When adults take the time to look carefully at what homework is given and why, they may realize that some assignments don't fulfill any important function and could be eliminated altogether. But good teachers use homework for several important reasons, and parents should do everything they can to support them.

A Few Good Reasons Why Teachers Give Homework

➤ A good homework assignment prepares the boy to learn well in the next class. *Example:* Read a short story that the group will discuss the next day.

➤ A good homework assignment underscores and sets into place skills and material the boy needs to know well, but which isn't suited to classroom teaching and learning. *Example:* Memorize a Spanish vocabulary list.

➤ A good homework assignment asks the boy to practice or demonstrate a skill learned in class, so that the teacher can see where the student needs more support. *Example:* Solve three difficult math problems.

➤ A good homework assignment asks the boy to brainstorm and think creatively on his own, to attempt to solve a problem that hasn't yet been addressed in class. *Example:* Design a paper airplane that flies in a loop, and try to explain why it works.

➤ A good homework assignment may involve sustained solo work like writing. *Example:* Write a one-page response to the class discussion that day.

➤ A good homework assignment may use resources that exist at home, but not at school. *Example:* Interview an elderly person about the Depression era.

If his homework exhibits any of these qualities, do everything you can to help your boy get it done in time. Have him do his homework in an environment free from distractions, but with people there to help if he needs it. (Could he come to your office after school and work alongside you? Could you make an agreement with another parent to supervise a homework period for two or more boys?)

SCHOOL OVERLOAD

Sometimes, however, a boy really does have too much homework—or the homework doesn't seem to have any purpose other than to keep him busy. If you feel a boy has too much work—for example, if he's staying up most of the night to do it and falling asleep in school—you need to step in and help. A boy who wants to do well in school may feel powerless against the system. You can be an important ally and at the same time show your empathy and respect for his emotional and physical health, including his need for other forms of activity.

If a boy you care about has too much homework:
➤ Confer with his teachers. Agree on how much time you can realistically expect him to work on his homework before it's okay for him to stop. Make a commitment to monitor his homework time so you know he's really tried.

➤ Ask yourself if you're contributing to his stress by expecting him to excel in too many different areas at once.

➤ Let him stay home from school for a day to catch up—and maybe take the day off work yourself to help him and talk about it.

➤ Help him organize his time. Have him prioritize his obligations—sports, work, extracurricular activities, family chores, homework.

➤ Ask him what you can do to make things easier. Make his lunch so he can sleep fifteen minutes later in the morning? Drill him on vocabulary in the car?

Remember, it's not the end of the world if your boy can't get everything done perfectly. An accepting, loving attitude that you trust him and you're on his side can work wonders for his stress level.

WHY BOYS DROP OUT

Bobby earned over $4,000 painting houses the summer after his junior year in high school, and spent much of it on a used Toyota he worked on every chance he got. An average student in a big public high school on the out-skirts of an industrial city, he got along well with his friends but made little impression on his teachers. But one day in October of Bobby's senior year, his mother came home from her insurance-company job to find Bobby's car gone and a note on the kitchen counter. "Don't worry about me, Mom," it read. "I'm taking off for a couple of months to look around and see the country. I know I can make it on my own, and school gives me nothing. I'll be back in touch when I find work and a place to live."

At fifteen, Gilbert was held back in eighth grade because he couldn't pass the district's standardized competency tests in reading. His school assigned him to a "transition class" that autumn, but Gilbert's Haitian immigrant family depended on him to contribute to their income, so he rose before dawn every day to work for a newspaper distributor, and by afternoon he was falling asleep in class over his worksheets. A big, likable young man with a beautiful singing voice, he grew discouraged as the year progressed and his grades were still falling short. One Sunday after church, Gilbert told his minister that he planned to drop out of school that week. "Maybe some day I can finish high school," he said. "Not now."

Many people think of boys who drop out of school as no-good delinquents who don't care enough about their futures to stick with their education. But in fact, the stories of these boys are often much more complicated, poignant with struggle and pain.

Like Bobby, the boy who drops out may have grown disillusioned with a school system that doesn't seem to know or care about him. He sees no point in studying academic subjects that have little relevance to his interests, and he is eager to get on with an independent life in which he makes his own choices.

Or like Gilbert, the boy who drops out may want the high-school degree but have adult obligations that make school an impossible bargain. Language issues may skew his test scores downward, and placement in classes with younger or lower-level students may dampen his feelings of self-worth.

Very bright students may feel disengaged because their school does not challenge them academically yet insists that they follow its lockstep procedures. Students of color may experience a kind of institutional racism that assumes they will not succeed, tracking them into classes with "dumbed down" curriculum and rigid teaching styles. Boys may experience prejudice just because of gender stereotypes.

Whatever a boy's academic record, as he enters high school he is particularly vulnerable to a profound feeling of disconnection between his emerging identity and the world of school. That grows even worse if he attends a large, impersonal school where he is not respected, listened to, or known well by even one adult. Even high schools with good reputations rarely offer the intellectual stimulation or the room for social and emotional development that young adults need.

Nationwide statistics show that ninth grade is the critical year in which students drop out or tune out from school. And "get tough" or "zero tolerance" measures that hold students back when they don't pass a standardized test often make matters even worse, as students give up and drop out altogether.

If schools are willing to take bold steps in school design and policy, they can have an enormous effect on this problem, however. Around the country, those that have reshaped their programs to support students throughout this critical period have shown dramatic increases in students' sense of belonging and reductions in their dropout rates.

WHAT CAN SCHOOLS DO TO HELP BOYS STAY IN SCHOOL?

Adolescent boys will do best in school when they feel like valued members of a group in which they fit in and are well known, and when the work they do connects to their interests and matters to someone outside the school. Here are some ways for schools to accomplish this:

> ➤ *Create ninth-grade teams or "academies," in which anywhere between 80 and 120 students spend all their classes with the same team of four or five teachers.* Especially in this transition year, the small size of this group creates a feeling of belonging.
>
> ➤ *Organize large schools into "houses" of up to 300 or 400 students, where students remain throughout their high-school years.* Some schools assign academic or career themes to these houses (communications, health careers, the arts, the law).
>
> ➤ *Link students with adults in the workplace and community as part of their academic work.* They could dismantle sets at a theater, carry out a community telephone survey, help analyze traffic patterns.
>
> ➤ *Link students with people younger than themselves as models and mentors.* Adolescents act at once more adult—responsible, diligent, considerate—and more childlike—curious, enthusiastic, jovial—when they are away from "the pack" with an important role to play on their own.
>
> ➤ *Try alternative means of instruction in basic skills.* Computer-aided instruction in reading or math? Music as a way to acquire language skills? Outdoor or experiential education that involves calculations, and can be followed up with writing? Helping out with younger students as they practice their skills with simple math and language materials?
>
> ➤ *Introduce multiple ways for students to demonstrate what they know and can do.* Can they create a board game or brochure? Have a debate or mock trial? Build a flying machine? Give a presentation on water quality to a local board? Assess them on the skills of communication and prob-

(continued)

lem-solving, not just how they answer multiple-choice questions on a standardized test.

➤ *Link students' after-school work to their intellectual and social development as young adults.* So many students have jobs outside school—65 percent of high-school seniors alone—that those jobs simply must nurture their intellectual and social growth. School should provide a place where students may come back and reflect on their experiences in the world.

The currently fashionable system of using a single standardized test for promotion decisions only reduces a boy's sense that he is valued for his individual qualities. If he is failing under the current means of instruction, moreover, forcing him to repeat the same instruction for a second year will not increase his learning, decades of research has proven. Nor will he benefit from "social promotion," in which a student without skills is simply kicked up the grades until he has spent enough years in school to leave.

Instead, schools should train all their energies on identifying the needs of particular students and finding new ways to address those needs. A caring and personal "arm" around each boy will go farther than any punitive approach can to make sure he graduates into a bright future.

12

Boys and Sports

What Sports Do for Boys • When Competition Takes Over • Coaches as Models • Boys Who Are Not Athletic

Sam and his cousin Trent, both eight years old, had been running around to-gether at family gatherings since their earliest years. So when Trent's father, Howard, suggested a softball game at the Fourth of July barbecue, Sam enthusiastically ran to recruit all the relatives he could round up. But the game had not gone on long before Sam turned up back at the picnic table where his mother and little sister were sitting.

"I just got sick of it," he told his mother when she asked about the game. "Uncle Howard kept trying to make me hit really perfect, like Trent. He said I need to work on my form if I want to be in Little League next year." He sat down and fiddled absently with a ketchup bottle. "Who cares about baseball anyway," he muttered.

"Wait a minute," said Sam's mother. "You don't have to hit home runs to have a good time playing the game. Uncle Howard doesn't understand that, because we didn't have Little League where we grew up." Cheerfully, she led Sam back to the game, along with his little sister. "Hey, Howie—since when are you coaching the Yankees?" she teased her brother.

Three cheers for Sam's mom! By emphasizing the fun of the game over the anxiety of proving his worth on the field, she is giving her boy a great start

on a lifetime of enjoying sports as play, whether they take place in an informal or a more organized setting. Without making a big deal of it, she has
also reminded her brother Howard that when boys play sports, there's more
going on than sheer competition. The Yankees they may not be—but when
they take to the field, boys are nonetheless learning important lessons and
expressing significant feelings.

WHAT SPORTS DO FOR BOYS

Whether in gym class, in informal games, or in organized competition,
when sports are approached as *play,* they give boys endless positive benefits, allowing them to express a broad array of emotions otherwise difficult
to show. For example, boys can:

➤ Discharge their enormous energy and assertiveness in the exhilarating phys-
  ical release of playing hard but fair against an opponent
➤ Act "aggressively" without hurting others
➤ Experience the pleasure of winning a fair struggle
➤ Learn to tolerate the disappointment of losing without humiliation
➤ Enjoy using their bodies, no matter what they look like
➤ Learn to accept themselves and other players
➤ Learn the importance of teamwork and respect for each other, their oppo-
  nents, and their coach
➤ Show their love and affection for one another without shame

Yet sports can also cause suffering for boys. Faced with a code that values
winning above everything—the "go out and kill," "win at all costs" mentality—a boy dons his emotional armor. When he feels most vulnerable, he
acts tough. Or he bolsters his own uncertain self-esteem by teasing other
vulnerable players.

Things can get even worse for boys if they have no natural inclination
toward sports. As long as the world equates masculinity with athletic competence and success, those who do not fit that mold must bury their feelings
of shame, humiliation, and anxiety and protect themselves against bullying.

In fact, some of the most severe teasing and bullying boys endure takes place in physical education classes and in competitive sports.

In the story that begins this chapter, Sam is still a young child when, like many other boys at this age, he gets his introduction to the pleasures and pressures of sports in a backyard family game of ball. Will sports for him turn out to be a transforming experience or a shaming one? The answer may lie in what comes next, as Sam encounters the world of organized, competitive sports.

WHEN A BOY PLAYS ORGANIZED SPORTS

In the United States today, organized sports for youngsters are growing at an unprecedented rate, and kids take part in them at an earlier age than ever before. An estimated 20 million to 30 million children participate in organized sports, coached largely by volunteers without formal training.

The following exercise will help you understand your role as a parent as it affects your boy's participation in organized sports.

What Do I Expect from My Boy's Playing Sports?

AN EXERCISE FOR PARENTS

What are the reasons you want your boy to play organized sports? Check all that apply from the following list.

___ I want him to learn self-discipline.

___ It's a chance for him to excel at something.

___ He has potential for a college scholarship or professional sports.

___ It's a way for him to make friends.

___ It will keep him busy and out of trouble.

___ It will channel his energy in a positive direction.

___ It's something that we can enjoy together.

___ It's something that's always been important to me.

___ It's important for him to learn teamwork and sportsmanship.

___ At his school it's very important socially to be an athlete.

___ Other_____

Of these, which is the most important to you? Why?

_____

_____

_____

_____

Finally, it's a good idea to notice how playing organized sports affects your boy's daily life, in both practical and emotional ways. The following exercise will help you sort out what you have observed about his responses to his athletic experiences. Again, your boy may want to complete it, too.

How Does Playing Sports Affect My Boy?

AN EXERCISE FOR PARENTS

When my boy is involved in competitive sports, I notice that:

His academic performance:
___ Improves because he must stay eligible for the team
___ Suffers because he doesn't have enough time and energy for schoolwork
___ Stays about the same
___ Other_____

His social life:
___ Becomes centered on the team at the expense of other connections
___ Improves because of his status in the school
___ Suffers because he's too tired to do anything
___ Other_____

His overall health:

____ Improves because of the exercise he gets

____ Suffers because of the intensity of the team's regimen

____ Stays about the same; he's always been active in sports

____ Other_____

His emotional life:

____ Goes up and down depending on how the team does

____ Benefits from the connections with teammates or coach

____ Suffers because his skills don't meet expectations

____ Other_____

Look at your responses to the items above. Were any of the items that you checked off things you hadn't previously considered as issues in his life? Were any of the behaviors you checked off things you hadn't previously linked to the boy's participation in sports? If so, write your thoughts and observations here.

_____

_____

_____

_____

_____

_____

YOUR ATTITUDE MATTERS

What makes the difference between a boy for whom sports are a happy, even transforming experience and one who feels shamed and hardened by his experience with sports? Very often, as the following examples illustrate, the difference is the *attitudes* that permeate the playing field. After reading each story, write your responses to the questions that follow.

As a new ninth-grade algebra teacher, Lou began to stop every day after school at the basketball court next to the parking lot and shoot some hoops with a ball he kept in the trunk of his car. "It didn't take long for a couple of

kids to show up and join me," he said. Before long, Lou had a regular pickup game going, and he began to get to know his students and their personalities in a friendly, low-stakes way. "The funny thing was," he observed, "my math class started to get a lot more successful, too. Especially with those kids who were having trouble, that time on the court gave me some new ways to tell them I knew they could do it."

For a boy, what's the difference between a basketball court and a math classroom?

_____

_____

_____

Do you think Lou would have seen the same results if he were coaching an organized team rather than playing a pickup game? Why or why not?

_____

_____

_____

Simon was always small for his age, and he tended to hang back from opportunities to try out for local or school sports teams. But the summer after his eighth grade, his older sister, Sarah, began dating an eleventh grader on the wrestling team. "You're strong, and you'd be a natural wrestler in your weight class," the older boy told Simon one day, after showing him some moves while Sarah looked on admiringly. Encouraged by the suggestion, Simon tried out for the team; four years later he had won regional honors, a varsity letter, and a new sense of confidence in his own athletic ability.

What might stop Simon and other smaller boys from trying out for athletics?

_____

_____

_____

How might adults encourage smaller-built boys to participate in athletics, without pressuring or shaming them?

_____

_____

_____

Austin began running alongside his father when he was in elementary school, just for fun. They both loved the feeling of being out in the early morning before other people were up, and they would keep a daily record of how long they took to run a mile. At the sixth-grade field day in June, Austin didn't win any of the events, but when he came home that night he wore a big grin. "Personal best!" he said, giving his dad a high five as he announced his seven-minute mile.

What did Austin's father do to foster his son's healthy attitude toward athletics?

_____

_____

_____

How do you imagine this might affect other areas of Austin's life?

_____

_____

_____

Every fall Saturday after the local youth-league football game, the coach of one team of middle-schoolers meets the boys at the local pizza joint. "It's not because we won the game," one youngster said when someone at the next table asked the reason for the celebration that day. "We just always get together after and talk about it."

What attitudes toward sports and competition are these boys building by this custom?

_____

How might those attitudes show up in other areas of their lives—for example, schoolwork or jobs?

In each of these cases, someone is teaching these boys not only to strive for excellence, but to risk making mistakes as they learn to do better. They are learning to pace their learning at a healthy rate, and to grow from losing as well as winning, from praise as well as criticism. Such mentors are essential to learning these things. Long after these boys' sports experiences are over, lessons like these will carry over into their everyday lives.

WHEN COMPETITION TAKES OVER

Sports can convey harmful messages, too. From coaches, parents, and the media, boys learn that our society expects obsessive competition from its males. They see how sports heroes are treated as gods at the expense of others. And they watch as we condone violence and even brutality in the interest of winning.

These attitudes come through not just in extreme situations, but in everyday rules and practicalities, as the following example shows:

The Eagle Valley Warriors were already headed for the state soccer championships for the fifth time when seventeen-year-old Luke, a first-string player, asked the coach if he could miss an important match to be in his sister's wedding, four weeks away. The coach was sympathetic but firm. "You know our policy—you skip a game and you're off the team," he told Luke. "If I let you off the hook, the next kid's going to want to go off on some family vacation. If we're going to stay a winning team, I just can't make exceptions."

Luke went home distraught after practice. "You know what being on the team means to me," he said to his parents. "Can't Stephanie just get married on Sunday instead of Saturday?"

Can you think of reasons for the coach to have a no-exceptions policy like this, given that he has charge of an elite team? If so, write them here:

_____

_____

_____

What is one important message Luke will take away from his situation?

_____

_____

_____

If you had a boy in this situation, what would you advise him to do? Why?

_____

_____

_____

LEARNING THE "KILLER INSTINCT"

When winning becomes the whole point of sports, boys are often rewarded for an intense drive to beat the opponent at any cost, as the following examples show:

Springville's football team hammered neighboring Wilton so badly in the first half of the game that Wilton had to forfeit due to the "forty-point rule" (if one team leads by forty points at the half, the game is over). Wilton's team took the loss cheerfully, coming over to congratulate their opponents. "No wonder they lose so badly," the Springville coach told his players after the boys had gone. "They don't have the killer instinct."

Dennis, an easygoing ninth grader, had grown up playing basketball in the park. Delighted when he made varsity in his first year at Martin Luther

King High, he angered the coach in his first game with his friendly wave to the crowd from the court. "You're not out there to have fun," said the coach. "You've got to keep only one thing in your mind: Destroy the other team."

Attitudes like this end up hurting everyone. They lead to a culture in which it's okay to go physically overboard in the game itself—pushing, checking, or tackling opponents too hard. Verbal assaults also escalate in a climate like this, and encourage boys to push past the rules of fair play.

What's Going Too Far?

A DIAGNOSTIC EXERCISE

In the following situations, small differences in the words and actions of the people involved make the difference between urging on players to win and going too far:

Before a game, the team joins for a huddle in which they yell out answers together to the coach's challenges: "Are we gonna win? Are we gonna go to the top?"

The pregame ritual of one football coach includes militaristic call-and-response patterns in which team members end by chanting, "Fight! Fight! Kill! Kill!"

In the first example, the team gets pumped up for the competition in a relatively positive way. In the second case, the ritual focuses on degrading and humiliating the other team. Words reflect attitudes, and "win" is different from "fight" or "kill."

At an ice hockey game, a group of fathers stands on the sidelines and cheers when one little boy knocks his opponent with his stick and steals the puck to make a goal. They don't notice that the fallen boy is crying and wiping blood from his nose.

At a middle-school baseball game, the first-baseman chases the runner as he sprints for second base, trying to tag him with the ball. Everyone watching screams encouragement, and both boys hurtle to the grass after the first-baseman lunges to tag the runner out.

In both cases, the boys are fighting as hard as they can to win. But the audience in the first case is cheering an act of violence, not of sport. The second case may be messy, but there won't be any dispute that both boys are playing fair.

Have you ever witnessed a scene like this? If so, describe it:

_____

_____

_____

Do you think the actions involved were going too far? Explain why or why not:

_____

_____

YOUR BOY'S HEALTH IS AT STAKE

"I was watching Charlie's football team at the end of practice on that very hot day last week," said Tamara, the mother of a high-school athlete. "The coach was making them do sprints in the heat, and I thought the boys were just going to pass out. He wasn't letting them take water breaks or anything. I guess he probably didn't feel the heat so much, since he was just standing on the sidelines. But isn't that dangerous?"

Charlie's mother is right to be concerned about her boy athlete's health. One of the dangers of the cult of masculine prowess in sports comes from the push to put training above a boy's need for balance in his physical habits. This boot-camp mentality can show up not just in football but in many different sports. For example:

➤ Wrestlers risk developing exercise obsessions or eating disorders in order to "make weight" in their competition class.

- Baseball players can injure themselves by pitching too much without resting their throwing arms.
- Runners can risk exhaustion from pushing themselves too far.

Parents like Tamara can wield important influence in this area by insisting on reasonable limits in a team's physical training. If necessary, consult a sports physician to back up your sense that the training has gone beyond a healthy limit. If you don't get results, go see the person to whom the coach reports, and share your concerns with other parents as well.

HEALTH ALERT: TOO MUCH, TOO SOON

Too much emphasis on athletic training too soon in a boy's life can lead to overuse injuries, whether he is a newcomer to sports or a seasoned player. Among the kinds of damage and inflammation caused by repeating the same movements over time are tendinitis, bursitis, "Little League elbow," shin-splints, and stress fractures.

When a boy's bones are still growing, he is at particular risk for some of these injuries. Fatigue also puts him at risk, as do improper footwear and playing before previous injuries are fully healed.

In the past decades, as systematic sports training for youngsters has increased, so has the incidence of overuse injuries. Some ways parents and coaches can help prevent them:

- Use preseason screenings to catch back problems, knee injuries, or muscle imbalances that can be remedied with strength training.
- Restrict the number of innings (or baseballs) pitched, yards swum, or miles run per week.
- Steer young athletes into training routines that build strength and flexibility and thus reduce the potential for injury.
- Avoid "boot camp" training routines that focus primarily on repetition of intense effort, such as wind sprints and thrust squats.

(continued)

We also now know that distorted body image is also a sports-related issue for boys, just as it has long been for girls. Some sports that enforce inappropriate weight loss or gain, or "beefing up" muscles, are more and more resulting in eating disorders and abuse of drugs like steroids.

Extreme training schedules and scare tactics aren't the only ways a coach can help a boy become the best athlete possible. The following exercise will help you come up with specific strategies that respect both a boy's physical and emotional needs.

Coming Up with Alternatives

AN EXERCISE FOR PARENTS AND COACHES

From the way their coaches train them, boys learn habits and attitudes about themselves and their bodies. After each example, use the space to write your thoughts about what's wrong with what the coach is doing. Then write your thoughts about what a boy learns from the suggested alternative.

Example: A football coach opens the weight room before- and after-hours for his team's use. Next to the door he posts a public record of each player's muscle size, the number of weights he lifts, and the times he came in to work out.

What's the danger?

_____

_____

Alternative: The coach could have each team member keep an individual journal of his weight training, then have regular one-on-one conferences to discuss their progress.

What's the benefit?

_____

_____

Example: The cross-country coach tells runners before the race, "If you don't collapse at the finish line, you haven't run hard enough."

What's the danger?

_____

_____

Alternative: At the start of the race, the coach encourages runners to run harder on the uphill sections, then rest on the downhill stretches.

What's the benefit?

_____

_____

Example: The wrestling coach turns the heat way up in the practice room and has wrestlers take saunas to dehydrate so they can "make weight."

What's the danger?

_____

_____

Alternative: The coach works with each boy to create a personal nutrition plan, and stays especially sensitive to a boy's growth spurts.

What's the benefit?

_____

_____

HOW PARENTS CAN HELP

At the beginning of this section we watched as Luke, a soccer player on a winning team, was forced to choose between his sister's wedding and remaining on his team. As in so many other dilemmas a boy athlete faces, Luke will need all the emotional support his parents can offer as he decides what to do.

How can parents help their boys experience the transforming power of sports without falling prey to the cult of male dominance that so often accompanies organized athletics?

➤ Help your boy find a sport or physical activity that he likes and can learn to do reasonably well. Don't limit the choices to organized or competitive sports—running, dancing, or skateboarding can all help a boy feel good about his body.

➤ Get directly involved in sports with your boy, in ways that emphasize fun, not winning. Whether on the court or on the sidelines, your attitudes matter.

➤ Whether you're talking about his team or about professional sports, make it clear that you value sports for how much fun it gives people, not for the sake of winning.

➤ Talk to your son's coach about what matters to you, and then monitor the messages the boys get from him at practice and in games.

➤ Insist that the school provide multitiered athletic programs so that boys of all abilities can play.

➤ If your boy is injured, make sure he doesn't go back into practice or play before the doctor says he's ready.

➤ Make sure gym classes include enough variety so that even nonathletic boys can play and exercise without feeling ashamed.

➤ Convey appreciation for all of your son's interests, not just sports.

Use the list above as a guide to help you answer the following questions:

What specific things do I already do that support my boy's healthy attitude toward athletics?

_____

_____

_____

What specific things could I be doing better to help my boy keep this healthy attitude?

_____

_____

_____

COACHES AS MODELS

A boy's coach—that is, any adult who supervises boys playing sports—often plays as important a role in his development as any other person in his life. Especially in adolescence, a coach may stand in for the parent in many ways, as a boy spends more time on his own away from the family, seeking his emerging identity.

Within the context of a close sports team, the coach creates a crucial emotional environment, which can develop and nurture a boy's sense of self-esteem and connection to others. The following exercise will remind you how powerful a coach's influence can be in shaping a boy's experiences and beliefs.

What Did I Learn from My Own Coaches?

AN EXERCISE FOR PARENTS AND COACHES

Think back on your own experiences with organized sports (teams or physical education classes). Which coaches stand out in your memory, and why?

_____

_____

_____

_____

_____

Choose one of the coaches you described above. How did that coach behave toward you:

During practice? _____

_____

During games? _____

_____

When you won? _____

_____

When you lost? _____

_____

How did that coach behave toward:

Your opponents? _____

_____

Referees and game officials? _____

_____

Parents and other spectators? _____

_____

_____

What did you learn from the coach that has stuck with you:

About sports? _____

_____

About life? _____

_____

About yourself? _____

_____

COACHES ARE TEACHERS

Because coaches teach boys so much about so many things, they need to be as thoughtful about their teaching methods as teachers are in other areas of learning. No good teacher would ridicule a boy struggling to master math, reading, or writing. Likewise, when a young athlete has trouble mastering the skills of a sport, a good coach will bring not just sports expertise but empathy and sensitivity to his task.

"Even in the middle of intense play, I try to watch how each kid is doing physically," says John, a parent who coaches a youth-league football team in his town. "Some boys won't admit when they're in pain—they're afraid they'll be letting down the team, and me, and their parents. I tell them they need to tell me when something hurts—and if it hurts, it's time to stop."

This coach is teaching his young players that part of playing well is to pace their physical efforts at a healthy rate. By establishing a setting in which it's safe for them to acknowledge pain, he bolsters both their athletic ability and their feelings of self-worth.

TIPS ON WINNING TACTICS FOR COACHES OF BOYS

Whether their teams win or lose, good coaches come up with many ways to support their learning. For example, a coach might:

➤ Call players by affectionate (not shaming) nicknames that have special meaning to them and the coach
➤ Say something in praise of every individual player at the sports awards banquet, not just the superstars
➤ Make sure training sessions keep kids' overall health as a top priority, with plenty of water breaks, warm-ups, and cool-downs
➤ Include noncompetitive drills and scrimmages in training sessions
➤ Give every boy as much chance to play as possible
➤ Strive for an ongoing personal connection with every boy on the team

Add your own ideas here:

_____

_____

_____

We've seen that coaches are powerful teachers. And while most coaches are caring adults who want the best for the boys they work with, some of them use tactics that reinforce the cult of masculinity and winning at all costs. A coach like this can devastate a boy's self-esteem—especially if the boy doesn't fit the "star athlete" description. Furthermore, even the strong athletes learn the wrong lessons when a coach displays or rewards these tactics. Some ways coaches do this:

They put winning before fair play.
Example: Alan, the junior varsity soccer coach, teaches his players to push the rules wherever possible, taking advantage of any chance to gain ground. "Sneak closer if you can when the ref isn't looking," he urges them when an opponent is taking a direct penalty kick, which requires other players to stay a certain distance away.

They value stronger players more than less skilled ones.
Example: Jeff's basketball coach only plays his top five players unless his team is ahead by a wide margin. The other players, like Jeff, sit on the bench, or get put in for a few minutes once the game is decided. In practices, first-string players merely walk through their moves "to save energy for the games," according to the coach. "You other guys aren't good enough to give these players a real practice anyway," he says.

They ridicule or humiliate players for their mistakes.
Example: "You throw like a girl," the physical education teacher tells Toby, a young boy trying to master throwing a baseball. Out of their own fear of being ridiculed like this, the other members of the class fall into the habit of goading Toby with the same taunt every day.

They promote a pecking order among players.
Example: New to the school football team, Joey endures the customary hazing of younger players in the locker room. After he is held under the

shower and snapped with towels time after time, he goes for help to the coach, who just laughs. "Next year it will be your turn," the coach says.

They blame others for mistakes or losses in games.
Example: At the annual sports awards banquet, the baseball coach takes the mike to praise his players, then uses the occasion to gripe about umpires' decisions that "cost us the game" in some cases. "We would have won the championship if it hadn't been for that ump," he says.

WHEN A COACH . . .	THEN A BOY . . .
➤ Derides or humiliates boys who make mistakes	➤ Feels ashamed
➤ Pushes boys beyond their natural skill levels	➤ Hardens himself against his feelings ➤ Hides behind a mask of self-confidence, swaggering, or aggressive action
➤ Offers encouragement only when the boys win	➤ Grows obsessed with how well he performs, risking injury to himself or others
➤ Disparages the abilities of the opposing team	➤ Focuses on beating his opponent at all costs
➤ Cheers on boys who show all levels of skill	➤ Feels that he really matters to the team
➤ Makes sure that sports include all boys	➤ Feels proud of what he can do and interested in improving his skills
➤ Leads boys to cooperate with teammates across skill levels	➤ Feels connected and bonded to his teammates

WHEN A COACH . . .	THEN A BOY . . .
➤ Openly relishes the fun of the game itself, whether or not the team wins	➤ Enjoys the effort to achieve his personal best ➤ Dares to make mistakes as he learns
➤ Models a sense of fair play	➤ Learns to make appropriate moral judgments
➤ Conveys to his players a loving sense of connection, not a rigid or punitive attitude	➤ Looks up to his coach as role model and mentor who can offer guidance, support, and encouragement

BOYS WHO ARE NOT ATHLETIC

Brothers with just fifteen months separating their ages, Nate and Evan have very different temperaments. Nate is a star athlete, while Evan has always preferred reading science fiction and playing his guitar. Despite their differences, the brothers have always had a close relationship and stuck together at school. But now that Nate has made the varsity basketball team as a sophomore, things have become tense between them.

One night at the dinner table, Nate casually asked if his parents could drive him to a party that Saturday. "Sure," said his father. "I can drop the two of you off on my way to the gym." Nate looked uncomfortable. "Dad, it's not really a party for freshmen." Evan flushed. "Except for Walt and those guys," he shot back bitterly. "Dumb jocks."

Nate gave his parents a pained look. "What am I supposed to do?" he said. "Evan just wouldn't fit in with that crowd." He turned to Evan. "You know you wouldn't have a good time." Evan stood up angrily. "Don't pretend you care how I would feel. You don't even talk to me anymore, now that you're such a big shot!"

Boys who aren't athletic often experience painful humiliation from school-mates and even family members—who usually don't realize how much shame the boy might be feeling inside. Though Nate is doing what he thinks will protect his brother, he can't shield Evan from the judgments of others—which only reinforce Evan's own internalized self-criticism.

Before the loving relationship between the brothers is damaged further, Mr. and Mrs. Paterson need to step in and start talking as a family about this issue. They should start by talking to each boy separately.

What they can say to Nate, the athlete:

➤ Why do you think the athletes in school tend to stick together and exclude people who don't play sports?

➤ Why do you think Evan said you don't talk to him anymore?

➤ Do you wish Evan played sports, too? Why?

➤ What do you like about Evan that's different from what you like about your friends from the team?

What they can say to Evan, the nonathlete:

➤ What's it like at your school for kids who don't play sports?

➤ Why do you think people value sports so highly?

➤ Do you think Nate's changed deep down, now that he's on the team?

➤ Do you know that we're just as proud of you as we are of your brother?

After talking to their boys separately, Mr. and Mrs. Paterson asked Nate to make the first move to patch up his relationship with his brother. At the same time, they assigned both boys to clean their old toys out of the garage where they had been stored for years. Mr. Paterson returned from an errand that weekend to find the boys crouched on the garage floor in the midst of dozens of action figures that they had lined up in a mock battle. "They both looked pretty embarrassed when I caught them playing," he told his wife. "But I haven't seen them laughing like that together in months. And Nate said they'd both rather go out for pizza and a movie tonight than go to that party."

It wasn't easy for the Patersons to step into this difficult situation between their boys, but in doing so they modeled how to connect empathetically with both of them. It's a lesson their sons can use not only with each other in the future, but also with other boys that might not fit the mold of athletic prowess. They are learning from their parents the skills to intervene when others are consistently picked last for gym class teams or taunted as "losers."

If instead the Patersons had fallen into the trap of comparing their sons' success in sports, they not only would have risked taking the fun out of sports altogether for Evan, but they would be devaluing other areas in which he might have interest or excel.

Some nonathletic boys may try to avoid athletic activities altogether. Others harden themselves against the pain of being persistently rejected and disgraced. Yet knowing how playing sports can open new worlds of physical release and self-esteem to all kinds of boys, adults may rightly seek a way to draw them into this potentially transforming experience.

How can we support boys' accomplishments in sports without making them seem more important than other areas of success? If you're the parent of a boy who is not an athlete—whether he is younger or older—use the following exercise to reflect on your own responses and feelings about sports in his life.

➤ What do you value about your boy?

➤ Do you ever wish your boy were more athletic? Why?

➤ Do you worry about your boy because he's not athletic? What are some of your fears?

➤ How might your responses be different if your nonathletic child were a daughter, not a son? Why?

➤ Do you think having a star athlete for a son reflects well on a family? Why?

➤ Do you think your boy feels bad about not being an athlete? Is there anything you do or say that might make him feel that way?

➤ Is there anything you could do or say to let him know how proud you are of him for who he is? (*Examples:* joining him in an activity he enjoys, asking him for help in an area he's good at.)

Perhaps most important for parents and teachers is to do everything they can to open up the world of athletics to all boys without shaming those who do not excel on the playing field. Just as all kids can expand their horizons through music and art regardless of their talents, all deserve to know the power and pleasure that sports can add to their lives.

In their "Bill of Rights for Young Athletes," four coaches set out their inspiring philosophy of what every youngster should be able to experience in athletics. One could easily expand the definition of "sports" here to include such energetic and playful activities as dance, chess, math competitions, cooking contests, and other playful activities that some boys might prefer. In all these cases, the same rights make equal sense:

➤ The right to participate in sports
➤ The right to participate at a level commensurate with each child's maturity and ability
➤ The right to have qualified adult leadership
➤ The right to play as a child and not as an adult
➤ The right of children to share in the leadership and decision-making of their sport participation
➤ The right to participate in safe and healthy environments
➤ The right to proper preparation for participation in sports
➤ The right to an equal opportunity to strive for success
➤ The right to be treated with dignity
➤ The right to have fun in sports

13

Boys and the Media

TELEVISION AND MOVIES • MEDIA, GENDER, AND TOYS • THE PRINT MEDIA • VIDEO AND COMPUTER GAMES • USING THE INTERNET • BOYS AND THEIR MUSIC

Wanting to set apart a special time to spend with his ten-year-old son, Mike, Barry asked the boy to choose whatever he wanted them to do together every Monday night, when Mike's mom was out at her weekly yoga class. But he was horrified when his son made his choice.

"He wanted us to watch WWF wrestling on cable TV together," Barry told Mike's fifth-grade teacher, Mr. Frost, when he saw him at the science fair. "I couldn't believe my eyes—the fighters were slamming each other against the fence, grabbing their crotches, making obscene gestures, taunting each other. Not only was it in horrible taste, but it was hypermasculine, violent, extreme . . . everything we've been trying to discourage in Mike as a boy."

Mike's best friend, Taylor, loves the show, too, Barry learned. "When they get together, I found out, they're playing WWF Warzone on Taylor's Nintendo. It's the same thing! The kids know all the characters inside out; they're even buying these merchandise spin-offs modeled after their favorite players."

Despite Barry's reluctance, Mike has his heart set on watching the Monday-night show during their time together. "You don't get it, Dad," he argues. "They're just pretending to hurt each other."

Barry is right to worry about Mike's fascination with this violent program. Even when programming is not aimed at kids, it influences their thinking and behavior. Over a third of WWF wrestling viewers are under seventeen, a recent study found, and many schoolchildren imitate the obscene behavior they see there.

Boys who watch a lot of TV may think of violence as normal by their middle years, expecting or tolerating it. Yet they also may not perceive media violence as "real," causing genuine pain or suffering. (As WWF reveals, sometimes they're right!)

In this chapter we will explore the ways that a boy's life reflects his involvement with television, movies, video games, computer games, the Internet, and music. But before we go into this complex media landscape, we will use the following exercises to figure out just where you and your family stand in relation to the most pervasive medium of our time, television.

TELEVISION AND MOVIES

Who's Watching What?

AN EXERCISE FOR PARENTS AND TEACHERS

Did you have favorite TV shows or movies when you were growing up? What were they?

_____

_____

_____

Pick one of the items on your list. What did you like about this show or movie?

_____

_____

_____

Did you usually watch it alone or with other people?

_____

Rate the violence content of that show:
___ Not violent at all
___ Some violence
___ A lot of violence

Do you have a favorite TV show now? If so, what is it? _____

_____

What do you like about it?

_____

_____

_____

Rate the violence content of that show:
___ Not violent at all
___ Some violence
___ A lot of violence

Do you know a favorite TV show or movie of the boy or boys in your life? If so, what is it?

_____

Have you ever watched it? _____ *If so, rate the violence content:*
___ Not violent at all
___ Some violence
___ A lot of violence

Do you think your boy has been exposed to significantly more violence on television and in movies than you were as a child? _____

STATISTICS ABOUT BOYS, TELEVISION, AND VIOLENCE

➤ Some studies have shown that by age ten, boys expect less disapproval from their parents for aggression than girls do. Older boys are less likely than girls to think that the victims of aggression actually suffer.

➤ Children watch TV for over twenty-three hours a week, on average, with 60 percent of nine-year-olds watching over three hours a day. In a 1999 University of Pennsylvania study, parents reported their children spent, on average, 3.25 hours per day watching television or videos; 48.2 percent of the children had television sets in their bedrooms.

➤ Programming and games aimed toward boys show winners using violence and aggression; those for girls have heroines escape from conflict with magic, kindness, and help from others.

Many parents do not realize the extent to which television is a presence in their children's lives. The following exercise will help you assess your family's watching habits.

Assessing Our Household's Media Consumption

AN EXERCISE FOR PARENTS

How many television sets are in your house? _____

Where are they? (List all rooms.)

_____

_____

_____

_____

_____

How many hours of television do you yourself watch in a typical day?

___ Less than an hour

___ One to two hours

___ Two to four hours

___ More than four hours

How many hours of television does your boy watch in a typical day?

___ Less than an hour

___ One to two hours

___ Two to four hours

___ More than four hours

___ I'm not sure

How many movies (including videos, but not movies on television) do you watch in a typical week?

___ None

___ One

___ Two to four

___ More than four

How many movies (including videos) does your boy watch in a typical week? Count all repeat viewings of the same video. If your boys have different viewing habits, make a separate list for each additional boy.

___ None

___ One

___ Two to four

___ More than four

Do you watch the news on television? _____

If so, when?

___ Morning

___ Midday

___ Evening

___ Late at night

Does your boy watch the news on television with you? _____

Do you usually watch television programs, videos, or movies with your boy,
or separately? _____

Of the toys in your home (including video or computer games), how many
have some connection to television shows or movies?
___ Very few
___ Quite a few
___ Most

Now look at your answers to the above exercise. Overall, how would you
rate the extent to which television or movies are present in your family's
life? (Check all that apply.)
___ Television and movies aren't very present in our life.
___ We like television and movies, but other things take up far more of our atten-
    tion.
___ Our boy watches a lot, but the adults in our household don't.
___ Our boy is too busy to watch, but the adults watch a lot.
___ We all watch a lot of television and movies, but they're not very important to
    us.
___ Our boy's pastimes mostly have some connection to television or movies.

How do you feel about your answers to the previous question?
___ I feel fine about it.
___ I'm worried about it.
___ I wish I knew how we compare to other families.
___ I don't like it, but I don't see how I can do anything about it.
___ Other _____

Boys learn dubious lessons from television, which can numb them not only to violence, but to stereotypes about race and gender. TV dramas feature male characters in a two-to-one ratio to females, with the "villains" most often male, young, lower class, and Latino or "foreign."

On the other hand, watching violent programming doesn't necessarily make a boy violent. Many of today's peaceful adults grew up watching everything from Western-style shoot-outs to *Star Wars*. Every boy is different, and there are no rules that can tell you what is going to hurt him and what is okay.

The best way for you to know how television affects your boy is to watch with him and talk with him about it so you know how he feels. This special exercise was designed for you to complete with your boy. The exercise will help you analyze a particular television show, so if you'd like to do it for more than one show, make copies of it before you fill it in.

Watching TV Together

AN EXERCISE FOR PARENTS AND THEIR BOYS

This exercise has three parts: one part to do before watching the show, one part to fill out while you're watching, and one part to work on after the show.

Part One: Pick a television show that you can watch together.
Record the basic information about the show here:

Name of show: _____

What time is it on? _____

What station is it on? _____

What kind of show is it?

____ Cartoon

____ Sitcom

___ Drama

___ Game show

___ Educational

___ News

___ Other_____

Is this show mainly for grown-ups or for kids?

___ Kids

___ Grown-ups

___ Both

What makes you think that?

_____

_____

Who do you think usually watches this show?

___ Male viewers

___ Female viewers

___ Both

What makes you think that?

_____

_____

Part Two: Watching the show

Now you're ready to watch the show. As you watch, fill out the chart below. You'll have to pay close attention to what's going on and be ready to mark the chart with information about all the characters on the show and what they do. You'll also have to keep track of all the commercials, so make sure you're really ready before you start watching!

COMMERCIALS

Make a mark every time you see the following kinds of commercials:

Food _____

Cars _____

Alcohol _____

Toys _____

Financial services _____

Household products (laundry, etc.) _____

Drugs/medicine _____

Movies _____

Other TV shows _____

Other _____

Keep count here of:

Male characters _____

Female characters _____

Make a mark every time:

Something violent happens _____

Something sexual happens _____

Part Three: After the show

What did you notice about what kinds of commercials were on during this show?

_____

_____

_____

Did you notice anything different about what parts men and women played in the commercials?

_____

_____

_____

Why do you think they chose those commercials to go with this show?

_____

_____

_____

Did you find any of the commercials tempting? (Did you want to buy the things that were advertised?) Which ones?

_____

_____

_____

Were there more male characters or female characters in the show?

_____

If there was violence in the show, who did the violent acts?
____ Male characters
____ Female characters

Who were the victims of the violent acts?
____ Male characters
____ Female characters

How was violence used on the show? Check all that apply.

___ Good characters used violence to make things turn out right.

___ Only bad characters used violence on the show.

___ Violence was funny on the show.

___ Violence was scary on the show.

___ Good characters and bad characters both used violence on the show.

___ Other _____.

What do you think the differences are between violence on this show and what you know about violence in real life?

_____

_____

_____

What kind of sexual content was on the show?

_____

_____

_____

If and when the characters acted in sexual ways, what did it mean?

___ They loved each other.

___ They liked each other.

___ It didn't seem important if they loved or even liked each other.

Do you think that's the way sex is in real life? Why or why not?

_____

_____

_____

Were there characters on the show who were:

___ Not white?

___ Not physically attractive?

___ Not athletic-looking?

___ Not interested in the opposite sex?

___ Not rich?

If there were any characters on the show like this, were they:

___ Funny?

___ Bad?

___ Scary?

___ Just the same as the other characters?

Do you think that's the way it is in real life? Why or why not?

_____

_____

_____

Do you think that people in real life should *act the way people in the show acted? Why or why not?*

_____

_____

_____

An afterword for parents

Doing this exercise with your boy may have brought up some new or uncomfortable subjects between you. Use the following space and questions to help you think about your own responses.

Were you surprised by any of the content of the show you watched? Explain.

_____

_____

Do you think the exercise helped your boy think in new ways about television? Explain.

_____

_____

Was there anything you felt very uncomfortable discussing with your boy?

_____

_____

Did you learn anything new about your boy through doing this exercise to-gether?

_____

_____

Did you learn anything new about TV's use as a marketing tool to reach youngsters?

_____

_____

WHAT THEY'RE WATCHING

A research group from the University of Pennsylvania reported in 1999 that one in five television shows aimed at young people had little or no educational value. Among the findings:

➤ One third of the shows classified as educational under FCC guidelines were "highly educational," 45.5 percent were "moderately educational," and 21.2 percent were "minimally educational."

➤ Twenty-eight percent of children's shows contained four or more acts of violence, and 75 percent of these high-violence programs did not carry the FV, or "fantasy violence," content rating for children's programs.

➤ Forty-five percent of children's programs contained one or more instances of problematic language and 12 percent of programs had one or more instances of sexual innuendo.

YOUNG BOYS AND VIOLENCE ON TELEVISION

"Colton used to love going to the corner store at supper-time if we were out of milk," said Jolene, the mother of an eight-year-old boy and two younger girls. "But last week he just hung back and wouldn't do it. At first I didn't think anything of it, but later that night he started asking me questions about this boy he had seen on the news, who was found dead three weeks after

he'd been kidnapped. I guess I didn't realize he was listening when I had the news on while I made supper."

It's easy to overlook how scary even seemingly harmless programs or movies can be for a younger boy. Watching the news, for example, might seem educational, and a cartoon version of a fairy tale might seem perfectly okay for a little boy to watch alone.

The following exercise will help you remember the kinds of programs that were overwhelming to you as a child, and become more attuned to what might bother your boy.

Was I Too Young for That?

AN EXERCISE FOR PARENTS

Do you remember seeing anything on TV or in the movies when you were young that scared or disturbed you? If so, describe it here:

_____

_____

_____

Did it affect you afterward in any negative way (nightmares, insomnia, fears of a particular thing you had seen in the program)? Explain:

_____

_____

_____

Were you alone or with other people when you saw it?

_____

Did you wish you hadn't seen it afterward?

_____

As an older child or an adult, did you ever see this same show or movie (or one similar to it) again? If so, how was your experience of it different?

_____

_____

_____

WHEN YOUNG BOYS WATCH TV: TIPS FOR PARENTS

➤ Make sure you check in with a young boy and give him the option of leaving without shame.

➤ If something seems scary or violent, talk about it afterward.

➤ Watch his body language. He may be ashamed to say how scared he was. Remember, he may play out his fear through "acting out" scary or violent parts, and it's important not to confuse this with misbehavior.

➤ Be alert to what's showing when you think your boy isn't paying attention (the news, commercials, your programs).

➤ If you use videos to keep your boy occupied when you need time, make sure you've viewed them together first.

AGREEING ON WHAT YOUR BOY MAY WATCH

"After I found my ten-year-old son watching Baywatch, *I decided it was time to put my foot down and I told him he could only watch TV when I'm there," said Dora. "But then I found out he's going next door every day to watch with his friend. He doesn't understand what the big deal is. How can we come to an agreement?"*

When adults come down hard on a boy's interests, he feels judged and demeaned, concluding that he must be bad for his "guilty pleasures." So it's particularly important, if you're thinking of setting limits on your boy's watching habits, to come to some agreement that he feels part of.

The following exercise will help you think through how you want to structure your boy's viewing.

Establishing Reasonable Guidelines

What do you feel is a reasonable amount of time for your boy to watch television every day?

Weekdays_____

Weekends_____

Are there other guidelines you'd like to see observed having to do with the amount he watches?

___ Not watching until homework is done

___ Not watching after_____ P.M. on weekdays

___ Other_____

What about guidelines as to the content of what he watches (for example, shows or channels he can't watch)?

_____

_____

_____

Looking at your answers above, is there anything you can imagine compromising about?

_____

_____

_____

Now show your boy your answers, and ask him the following questions.

➤ Do you think these guidelines are reasonable? Why or why not?

➤ Do you understand why I feel the way I do?

➤ If you could change one of these rules, what would you change? Why?

Now that you've talked with your boy about guidelines, you might want to draw up an agreement about television watching. Boys often appreciate having clear rules, even if they disagree with them, especially if they feel they are part of the negotiation about them. Make sure there's a policy about exceptions, but establish fair consequences if he breaks the rules without permission. (For example: If he watches for too long one day, he can't watch at all the next day.)

TIPS FOR PARENTS

➤ Watch television with your boy. The shows he likes have meaning to him, and he needs to know you respect that. Make a deal: He chooses this time, you choose the next.

➤ Ask questions, and don't dismiss his responses. Why do the characters act the way they do? Would he ever act that way? What might the consequences of their actions be?

➤ Tell him your own reactions honestly, but without judging him. Wonder out loud why he doesn't share your responses, but be careful not to shame him.

➤ Choose alternatives. For your turn, pick a program or game with action that doesn't glamorize violence. Introduce him to your favorites, and get him talking.

TIPS FOR TEACHERS

➤ Use media as an opportunity to teach critical thinking. Kids can learn early to identify programming elements and think about their underlying purposes (like marketing toys) and hidden elements (like gender stereotypes).

➤ Make connections from popular media to academic subjects. Get kids to gather and analyze viewing statistics, compare plots, or write episodes for various shows.

MEDIA, GENDER, AND TOYS

"We've always given Bobby and his sister playthings that didn't encourage gender stereotypes," said Bruce. "But at Bobby's sixth birthday party, his

pals gave him practically everything we'd been avoiding—action figures from violent TV shows and movies, and all the dumb accessories that go with them. Wouldn't you know that those were his favorite presents! Now he never wants to play with his other stuff anymore and he keeps bugging us to buy him more of these violent toys. We can't raise the kid in a vacuum—what are we going to do?"

Bruce's problem is typical these days, when children are bombarded with billion-dollar advertising campaigns aimed at getting them to demand products that are closely linked with mass-media entertainment. No matter how hard parents try to shield their sons from it, the message will eventually reach them: "Boy toys" are about violent action and destruction, and "girl toys" are about love, cuddling, attractiveness, and relationships.

You don't need to urge your boy to play with Barbie in order to raise him free of the Boy Code's restrictions. But the toys you supply do have a big effect on helping him develop all the sides of his personality and character—not just the strong, tough parts that reflect the code. Because Bobby has been playing since early childhood with non-gender-specific toys, he probably already has a sturdy sense of his own creativity, imagination, and emotions in play situations.

Bruce and his wife should talk to Bobby now about what messages his new media-action toys are sending about boys and how they should be. Their son will have questions, too, and they should listen with open minds and be ready to respect his point of view.

Questions to ask boys about toys that seem gender-biased:
- ➤ Do girls play with toys like this? Why not?
- ➤ Do you think boys should be like these superheroes?
- ➤ What do you think would happen if somebody really shot and killed somebody?
- ➤ Why are the bad guys bad? How do you think it would feel to be one of them?
- ➤ Do you think this superhero ever makes any mistakes?

Some questions boys might have about this kind of toy:

➤ Everyone else plays with these toys, so how come you don't want me to?

➤ I like these toys better. Why can't I have the toys I like?

➤ How can I play right if I don't have the right stuff?

Bruce and his wife might want to work out a compromise where Bobby can play with the toys he got for his birthday as long as he sometimes plays with his other toys, too. They might also sit with him when he watches television shows they have concerns about, or plays with toys they don't like.

The most important thing they can do is to have a conversation, sharing their feelings as a process, rather than have a continuing series of confrontations about the subject. If Bobby keeps talking with his parents about his toys and how he likes to play, he's already reflecting on his actions in a way that will foster his healthy development.

TIPS TO REMEMBER

➤ *Provide toys that promote nonspecific, open-ended, creative play.* For example, a ball is good because it has many uses and possibilities, and doesn't come with instructions.

➤ *Notice how your boy is using his toys, not just which toys he's using.* For example, he might be tucking his toughest-looking action figure tenderly into bed with him at night. Don't take away toys that he has obviously formed an attachment to.

➤ *Let your boy help decide on policies about toys.* This is an important way for him to learn not only about the issues of gender stereotyping, but also about how to work through conflicts respectfully.

Some good toys for boys:

➤ Dinosaur or other animal figures

➤ Balls

- Legos
- Playmobil
- Clay, paints, other art materials
- Blocks
- Stuffed or model animals
- Trucks, cars, trains, and planes
- Puppets, dolls, and tools for dramatic play
- Music-making materials (pot lids, toy drums, wind-up music toys, rattles)
- Large-motor play equipment (slides, swings, rocking-horses)
- Small-motor playthings (yo-yos, puzzles, bubble toys, workbench toys)
- Bath and water toys (turkey basters, squirt and spray bottles, sponges, colanders, buckets)

Some not-so-good toys for boys:
- Highly realistic media-linked toys that spell out exactly what children should do with them
- Toys with explicit sexual imagery (for example, action figures with exaggerated breasts)
- Toys that require explicitly violent play
- Toys with distorted masculine bodies (action figures with huge biceps, for example)
- Toys that reinforce sexual stereotypes of how boys "should" play (tough, aggressive, violent superheroes)
- Toys that require or encourage accumulation of unlimited accessories (clothing, videos, other toys)
- Toys that require exclusive use, and discourage imaginative play with a variety of materials

THE PRINT MEDIA

"I was cleaning the house last week when I noticed a pile of magazines in Roger's room," said Barbara, the mother of a thirteen-year-old boy. "I don't like to snoop, but I couldn't help noticing what they were about—and I was pretty horrified. Mixed in with those awful sci-fi comic books he likes

to read was some stuff that must have come from one of those skinhead-type groups—all kinds of bigotry that I wouldn't want him even exposed to, if I could help it. How can I bring up the subject with him—and is it okay for me to tell him I won't have that stuff in my house?"

Barbara faces an issue that many parents of young teenage boys confront for the first time when they discover their youngster is reading material they find objectionable on any number of counts. It's not uncommon, for example, for boys at this age to peruse extreme reading matter like the following:

➤ Pornographic magazines
➤ Violent or sexual science-fiction material
➤ "Zines" (small self-published underground magazinelike publications, which sometimes, but not always, have an extreme point of view)
➤ Comic books with violent or sexual material

Any of these materials might be interesting to a boy as he tries to find out for himself who he is, what he believes, and what his sexuality consists of. Yet just as with your boy's other interests, if you come down hard on his private choices of reading material he will feel invaded, judged, and demeaned.

Moreover, unlike with television, a parent may find it impractical to attempt to try to control what a boy may and may not read. Though adults can certainly make it clear what kinds of reading matter is unacceptable in public areas of a household, they may not feel comfortable extending such control to a boy's private spaces.

The key is to open up opportunities for respectful dialogue with your boy, and listen well to what he says, even if you disagree with him. Rather than have Roger conclude that he is a bad person for reading materials that his mother disapproves of, for example, Barbara should engage him in conversation about them, finding out what he thinks of the ideas they contain, and why.

Try to keep the conversation as open-ended as possible. The point is not to come to a right or wrong answer, but to think broadly together about what this material means to him. Some possible questions Barbara could ask her son about what he is reading:

➤ Who do you think mostly reads this material?
➤ What do you think they find interesting about it?
➤ What do *you* think is interesting about it?
➤ Do you agree with what it's saying (or implying) about its subject(s)? Why or why not?
➤ Is there anything that disturbs you about this material? (If so, what?)
➤ Can you think of any people who would find this material disturbing? Why?
➤ Do you think this material accurately reflects the way things are in real life?
➤ If so, do you want real life to be that way?

If you have other questions you'd like to ask in such a conversation, write them here:

_____
_____
_____

After you've talked with your boy:

What did you learn that you hadn't realized before?

_____
_____
_____

How did you feel about what you learned?

_____
_____
_____

VIDEO AND COMPUTER GAMES

"Van and about three of his friends play video games almost every day together," says Phyllis, the mother of an eleven-year-old boy. *"But they hardly*

talk to each other at all—except for yelling out when they score points, and cheering when they knock someone out of play. Isn't this a kind of antisocial way to have fun?"

Phyllis has a good question. Starting around ten years old, boys often stop playing together in the ways they did when they were smaller—running around outside, for example, or acting out imaginary bad guy–good guy scenarios. Instead, when they get together outside of school, boys in their preteen years often turn to Nintendo, PlayStation, or similar computer games for this same kind of stimulating dramatic play.

But is it the same? When boys are interacting with real people in their early cops-and-robbers scenarios, they can't help but notice if their pretend opponent really bleeds when he falls down, really cries when he hurts himself, really has feelings about whether he wins or loses. On the screen, the game-players are pretending, too—but no human reality intrudes.

WHAT THE GAMES DO

But before coming to judgment, any parent whose boy is spending time with video or computer games needs to know firsthand the content of the games he plays. Played sometimes on a video game system dedicated to this purpose, sometimes on a computer that also performs many other functions, sometimes on the Internet, and sometimes on larger machines in a video arcade, these games fall into several broad categories:

➤ *Shoot-'em-up and martial arts games.* The main point of these games is to kill opponents on the screen; boys usually play them with other people. Doom and Quake III are examples of this kind of game.

➤ *Fantasy adventure and role-playing games.* Usually played alone, these games have the boy take on a character who goes on a quest or otherwise solves puzzles. Tomb Raider and Riven are examples of this kind of game.

➤ *Systems simulation games.* These involve the players' skills in modeling complex systems, and take large amounts of time and intelligence to play; they are so involving and complex that the player runs the risk of not being able to stop. Civilization and Sim City are examples.

- ➤ *Sports games.* On-screen basketball, football, soccer, and the like, these games allow a player to control the action of a team member and compete to win the game. A variation on the sports game is WWF Warzone, a virtual replication of the World Wrestling Federation program.
- ➤ *Vehicle simulation games.* The player controls a motorcycle, car, boat, airplane, or spaceship, either in a race or in a competition to destroy his fellow players. The X-Wing Pilot series (a spaceship flight simulation) and Rally Cross (a cross-country race car simulation) are examples of this kind of game.

WHAT'S THE PROBLEM?

It's easy to see how a boy could be interested in any of the games we just described. And one might argue that playing these games could foster a number of positive skills. For example:

- ➤ They can give boys experience manipulating computers and other technology.
- ➤ They can give boys practice integrating visual and motor skills.
- ➤ They can provide a safe outlet for boys' competitive and "aggressive" energies.
- ➤ They sometimes can provide practice in analyzing and creating models of complex systems, and in solving problems.
- ➤ They sometimes have an imaginative element that interests and engages boys.

Have you noticed any other positive effects on your boy from playing video or computer games? If so, write them here:

_____

_____

_____

On the other hand, video and computer games also can have quite *negative* effects on a boy's development. For example:

- They can consume a great deal of time that might be spent interacting with people or doing more active pastimes.
- They can dehumanize and trivialize aggressive or violent acts and numb boys to their consequences.
- They can be hard to stop playing.
- They can isolate boys from companionship and dialogue, especially if the games are played alone.

Have you noticed any other negative effects on your boy from playing video or computer games? If so, write them here:

_____

_____

_____

WHAT CAN PARENTS DO?

It's not always practical for a parent to sit down and play a video game with a boy in the way they can watch a television show together. Video games take so much concentration, for one thing, that it's unlikely your boy will be able to talk to you at all during the game, as he might during a television show.

Still, you can open a dialogue with your boy before he begins to play a particular game. Just as with your boy's reading or television watching, listening to his point of view here will foster the vital connections he needs as he grows up. For example, you might keep track of his answers to questions like these:

Is the point of a particular simulation game:
____ To conduct a war and annihilate all the rivals?
____ To create a flourishing city?
____ To practice diplomacy and negotiation among states?

Is the point of a particular sports game:
____ To follow the normal rules of the sport?
____ To subvert the rules of the sport with secret weapons?

In a particular war game or martial arts game, are the targets:

___ Spaceships, robots, or other nonhuman opponents?

___ Realistic-seeming soldiers?

Once you find out more details about the games your boy wants to play, you can better decide what guidelines you want to set. For example, ask yourself:

Would you be uncomfortable with a video game in which your boy:

___ Flies in a plane shooting down other planes?

___ Shoots at monsters?

___ Shoots at people?

Would you be uncomfortable with a video game in which your boy:

___ Races a vehicle against other vehicles for speed?

___ Sets traps to demolish other vehicles in a race?

___ Pushes other vehicles off the road in a race?

After considering this information, are you comfortable with your boy play-ing any of the games you learned about? If so, which ones, and why? Write your thoughts here:

_____

_____

_____

Many parents set guidelines for what kind of video games their boys may play, limiting them to certain sports games, for example, or to games with nonviolent content. Since many boys will go on playing video games for hours on end, parents also often set time limits on this activity. If they do, it's important that they help the boy find alternative activities that he finds satisfying.

In the space below, write down what guidelines you think are fair for your boy's video game activities:

What do you feel is a reasonable amount of time for your boy to play video games every day?

    Weekdays_____

    Weekends_____

Are there other limits you'd like to see observed having to do with the amount he plays?

___ No playing video games until homework is done

___ No playing video games after_____ P.M. on weekdays

___ Other_____

What about guidelines for which games he plays (for example, particular games or types of games he can't watch)?

_____

_____

_____

Looking at your answers above, is there anything you can imagine compromising about?

_____

_____

_____

Now show your boy your answers, and ask him the following questions.

➤ Do you think these guidelines are reasonable? Why or why not?

➤ Do you understand why I feel the way I do?

➤ If you could change one of these rules, what would you change? Why?

WHEN TO WORRY

If your boy is spending almost all his free time playing video games, you may have reason to worry. They may be serving as his escape from something else that is going wrong in his emotional life. If he is uncomfortable with other youngsters, for example, playing a complicated role-playing game by himself might fill the lonely gap he feels. Or the obsessive activity of video game play may be signaling that he is depressed.

Use the chart in chapter 8 of this book (page 168) to get a sense of whether your boy's activity is a symptom of depression, for which you should seek professional help. In addition, you might write down your thoughts on the following questions:

What else is going on in his life right now?

_____

_____

_____

Are his video game habits interfering with the activities that formerly occupied his time (school, sports, hobbies, etc.)? If so, describe how:

_____

_____

_____

Does he show other signs of depression (such as irritability or anger at limits on his game playing)? If so, describe here the symptoms you notice:

_____

_____

_____

USING THE INTERNET

"When I got Brian his own computer, I thought it would help him with schoolwork," said Harry, the father of a fifteen-year-old high-school sophomore. "Since then I've been kind of horrified at how he uses it, though. Every time I go in there he's talking to his friends on this Instant Messenger thing, and he's on-line for hours, I think. He says he's 'doing his homework,' but I'm worried that it's a lot more than that. But how can I supervise him on-line? I can't always be looking over his shoulder!"

Once a parent might have been happily surprised that a boy like Brian was spending so much time in written communication with his friends. But parents like Harry have a whole new world of questions now that the Internet has become a fact of life in many homes. Among their worries:

➤ Whether and how to try to affect what a boy is exposed to via the Internet
➤ How to protect a boy from potential harm from his Internet use
➤ How to keep a boy from letting his Internet use dominate his time to the exclusion of other activities

Like television, video games, and so many other technological media, the Internet can be a good resource for a boy who uses it with restraint. But just as with adults, it can take over huge amounts of a boy's time, so it's important to limit his use to a reasonable amount. The exercises in this section may be used either by parents at home or as a basis for discussion with the boy's school.

The following exercise will help you think about the extent of your boy's current use of the Internet.

Diagnosing a Boy's Internet Use

AN EXERCISE FOR PARENTS AND TEACHERS

Where is the computer your boy uses located?
____ In a public area where people come and go
____ In his bedroom
____ At school

Is the computer your boy uses:
____ Primarily for his own use?
____ Shared with others in the family?
____ Shared with schoolmates?

Does the computer your boy uses have:

___ A filter for material you consider objectionable?

___ No filters for different types of material?

___ I'm not sure

Does your boy use:

___ E-mail with an address not shared by others

___ A shared e-mail account

___ An address at school only

___ A Web-based e-mail account (such as Hotmail) that leaves no records on your hard drive

___ I'm not sure

In a typical week, how much does your boy use the Internet for homework?

___ Not at all

___ Sometimes; a few times a week

___ Practically every day

___ I'm not sure

In a typical week, how much does your boy use the Internet for nonschool purposes (chat, surfing the Web, on-line gaming, social e-mail)?

___ Not at all

___ Not much; a few times a week

___ Practically every day

___ I'm not sure

From what you know, who does your boy communicate with over the Internet?

___ His friends or relatives

___ His teachers

___ Participants in interest-group list-serves or chat rooms (Describe here:

_____)

___ I'm not sure

How skilled is your boy on the computer?

___ Not very skilled

___ He knows a lot, but he's not an expert

___ He knows much more than most of us

___ I'm not sure

Looking over your answers to the above questions, what positive benefits do you see your son taking from his Internet use? Write your thoughts here:

_____

_____

_____

Looking over your answers to the above questions, what negative effects do you see on your son from his Internet use? Write your thoughts here:

_____

_____

_____

INTERNET SAFETY FOR BOYS

While respecting his right to privacy, adults also need to make boys aware of how this medium can capitalize on a user's vulnerabilities, involving him in costly, dangerous, or illegal activities. Just as you would warn your boy about possible predators on the streets, talk seriously with your boy about those who use the Internet as their territory.

Most important, make sure he knows *not to give his real name, telephone number, or address* to any unknown person over the Internet without your approval.

Other possible dangers include the many on-line games that take place over the Internet. Sometimes role-playing games, for example, can spiral into unintended dangers for an unwary boy lured by an on-line stranger into taking on a perverse role.

Many Internet access providers, such as America Online, provide a "family filter" intended to prevent certain kinds of material—pornography, for instance—from getting through to a user's computer. If you choose to use such a filter, you should know that:

➤ Though reasonably effective, such filters are not foolproof; your own boy may be able to sidestep it. Some material you don't want will still make its way through.

➤ These filters also block educational or other material to which you might not object, but which may share "key words" with objectionable material.

A preventive approach to Internet safety can take other forms, too. Many families put their computer in a family living area, to quench the temptation to use it unwisely and to counteract the isolation of Web surfing. Others set limits on how much time their boys may spend on-line. Use the following space to think about what guidelines might make sense in your situation:

What do you feel is a reasonable amount of time for your boy to use the Internet every day?

Weekdays_____

Weekends_____

Are there other guidelines you'd like to see observed having to do with the amount of his Internet use?

___ Not using the Internet for nonacademic purposes until homework is done

___ Not using the Internet after_____ P.M. on weekdays

___ Other_____

What about guidelines for how he uses the Internet (for example, types of sites he can't visit)?

_____

_____

_____

Looking at your answers above, is there anything you can imagine compromising about?

Now show your boy your answers, and ask him the following questions.

➤ Do you think these guidelines are reasonable? Why or why not?

➤ Do you understand why I feel the way I do?

➤ If you could change one of these rules, what would you change? Why?

BOYS AND THEIR MUSIC

"I just don't get what Jed likes about that music!" said Eugene, the father of a high-school junior whose band practices in the family's garage. "God only knows what the words are saying, and I can barely make out a tune. I worry that the kid'll lose his hearing by listening to it through earphones, but when he plays it over the speakers I can't hear myself think. Yeah, my parents probably said the exact same thing when I used to listen to the Rolling Stones—but this stuff just sounds like screaming to me. Is Jed sending me a signal that something's very wrong in his life?"

Whether it's heavy metal or hip-hop, hard rock or blues tunes, a boy's music may come closest of any popular medium to reflecting his emerging sense of self. More than any other art form can, listening to music helps boys connect directly and powerfully with their feelings—sadness, loneliness, joy, passion, anger, confusion, and many other emotions he might otherwise find very hard to express.

A boy who is drawn to sad or angry music, however, isn't necessarily sending a signal that he's in emotional trouble. As he tries to carve out his own identity, he may just like the idea of listening to something different or rebellious, something that puts off adults and separates him from their values. Sometimes he wants to fit in with what all the other kids are listening to. And sometimes he just likes the way certain music sounds, no matter how horrendous it may seem to an adult.

To remember that feeling, Eugene need only think back on his own adolescence, as the following exercise reminds us:

What Did I Listen To?

AN EXERCISE FOR PARENTS AND TEACHERS

Think back on the music you listened to in high school, and then write the answers to the following questions:

What was your favorite musician or musical group?

_____

What did you like about that music? (Check all that apply.)
____ The particular meaning or message of its lyrics
____ Its melody, harmony, rhythm, or other musical qualities
____ It was popular among people I liked or wanted to be like
____ Other_____

How did your parents react to that music?
____ I don't know; they never listened to it.
____ When they listened, they didn't like the way it sounded.
____ When they listened, they didn't like the lyrics.
____ They liked it, too.

If your parents didn't like your music, explain why you think that was.

_____

_____

_____

If you could talk to your parents now about what that music meant to you, what would you like to be able to say?

_____

_____

_____

When you talk to your boy about his music, do you find yourself echoing any of the things your parents used to say to you?

_____

_____

_____

Do you see a difference between your situation back then and the way you and your boy are interacting now? If so, what are they?

_____

_____

_____

Now that you've thought about your own adolescent experiences with music, do you feel differently about your boy's current experiences with music? How?

_____

_____

_____

WHEN HIS MUSIC OFFENDS YOU

"I was horrified when I realized what my boy was listening to," said Gretchen, the mother of a high-school sophomore. "The only lyrics I could actually make out were outright obscene. Should I tell him he can't listen to this garbage?"

Gretchen shares this question with many other adults: What if the music your boy likes, or the way he uses it, seriously offends or disturbs you? There are many ways this might occur:

- The lyrics might be sexually explicit or violent.
- The content may be politically offensive to you (antigovernment, antipolice, advocating drug use).
- The sound may be too loud or otherwise difficult to listen to.
- The boy may use the music to isolate himself, listening with headphones and tuning out every other connection.

But rather than coming down hard on her boy's choice, Gretchen might view the music instead as a chance to open up a dialogue with him about what he believes, what he likes, and who he is. Whether an adolescent boy is drawn to the music itself or to its words, his choice of music is very personal—and it can be a valuable window into his life and emotions.

STEPS ADULTS CAN TAKE

Step one: Listen to his music.

- Tune in to the top 40 or another station he likes when you're driving with him in the car.
- Ask him to take off the headphones and share his CD with the rest of the room.
- Don't jump to conclusions based on what the music sounds like. Surprisingly, even if a band's music seems like violent or offensive noise or its image is aggressive and ugly, its lyrics may present another picture, advocating social justice or protesting against inequities or brutality.

Step two: Read the lyrics.

- Look for the lyrics in the liner notes. (If the music was downloaded via the Internet, however, no liner notes will accompany it and you may have to figure out on your own what the lyrics are saying.)
- If you find them offensive, don't assume that your boy doesn't care what they mean. He may not even realize what they say. Younger kids especially are often drawn to a band's "cool" image, not realizing what they're singing about. Lyrics about drugs, sexual abuse, and other offensive subjects may be masked by loud, shouting choruses with ambiguous meanings.

Step three: Talk to your boy about his music.

Ask him in a relaxed moment what he thinks of its message.

In many ways, this is similar to talking with a boy about his choice of reading material. For example, some possible questions Gretchen could ask her son about the music she heard are:

➤ What are they singing about in this song?

➤ What does it mean?

➤ Who do you think mostly likes this music?

➤ What do you think they like about it?

➤ What do *you* like about it?

➤ Do you agree with what it's saying in its lyrics? Why or why not?

➤ Is there anything that disturbs you about this song? If so, what?

➤ Can you think of any people who would find this song disturbing? Why?

➤ Do you think this song accurately reflects the way things are in real life?

If you have other questions you'd like to ask in such a conversation, write them here:

_____

_____

_____

Watching MTV and other top 40 music videos is another way to stay in touch with what's popular among the adolescent crowd. These very sexualized videos primarily exist to sell the image of the band and promote album sales. If you find them offensive, talk with your boy about limits on his viewing, just as you might structure his other television viewing. It's not the same as censoring what music he listens to. (In fact, a boy's overuse of what we might regard as inappropriate videos may signal that he is trying to ward off depression through withdrawal and obsessed behavior. Stay alert to this possibility.)

ROCK CONCERTS AND CLUBS

Rock concerts are now part of the popular music scene of adolescence, and well worth investigating if your boy wants to attend one. Popular bands have widely different reputations for different kinds of concerts. Some are violent shows, with mosh pits near the stage where a younger boy could get scared or hurt. Some are occasions for audiences to use drugs.

When your boy first shows an interest in going to a rock concert, take the opportunity to go along to a few if you possibly can. You don't have to embarrass your boy by sitting with him and his friends, but you will find out a lot by just keeping your eyes open.

If eventually your boy goes to rock concerts with friends on his own, talk to him about safety issues before he goes. It's common for drugs to be sold at such concerts, and narcotics officers will be looking for any opportunity to arrest those who sell or buy them.

Drugs are also part of the club scene that attracts many older teenagers, who get into such clubs with forged identification cards. Chapter 9 of this book ("Boys and Drugs") will help you familiarize yourself with the warning signs that he may be falling into this scene.

LET HIM BE HIMSELF

These are scary areas for boys and their parents to navigate, but it's important to realize that the music itself is not the problem. In fact, music provides an important way for a boy to connect with and release his emotions, evolve an aesthetic sense, and act as a creative person. It's also a way for him to practice his developing critical intelligence, if adults will pay respectful attention to his choices and tastes. If a parent can possibly stand not to set limits on a boy's musical choices, it's an especially good place to back off and let him be himself.

14

BOYS' FRIENDSHIPS

HOW BOYS MAKE FRIENDS • STAYING CLOSE • FRIENDSHIPS WITH GIRLS

"Every morning before homeroom, this one group of boys sits in the back and insults each other," says Ms. Timmons, a young ninth-grade teacher at a large regional high school. "Two of them constantly pick on each other for the clothes they're wearing. Yesterday I heard one saying, 'Tyrone, we know you're hiding your skinny ass in those baggy jeans!' I try to teach the kids to respect each other, but they just laugh at me when I tell them to stop. Should I tolerate this kind of insulting behavior?"

Ms. Timmons is right to teach respect, and she may not want to permit certain language in her classroom. But what seems like "insulting behavior" to her may actually be a sign of these boys' close and loving friendship.

Unlike many girls, boys often express their love for each other through mutual teasing, jostling, and even insults. Hampered by the Boy Code from openly revealing their feelings, they find ways to "speak in code."

Adults, especially women whose experience of intimacy may be very different, sometimes need help translating that code. In this chapter, we'll look at the special forms that boys' friendships take, both with other boys and with girls. And we'll explore ways that adults can encourage these friendships to flourish.

HOW BOYS MAKE FRIENDS

"There's a big difference between how my daughter plays with her friends and how my little boy does," said Nona, the mother of a seven-year-old girl and a five-year-old boy. "Leah likes to play Mommy; she always makes her friend be the baby. But Adam and his friend spend hours making airplanes out of Legos. While they work they talk about whose airplane is going to fly faster and win the battle. Then they run around with the airplanes, making shooting sounds and crashing to the floor."

Even at this young age, Leah and Adam are examples of the broad differences between boys' and girls' friendship patterns. While there are many variations from the norm, this is how the patterns tend to look:

BOYS' FRIENDSHIPS	GIRLS' FRIENDSHIPS
Play games with structure and rules	Revolve around relationships
Test skills in a mutual challenge	Focus on hierarchies like "best friends"
Jostle and compete with each other	Openly express tenderness and affection, and express their competition verbally

Think about the ways your boy relates to his friends. Do you notice any of these patterns? Describe:

_____

_____

_____

Do you notice ways in which he breaks these patterns? If so, describe:

_____

_____

_____

In friendships especially, remember, we see a lot of variation among boys with different temperaments. It would not be unusual for some boys to be more openly sharing and affectionate, using fewer physical signals than other boys do with their "best friends." We should learn to honor the full range of diverse expression of friendship among boys. Being more sensitive and open does not make him "less of a boy," and being more active and physical does not make him less of a real friend.

UNDERSTANDING THE RULES OF BOYS' FRIENDSHIPS

In the movie *Stand by Me,* a group of middle-school boys goes on a quest together and helps one another through difficult emotional situations. The boys in the movie express their love and respect for one another through teasing and action. They obey the hidden set of rules that govern boys' relationships with one another:

1. Stand up for your buddies.
2. Actions speak louder than words.
3. Be there when your friends need you.
4. Stay cool no matter what.
5. Teasing is affectionate; just don't go too far.

Many boys of all ages—and even some men—follow these rules in their friendships. In the following exercise, you will have the chance to practice recognizing these rules in action.

Staying Within the Rules

AN EXERCISE FOR PARENTS AND TEACHERS

After each story, look at the list of rules above. Write the numbers of the rules the boys are following in the space provided.

Wright, eleven, has just been diagnosed with juvenile diabetes and has to follow a strict diet. On the bus home after the big soccer tournament, the coach passes out doughnuts and cookies to the players. Wright's friend Frank, sitting beside him, passes the box back without taking anything. "I don't really like that stuff either," Frank says to Wright. "Do you have an apple or anything?"

Frank is following these rules: _____

Have you ever witnessed or experienced this rule in action? Explain:

_____

_____

_____

Tanner was wait-listed at his first choice of colleges, and his only acceptance came from a state school where none of his friends would be going. Although very upset, the next day at school he tells his friends casually where he'll be going. "That's cool," says his best friend, Cole, who had been accepted early to his own top choice. "It's pretty close to where I'll be, so we can hang out sometimes on weekends."

Tanner and Cole are following this rule: _____

Have you ever witnessed or experienced this rule in action? Explain:

_____

_____

_____

Nine-year-old Thuy brings his violin to school every Wednesday, and stops for his lesson on the way home. As he's leaving one Wednesday, an older boy stops him and grabs his violin case, holding it out of reach. "Does the little Tweety Bird want his faggy toy back?" the older boy taunts. Thuy turns red and says nothing, but his friends Benjy and Liam step closer to him. "Shut up and give it back," says Benjy. "If you mess up his violin we're going to tell!"

Thuy's friends are following this rule: _____

Have you ever witnessed or experienced this rule in action? Explain:

_____

_____

_____

When fourteen-year-old Eric's father left the family, Eric and his mother had to move to a much smaller apartment with a no-dogs rule. "Chief's too old for anyone to want to adopt him," Eric told his friend Ryan with a catch in his voice. "My mom says they might have to put him to sleep." The next day, Ryan called Eric. "I talked to my parents and they said we could take Chief for you if you want," he said. "As long as you can help out with taking care of him."

Ryan is following this rule: _____

Have you ever witnessed or experienced this rule in action? Explain:

_____

_____

_____

At the last two sophomore class parties he's been to, Andy has spent most of his time in a corner with Stephanie, the first girl he's "gone out" with. Now the two often hold hands in the halls at school, and his friends rag on him mercilessly about it. "Hey, Andy, where's your boss?" they call to him between classes. But at "their" cafeteria lunch table, they move aside to make room for Stephanie to sit next to Andy.

Andy's friends are following this rule: _____

Have you ever witnessed or experienced this rule in action? Explain:

_____

_____

_____

Once you recognize these patterns in your boy's friendships, you'll see that many of his actions connect to his need to safely express his closeness and affection.

HELPING YOUR BOY MAKE FRIENDS

"It seems like Sam and Mo's friends always end up at our place," said An-jali, the mother of fifteen-year-old twin boys. "We've got this old pool table in the basement and an extra refrigerator down there, too, because our boys eat so much. I don't want them hanging out down on the corner, so I go to the food warehouse and buy snacks and drinks in big cartons. And I don't really care how much noise the boys make down there, so they've started bringing their guitars and playing. Now they say they're going to start a band."

Anjali has done just the right things to encourage her boys' friendships:

➤ She provides a place where they can gather safely but privately.
➤ She doesn't object to their activities.
➤ She makes her welcome clear by providing plenty of food.
➤ She provides access to activities that boys like to do, such as playing pool.

The following exercise will help you think about how to make your house a welcoming environment for your boy and his friends:

Is My House Boy-Friendly?

AN EXERCISE FOR PARENTS

Check any of the conditions below that apply to your living situation:
___ There is a place where boys can gather comfortably.
Describe:

___ You have food and drinks they like and are allowed to snack on.
Describe:

_____

___ There are things they like to do (pool table, water play, games, music, basketball hoop).
Describe:

_____

___ You are there at times when they like to gather.
Describe:

_____

___ You know your boy's friends and enjoy having them around.
Describe:

_____

EXCLUSION AND REJECTION

"Ethan never fit very well into any group," said Harold, the father of a twelve-year-old boy. "He doesn't really play sports or an instrument, and he never liked Scouts that much either. He likes to read, and I guess that's not so popular these days. Now that he's in seventh grade, it's starting to worry us. Last week they had a dance at school and we learned later he was the only boy who didn't go. What can we do to help?"

Not every boy has a whole group of pals to "stand by him." But if Ethan doesn't have any close friends at all, his parents are right to be concerned. It's possible that Ethan is withdrawing from his peers because he is depressed, and if so, he may need help from an outside professional.

But if Ethan is being excluded or rejected simply because he doesn't fit the mold, his parents can support him in other practical ways. First, they need to think through what brought Ethan to this place, and what he needs to help him out of it.

Why is Ethan being excluded?

➤ Ethan may not know the basic skills of friendship.

➤ Ethan may be too shy to have established a close friend.

➤ Ethan may not be interested in doing the things the boys around him do.

➤ He may be finding it hard to break out of a label others have placed on him.

How could adults help Ethan learn to make friends?

➤ His parents and teachers could point out specific friendship skills and praise him in private when he tries them.

➤ He could work with a younger boy or a girl on some regular activity.

➤ He could start participating in a project that involves an unrelated circle of people (drama, photography classes, rock climbing).

➤ He could find a pen pal in another place.

➤ He could link up with an older mentor to pursue an interest he may have.

➤ They could help him find other boys with similar temperaments and shared interests, with whom he would feel more comfortable.

Without shaming Ethan, his parents can give him chances to make a fresh start among people who haven't already labeled him as an outsider. In a matter-of-fact and supportive way, they can also show him what people do when they reach out to make a friend. Especially at this awkward stage of a boy's adolescence, friendship skills don't always come naturally. Sometimes, caring adults need to teach them explicitly.

Most important of all, boys who feel excluded by their peers need to feel complete love and acceptance from their families, and need to know there's nothing "wrong" with them. There's no such thing as too much parental love and support. Point out and praise his strengths, and let him know you'll always be there for him.

TEACHING THE SKILLS OF FRIENDSHIP:
TIPS FOR PARENTS AND TEACHERS

TEACH A BOY TO:

➤ Move into a group without drawing immediate attention to himself.

➤ Listen to what's going on and size up the situation.

➤ Ask questions that have to do with what's going on.

➤ Find something he can agree with and enter the conversation.

➤ Avoid disagreeing with other group members too often, even if he thinks he's right.

PRAISE A BOY WHEN HE:

➤ Starts a conversation with someone he doesn't know very well.

➤ Tells someone when they hurt his feelings.

➤ Asks someone their opinion on something.

➤ Cooperates on a project or a game.

➤ Listens when someone needs to talk.

➤ Tells someone how he feels about them.

➤ Tells someone he liked what they did.

➤ Does something nice for someone spontaneously.

INTERVENE WHEN A BOY:

➤ Dismisses somebody's opinion.

➤ Excludes somebody from a game or project.

➤ Always interrupts other children.

➤ Hurts somebody physically.

➤ Acts like a bully (see chapter 6, "Bullies and Troublemakers").

STAYING CLOSE

Some boys have a special way of showing their affection and solidarity with each other without exposing their vulnerability:

- They keep their physical expressions of love quick and active (a slap on the back, a high five).
- They don't talk to friends about problems, but they acknowledge them in other ways.
- They express their closeness and empathy indirectly, through acts of loyalty.

Sometimes adults may not recognize when boys are "speaking in code" to express their mutual closeness. The following exercise will give you practice "translating" boys' coded messages, so that you can better understand their friendships.

Translating the Code

AN EXERCISE FOR PARENTS AND TEACHERS

After each example, pick what you think the boy really means:

1. After a lost game, a boy tells a teammate who fumbled a key play:
   "Bad luck—I think the ref called that wrong."
   He really means:
   ___ I think the referee was unfair.
   ___ I don't blame you for messing up; I still like you.
   ___ It's your fault we lost.

2. One boy has a date for the prom; his best friend gets turned down by the girl he asks. The first boy says:
   "We're going to hang out at the postprom party, right?"
   He really means:
   ___ You're still part of our crowd; it doesn't matter to me what girls think of you.
   ___ Am I going to have to hang out with you the whole night?
   ___ It's weird that you don't have a date.

3. A crowd of boys is hanging out in the empty lot. One boy jumps on another's back, saying:

> "Hey, dainty boy—do you want me to call your mommy to rescue you?"

He really means:

___ You're a mama's boy.

___ I want to prove I'm stronger than you.

___ I like you and want to play.

You may have had doubts about what the boys in these examples really meant. But between friends, boys rarely misinterpret each other's coded messages. Through tone of voice and small physical signals, they let each other know that they love and support each other, even in rough times.

PRESSURE AND RISKY BEHAVIOR

Sometimes a boy can't stay close to his friends without risking harm to himself. Adults can help boys figure out whether to stick with the crowd or break away.

"I knew Ricky was old enough to choose his own friends, but I really didn't like the crowd he was hanging out with," said Donald, the father of a fourteen-year-old. "The whole group got in trouble with the police last fall for knocking down mailboxes on our block." Donald made Ricky pay for the damage he did, but he knew he wouldn't get anywhere if he simply forbade Ricky to hang out with his friends anymore. After a few days had gone by, at a quiet time when they were alone in the car, he struck up a conversation instead.

"I asked Ricky why he wanted to hang out with kids who would destroy property like that. At first, Ricky didn't say much of anything. Then I asked what he would do if the kids decided instead to hurt a person—to push over an old lady or something. Even if Ricky weren't exactly the one doing it, how would he feel about being part of a group like that? And if the police got involved, he would probably be held legally responsible anyway." Ricky and

Donald ended up in a good conversation about how hard it is to control what other people do. "Lately, he seems to be mostly avoiding that crowd," Donald said. "I think I managed to get through to him without taking away his feeling that he was making the choices about his life."

Donald found a good way to help Ricky make safe choices of friends, without taking away Ricky's dignity as he grows more independent. But it's not always easy for a boy to choose wisely. And parents may not always know when a boy's friends are pressuring him to engage in risky behavior.

That's why it's so important for adults to talk with their boys early about pressure, giving them words to say in situations like these. Boys need to learn how to say no without losing face.

Some ways a boy can say no:
➤ I'm doing something else that night.
➤ The coach says drugs will hurt my game.
➤ My parents will kill me.
➤ I'll lose my job if I test positive for drugs.

It helps if the excuse doesn't turn the boy into an outsider. In front of his friends, it's okay for him to put the responsibility for his choice on someone else.

Can you think of other words your boy could use to retreat from a risky situation without shame? Write them here:

_____

_____

_____

Boys have a natural desire to participate in things that seem exciting or even dangerous. But there are plenty of safe alternatives for boys and their friends that can provide that thrill.

Some alternative thrills adults can help set up for boys and their friends:

➤ Midnight basketball or indoor soccer tournaments

➤ Whitewater rafting or canoeing

➤ Wilderness trips to off-trail areas

➤ Circus skills training (trampoline, juggling, trapeze, etc.)

➤ High diving at a pool

Can you think of other exciting activities you could arrange? Write them here:

_____

_____

_____

Boys also have the urge to protect and stand up for their friends. Talk with your boy about ways he can intervene when his friends are in harm's way. He might say, for example:

➤ You shouldn't be driving. My dad's cool; he'll come pick us up.

➤ This place is sketchy. Let's get out of here.

➤ I think [Tommy's] sick. We should take him home.

A boy who feels that he's protecting and watching out for his friends is more likely to refuse to take risks like drugs and alcohol himself.

FRIENDSHIPS WITH GIRLS

So far we've focused on boys' friendships with other boys. But adults are often surprised to learn that many boys find some of their closest friendships with girls, from an early age.

"Benson always played with my friend's daughter, Nell, since they were born," said Mary Ann, the mother of a fourteen-year-old boy. "Around third or fourth grade they grew apart a little, but for the last couple of years

they've started talking on the phone and hanging out sometimes after school. He says that Nell is like his sister."

WHY BOYS NEED GIRLS AS FRIENDS

A nonromantic friendship with a girl can free a boy from the gender strait-jacket in several important ways:

A boy doesn't feel competitive with a girl in the same way he does with other boys.

"With the other guys, I have to worry about staying cool," said Darren, fifteen. "Rosa doesn't care if I make varsity soccer or if I'm acting tough. We just hang out and listen to music, and she helps me with my Spanish homework."

Girls make it safe for a boy to express his feelings.

"Minh is the one I can always call when things are rough with my dad," said Peter, thirteen. "The guys don't really know what to say, but somehow just talking to her makes me feel better."

Girls can be powerful allies at school in social situations.

"When I was in middle school, I wasn't really popular," said Freddie, sixteen. "But this one girl in my math class, Olivia, always sat next to me and we would pass notes. It made it easier, like at parties, to know she would talk to me. I didn't feel so weird."

Having a nonromantic friendship with a girl teaches a boy to understand girls without the pressure of sex.

"Alissa is the first girl I've ever really been friends with," said fourteen-year-old Simon. "Sometimes I don't get why she freaks out when I don't talk to her for a couple of days, or something. But I guess that matters more to girls."

Girls need boys as friends, too. With boys who are friends girls can practice asserting themselves, for example. And girls, too, learn what boys are like in relationships from such friendships.

Crossover Friends

AN EXERCISE FOR PARENTS AND TEACHERS

When you were growing up, did you have a friend of the opposite sex who was not a romantic interest? If so, what was this person's name?

_____

How did you spend your time together?

_____

_____

_____

How was that friendship different from your same-sex friendships?

_____

_____

_____

Do you have good friends of the opposite sex now? If so, list them here:

_____

_____

_____

What's special about your current opposite-sex nonromantic friendships?

_____

_____

_____

"HANGING OUT" WITH GIRLS

"My Andrew doesn't have a girlfriend yet—at least, I don't think so!" said Martha, whose fifteen-year-old boy attends a school where students come from all over the city. "He and his friends hang out socially on weekends in mixed groups of girls and boys, mostly at one another's houses." But lately Andrew and his friends have been asking to spend the night together, instead of coming home late on public transportation or depending on rides. "They're having co-ed sleep-overs!" Martha exclaimed. "Andrew says they're not 'doing anything'—and really, I guess I believe him, these are such good kids. But should I be worried, or not let him do it? This is all so different from what I ever expected!"

Martha and other parents may be worried about several things:

➤ They worry that children will be having sex with each other at these gatherings.

➤ They worry that all-night parties will include drinking and lead to other dangers like unwelcome sexual encounters.

➤ They worry about their own reputation and that of their children.

➤ They fear that they are not setting proper limits for what teenagers should be allowed to do together.

Do you have any other fears about what could go wrong in situations like this? Write them here:

_____

_____

_____

Before she decides what to do, Martha should talk openly with her son—and with the parents of the other kids involved—about these fears. She could ask Andrew these questions:

➤ Do kids ever fool around at these parties?
➤ Are there private rooms, or is everyone hanging out together?
➤ Will there be any adults around? Who?
➤ Do you understand why I feel uncomfortable with this idea?

Of the other parents, she could ask these questions:

➤ Are you going to be there?
➤ Are you going to make sure there's no drinking or drugs?
➤ Will you make sure everyone's hanging out together, not in private rooms?
➤ Tell me why you're comfortable/uncomfortable with this idea.

Different parents have different levels of comfort with these kinds of parties. While you should not be afraid to trust your own judgment, it's important to question where it comes from; the rules you learned growing up may need to change in the world where your own boy lives. Try to seek input from other trusted adults before you finally set the rules about what your boy may do. But it's important for you to talk through your reasons with him, respecting the fact that he may disagree while reserving your right to say no.

I think it's okay for my boy to "hang out" with girls as long as:

_____

_____

_____

I wouldn't feel comfortable with my boy "hanging out" with girls if:

_____

_____

_____

If you're uncomfortable with co-ed sleep-overs, you could:
➤ Offer to host a co-ed party that's not a sleep-over, and arrange transportation with other parents for everybody who wants to come.
➤ Offer to attend the co-ed sleep-over as an extra chaperone.
➤ Offer to help organize a co-ed sleep-over at school or some interesting place (a science museum, a roller rink, a campground, a library), with plenty of adults as chaperones.
➤ Other ideas:_____

_____

_____

For boys who aren't ready yet for sexual relationships, "hanging out" with girls in groups is an easy way to get comfortable around girls. Remember, in just a few years they will probably be living away from home, surrounded by girls and often in co-ed college housing.

Allowing your boy to "hang out" with girls now, in supervised settings, may help him take small steps toward strong, healthy, and sensitive romantic or sexual relationships when the appropriate time arrives. In the next chapter, we'll look more at how parents can guide their sons to make good decisions as they begin to explore their sexuality.

REMINDERS ABOUT SUPPORTING YOUR BOY'S FRIENDSHIPS

Do:

➤ Get to know his friends and their families.

➤ Share outings and projects with friends.

➤ Attend special occasions or events that involve his friends.

➤ Give him plenty of chances to play active, structured games with his friends.

➤ Tell him stories about your own close friendships.

➤ Praise his acts of friendship openly.

➤ Recognize that friendships between boys and girls don't have to be romantic or sexual.

➤ Let the band practice at your house.

➤ Have plenty of the "right" food—soda, chips, snack food—and welcome his friends.

➤ Make it easy for them to do active, fun things (water play, basketball, billiards).

Don't:

➤ Judge or criticize his friends.

➤ Assume that a girl he likes is necessarily a romantic interest.

➤ Label his physical expressions of affection as "gay."

➤ Interpret his competitive or insulting play as necessarily aggressive.

➤ Object to his talking on the phone to friends.

➤ Object to his making music with friends in a loud band.

15

SEX AND RELATIONSHIPS

BOYS AND THEIR SEXUALITY • SEX EDUCATION • "GOING OUT" AND FIRST LOVE • WHEN SEX CREATES DANGERS • HOMOSEXUALITY AND HOMOPHOBIA

"Tucker used to love to talk to us about what he and his friends were doing," said Bob, the father of a fifteen-year-old. *"This year, though, we can't get him to say a thing. If we ask him questions, he says a word or two and shuts up. I know he and the guys are starting to go to parties with girls, and I want to be able to give him some guidance about sex if he needs it."*

As a boy approaches adolescence, his emerging sexuality presents an entirely new set of issues, both for him and for the adults who care about him:

➤ Society's rules about masculinity grow more complicated as romance and sex enter the picture.

➤ There is more potential for shame than ever.

➤ The culture glorifies sexual conquest and romance, yet warns of new dangers, too.

A boy is in uncertain territory with practically every choice he makes. At the same time, as he tries to establish his own identity, he is less willing to allow his parents to help him with these choices.

It's common for a boy to clam up completely about such matters in the high-school years. Whatever his romantic and sexual life might consist of, he puts on a mask to protect it from scrutiny.

In this difficult time, strong and trusting connections between adults and boys are more important than ever. Tucker's parents don't need to invade their son's privacy in order to support him as he confronts these new choices and complications. The home can become a haven, where a boy can feel safe from shame as he forges his identity as a man.

The exercises in this chapter will help you guide boys through this period, clarifying their confusions without intruding into areas that belong to them alone.

BOYS AND THEIR SEXUALITY

By the time he reaches high school, a boy may feel reluctant to share much about his sexual life with his parents. Still, adults have many opportunities to positively affect a boy's values, beliefs, and actions about sex and romance.

In the story above, Bob can keep providing matter-of-fact opportunities to talk about important things in a safe context. Without prying into Tucker's affairs, for example, he can express his interest in the parties his boy goes to.

"On the ride home last Saturday night I asked him what he might like to do to celebrate his sixteenth birthday with his friends," Bob said later. "That led to a long conversation about what he thought a 'good party' was. I didn't say much, but I learned a lot just by listening."

MIXED MESSAGES ABOUT SEX AND ROMANCE

Along with adolescence comes a new pressure for boys—the feeling that they must have sex in order to prove their manhood. Even if their families or their school sex education courses are teaching abstinence, our entire culture is sending him the opposite message through television, movies, music, and other media.

The following exercise explores just a few of the contradictions the typical boy encounters:

What Message Is He Getting?

Check all the messages you think your boy might be getting, even if they contradict one another.

What messages about sex does your boy get from television and movies?
___ Everybody's having sex.
___ Anything is permitted.
___ Protection is unimportant.
___ Other messages:_____

What messages does he get from rock music and music videos?
___ Girls are sexual objects.
___ Love is important in a sexual relationship.
___ Love is not important in a sexual relationship.
___ Other messages:_____

What messages does he get from you?
___ Sex is a natural part of a living relationship.
___ You are not ready for sex.
___ It is not possible to speak comfortably about sexual feelings.
___ Other messages: _____

What messages does he get from school sex education?
___ Unprotected sex leads to pregnancy or sexually transmitted infections.
___ Sex is always dangerous for teenagers.
___ Sex is sometimes healthy and good.
___ Other messages:_____

What messages does he get from the law and from school rules?
___ Any comments about sex could get you in big trouble.
___ Don't talk about sex.

____ Always talk about sex before having it.

____ Other messages:_____

What messages does he get from his male peers?

____ Real men have sex all the time.

____ It's not cool to be a virgin.

____ Sex is cool, but don't act like you love the person.

____ Girls don't want sex—you have to persuade them.

____ Other messages:_____

What messages does he get from his female peers?

____ Nice boys are respectful and don't push for sex.

____ Nice girls don't have sex, ever.

____ Sex is fine if you're in love.

____ Other messages:_____

What messages does he get about homosexuality?

____ Being gay is the worst thing that could happen to a boy.

____ Treat all people with respect, no matter what their sexual orientation.

____ It's okay to tease people about "acting gay."

____ Gay sex is something very scary.

____ Other messages:_____

Look at all the different messages you checked. Now write them out here, one after the other, in a paragraph:

_____

_____

_____

_____

_____

_____

Read your paragraph out loud. What are your reactions?

___ I think it's funny.

___ I think it's very confusing.

___ It makes me mad.

___ I feel worried.

Explain a little more about your feelings here:

_____

_____

_____

HOW A BOY ACTS

Boys often react to the pressures of these mixed messages with a mixture of fear and confusion, which is not always obvious:

➤ Some boys look for closeness and warmth in less dangerous settings. They may seek out the strong but nonsexual friendships with girls that we talked about earlier.

➤ Some boys may treat sex as a casual, emotionally disconnected activity—what some observers have called "body-part sex." They may start with kissing games in grade school and only a few years later be getting girls to give them oral sex for "fun," even before they have tried intercourse.

➤ Some boys yearn for sexual closeness with a romantic partner, but fear the risks of intimacy—shame, rejection, dependence, or failure. (Will he be shamed in front of his peers by failing to "score"? Will his romantic interest reject him if he goes too far, or will he be unable to understand what his partner wants from him?)

Anxieties about sex may lead boys to use alcohol or drugs—which, in turn, increases the probability of having unprotected sex, multiple partners, or violent sexual encounters.

To sidestep this miserable spiral, boys need *positive connections with adults* who respect their growing independence and who can guide them toward wise choices.

EMERGING SEXUALITY

What parents say, and how we say it—as well as what we don't say—send messages to our boys from an early age about our values and beliefs about sexuality and romantic relationships.

"I guess my little Pete is getting to be a man," said Ceronne about her ten-year-old son. "He used to take a bath with his little brother, but now he locks himself in the bathroom to shower and he won't come out unless he's covered up. I don't say a word about it, just give the little one his bath alone these days. But I wish he had a father to tell him the facts of life."

Ceronne is right to respect Pete's newfound modesty as puberty approaches. And she is also right that this is the signal to talk with him about the "facts of life." Pete needs to know what the changes in his body are all about, and have the chance to ask questions freely. But he may or may not be comfortable having the conversation with his mother.

Sometimes another person may be more suited to give your boy the information he needs. Instead of pushing a conversation that Pete isn't ready for, Ceronne might:

- Arrange for an uncle, or another male or female adult that Pete trusts, to talk with him.
- Ask his pediatrician to talk privately with Pete about his changing body.
- Provide a good book for him to look through on his own.

Many mothers are taken aback by the sudden distance their boy puts between them as he approaches puberty. Filled with confusing and free-floating sexual feelings, and picking up society's message that they should push away from their moms, boys this age typically go through a phase when the mother's presence is particularly irritating.

"When he was a little boy, Carl used to love to cuddle with me on the couch before bedtime," said Lisbeth, the mother of a twelve-year-old boy. "But lately, any time I put my arm around him, he recoils or goes rigid. Should I take this as a sign of something wrong?"

This can be hard for a mother who has tried hard to keep emotionally connected with her boy. But if Lisbeth gives him space now, not disconnecting but allowing him both privacy and the later possibility of talking, her boy will reconnect with her when he's ready.

WHAT HE MIGHT BE ASKING

Parents can learn a lot about their boy's questions by listening for what might lie beneath the things he says in casual conversation. For example:

> *If he says:* "How tall were you when you were my age?"
> *He might be asking:* "Is it okay that I'm not as big as the other boys?"

> *If he says:* "Do you think it's weird if I bring Ms. Hermann a present?"
> *He might be asking:* "Is it okay that I have a crush on my teacher?"

> *If he says:* "I hate this family—no one ever leaves you alone for a second!"
> *He might be asking:* "I need more privacy in my room now that my body's changing."

If he says: "How did you guys know when you were in love?"
He might be asking: "How do I know what my sexual feelings mean?"

Remember, sometimes our biggest mistake when adolescent boys tell us "Leave me alone!" is that we do.

SOME GOOD TIMES TO TALK ABOUT SEX WITH YOUR BOY

➤ After you've seen a TV show or news broadcast that deals with a sexual topic
➤ If someone you know has become pregnant unexpectedly
➤ When you hear someone use a sexual slur ("faggot," "slut," etc.)
➤ After a movie that includes romantic or sexual interludes
➤ When you're talking about your own early crushes or romances, or your parents' rules and values
➤ If you can ask him to help you explain something about sex to a younger child

AVOID TALKING ABOUT SEX WITH YOUR BOY IN THESE WAYS

➤ Talking about your own sexual experiences with his other parent or someone else
➤ Asking him direct questions about his sexual experiences
➤ Implying or directly making criticisms of his friends or their behavior
➤ Delivering rules to him about what you expect of his sexual behavior
➤ Sounding like you know it all, or implying that you had no anxiety or confusion about sex when you were his age

---

SEX EDUCATION

Alice and her husband, Jim, were making love at about ten one night when their four-year-old son burst in on them to say he couldn't sleep. "By the time I realized he was there, it was too late—he had already seen what I wouldn't want him to see," said Alice. "The next day at breakfast he told me he had a bad dream about a big fight. It took me a while to figure out what he was worried about—turned out the poor kid thought Jim had been trying to hurt me! I sat with him for a while and talked about how mommies and daddies show their love for each other by getting very close with our bodies in bed."

Alice is giving her son an important early message that it's okay for him to talk to his parents about sex. She is giving him information, but also much more—by passing along her attitude that sex is a way for a couple to show love, that other people need to respect a couple's privacy in sex, but that she is not embarrassed to speak about it.

Jimmy was twelve years old when his father, Roland, unintentionally surprised him in his bedroom one day as he was masturbating on the bed. "I apologized and got out of there in a hurry," Roland said. "But later I was thinking about how embarrassed he must have felt, too." That night, Roland knocked on his son's door to apologize again, and then sat down to talk with him. "I told him that masturbating is really normal for kids and for grownups, too," he said. "I said it was a good way to get sexual pleasure by yourself, and I told him it couldn't hurt him at all. It was hard to get myself to talk about it, but I think Jimmy felt a lot better afterward, and so did I."

As your boy gets older, don't wait until he asks questions to bring up the subject of sex with him. Many boys will never bring up the subject on their own. Or they will respond to your overtures by saying, "I know all that stuff," and walking away.

But if you remain alert to what seems to interest him, you can find other ways to convey both information and your own beliefs and values.

What Should a Parent Say About Sex, and When?

As Early as He Begins to Ask

➤ Ask him to tell you what he thinks about how male and female bodies work.

➤ Correct any misinformation in language appropriate to his understanding level.

➤ Explain how and why male bodies are different from female bodies.

➤ Tell him how and why a boy's body is different from a man's body.

➤ Tell him how and why a girl's body is different from a woman's body.

➤ Explain how babies are conceived and born.

Before He Begins to Mature

(*Varies by child, beginning roughly around nine or ten years old*)

➤ Tell him that his body will be changing over time to look like a man's body.

➤ Talk about what he can expect from his changing body (feelings, erections, masturbation, nocturnal emissions, etc.).

➤ Invite him to ask you any questions he might have, and answer them directly.

➤ Give him a good book about his changing body and sex.

➤ If he has a good relationship with his doctor, ask his pediatrician to bring up the subject and answer your boy's questions at a routine physical exam when you are not in the room.

➤ Make sure his school offers sex education in a form with which you are comfortable.

➤ In your own behavior, model respect for the feelings and rights of others.

➤ Intervene directly when he interacts with others in disrespectful, thoughtless, or exploitative ways.

(continued)

"We were watching a show on TV where these younger kids were acting pretty sexy with each other," said Joanna. *"I said to my thirteen-year-old, Sam, 'What do you think would happen if kids really got that involved with each other?' We had a long conversation, but keeping it kind of at arm's length, about what 'some kids' might do and about whether movies and TV exaggerated the way kids really act. It seemed like that was the safest way for him to talk about his questions and opinions—and he had plenty of them!"*

Joanna is providing a shame-free way for Sam to bring up his concerns without feeling as if his mother is invading his private life. TV, movies, music, news, and many other media supply dozens of such openings for adults to ask a boy what *he* thinks and talk naturally about their own attitudes, too.

Research shows that conversations like these have a strong effect on a boy's decisions about matters concerning sex—as well as a strong effect on how open and direct they are with their parents later, when they may begin engaging in more sexual activity. Of course, a boy will always be affected by what his peers think and their pressures on him—but even then, your boy will probably remember what you have said.

TIPS FOR HIGH-SCHOOL TEACHERS:
TALKING ABOUT SEX AT SCHOOL

➤ Use your academic subject area as a starting point for thoughtful dialogue about responsible sexual behavior. Social studies classes might look critically at sex-related behavior patterns across cultures or at the use of sexual violence in war. Science and math classes might explore the biology or statistics of sexually transmitted infections.

➤ Use the student government to think through guidelines or rules on sex-related behavior, such as whether (and which) "public displays of affection" are appropriate in a school setting. Suggest a schoolwide conversation or "teach-in" on a topic of particular interest or controversy, alternating larger assemblies with small-group discussions.

➤ Demonstrate that you value respectful and open participation in difficult decisions, including when situations involve sexual behavior. Take every opportunity for dialogue among teachers, students, and parents about value-laden subjects like condom availability or sexual harassment.

"GOING OUT" AND FIRST LOVE

"Of course I expected Aaron to start going out when he was a teenager,"
said Toni, the mother of a tenth-grade boy. "But nothing prepared me for
seeing him all dressed up for the school semiformal, holding a corsage for
the girl he had asked. It took me right back to my own high-school days."

Most parents have their own inner timetable for their boy's sexual experiences—what they believe is "on track" and what is "off track." As the following examples show, much of that inner timetable is based on their own youthful experiences:

"Even though I had plenty of chances, I didn't have sex until I was seriously involved with someone in college," said Michael. "I wouldn't want my boy to be sleeping with girls before that—it would be a disaster if something went wrong and the girl got pregnant."

"I was too shy in high school to even ask a girl out," David said. "I hope my kid has more confidence in himself than I did at that age—I want him to be able to have fun at school dances. It's important that he get some experience with romance as a teenager—no one says these things have to last."

Michael wants his boy to follow the same timetable that worked for him. David, though, had bad feelings about his own youthful timetable and hopes it will be different for his boy. Either way, their opinions about their boys' sexual behavior come from a very individual context, which typically differs based on all kinds of factors—your family or community, other people's expectations, and similar pressures.

The following exercise will help you clarify how your own experiences have shaped your expectations for your boy.

What I Did and Why I Did It

AN EXERCISE FOR PARENTS

I first became interested in another person romantically at about the age of ____

Describe the situation:

_____

_____

_____

I first became interested in another person sexually at about the age of ___

Describe the situation:

_____

_____

_____

I first spent time alone with a romantic or sexual partner at about age ___

Describe the situation:

_____

_____

_____

What outside expectations surrounded your seeing a person romantically?
(Check all that apply.)

___ It was expected that we would see each other in group settings only.

___ It was expected that we would go out on dates alone.

___ My family expected that we would not become sexually intimate.

___ My family didn't care whether we became sexually intimate.

___ My peers expected that we would become sexually intimate.

___ My peers expected that we would not become sexually intimate.

___ My interest in this person was unacceptable to my family because

_____.

___ My interest in this person was unacceptable to my peers because

_____.

What internal pressures affected your decisions about sexual intimacy?
(Check all that apply.)

___ I wanted to fulfill the expectations of my family.

___ I wanted to reject the expectations of my family.

___ I didn't want my family to know anything about my choices.

___ I wanted to fulfill the expectations of my peer group.

___ I didn't want my peer group to know about my choices.

___ I wanted to fulfill the expectations of my romantic partner.

Whom could you talk with about your decisions regarding sexual intimacy?
(Check all that apply.)

___ My parents

___ My siblings

___ My friends

___ Another adult (describe role:_____)

___ My romantic partner

___ No one

___ Other (describe:_____)

Looking over your answers, think about any differences between the social pressures and expectations you experienced in this area and those that your boy might experience. Describe those differences here:

In our family, it might be different for my boy because:

_____

_____

_____

In the larger social setting, it might be different for my boy because:

_____

_____

_____

TAKING THE PLUNGE

Once a boy starts having sexual intercourse—and four out of five will before they leave their teens—he may not want to talk about it with adults. But if they know about it, parents often feel conflicting emotions.

"I just love the girl my son, Charlie, goes out with," said Rebecca, the mother of a sixteen-year-old boy. *"She's like the daughter I never had. And*

Charlie and I have always been able to talk, so I shouldn't have been so taken aback when he came to me to ask if I could help her get the birth-control pill. I just kept thinking of my own first time—it was in college, and the guy dumped me soon afterward. I'm amazed at how upset the whole thing with Charlie made me feel."

"I got married too early because we were going to have a baby, and that marriage ended in just a few years," said Bill, a divorced father who has since remarried and sees his seventeen-year-old son on occasional week-ends. "When I saw condoms in my kid's shaving kit last week, I flipped out. Even if my boy thinks he's having safe sex, anything could happen."

Rebecca and Bill found that their own early sexual experiences powerfully affected how they responded to their boys' situations. The following exercise will help you think about how such memories might affect you:

My First Time

AN EXERCISE FOR PARENTS

If you feel more comfortable doing so, use a separate sheet to write down the answers to the following private questions, so you can dispose of it when the exercise is finished.

How old were you when you had sexual intercourse for the first time? ____

Describe the person and the situation briefly:

_____

_____

_____

How did you feel about it at the time?

___ It was a good experience; I wouldn't change anything.

___ It wasn't a good experience because_____

_____

_____

If you could go back and give yourself advice at that time, what would you say?

_____

_____

Do you think you would have taken that advice? Why or why not?

_____

_____

DIFFERENT PEOPLE, DIFFERENT CHOICES

When parents object to the partners their boy chooses or the choices he makes, it makes his feelings even more difficult.

"My son, Scott, is a sophomore, and he's fallen hard for a senior girl," said his mother, Gayle. "You can tell that she's too old for him just by the way she dresses—and she has her own car, so I never know what they're doing. I know it's not going to last—she's going off to college next year, for one thing. But can't I do something to keep him from getting hurt?"

Gayle's best chance to help Scott is to respect his privacy in this romantic involvement. If she doesn't judge or shame him for his choices, he will feel safe coming to her later if things do in fact go wrong.

But she shouldn't assume that her son is making the wrong choice just because it isn't what his mother dreams of. People are drawn to romantic partners for many reasons, and maybe this older girl is just what Scott needs right now, giving him security or support he can't find elsewhere. By identifying positive aspects to the relationship, Gayle will send a message to her boy that she respects and values his opinions and needs.

When you show or tell your boy your own feelings, values, and beliefs about sexuality and romance, he absorbs this information in a very powerful way. But even within the same family, parents approach these topics from very different perspectives. The following exercise will help you identify where you stand:

What I Believe About Sex and Romance

AN EXERCISE FOR PARENTS

Following are some of the beliefs adults might hold about sex and its place in a youngster's life. Check off any that you agree with:

___ It's okay for kids to start dating as a couple when they're in middle school.

___ Middle school is too young for a person to be sexually intimate in any way.

___ High school is too young for a person to have sexual intercourse.

___ Sexual intercourse should be reserved for marriage.

___ Sexual intercourse should be reserved for a serious commitment.

___ When to have sex is a personal choice, but it should always be conducted in a safe manner.

___ Masturbation with another person is something I object to.

___ Mutual masturbation is a substitute for sexual intercourse and it's all right to do it before people get further involved sexually.

___ Oral sex is a substitute for sexual intercourse and it's all right to do it before people get further involved sexually.

___ Oral sex is taking sexual intercourse one step further and shouldn't happen till later, if at all.

___ It's okay to have sex with a number of different people before you settle down.

___ Sex should be reserved for one special person.

Add any other beliefs here:

_____

_____

WHEN SEX CREATES DANGERS

Along with a boy's growing interest in sex comes a growing vulnerability to risk. As soon as he enters adolescence, he needs information about sexual harassment, unwelcome sexual actions, sexually transmitted infections, and other hazards to himself and others.

"My boy, Wylie, and the guys he hangs out with are always throwing around insults at each other," said Carmella, the mother of a twelve-year-old. "They're just having fun and I don't do anything about it. But when I came home from work yesterday they were out on the steps, and I heard them pestering these two girls going by, making fun of their clothes and the way they were walking. I felt like yanking Wylie right inside and telling him I never wanted to hear him talk that way."

Carmella's instinct is right to step in here—but how she does it will make all the difference. Merely forbidding her son, or showing how upset she is, unfortunately won't lead to genuine change. Without shaming Wylie, she needs to help him understand how hurtful this seemingly "normal" behavior is. In a private time and place later, for example, she could ask him, "How would you feel if adult men were doing that kind of thing to me?" Or, "How would you feel if girls were making fun of you and your body in front of other people?"

When they are aimed at a girl, the friendly insults boys use to express solidarity and friendship with one another easily cross the line into sexual harassment. Younger boys may have trouble comprehending this distinction at first, and need to learn to see it from the perspective of the other person. But it is a serious matter. If it occurs at school, for instance, charges of sexual harassment may result in suspension or other disciplinary action. But even if consequences like this do not follow, it will hurt their chances for healthy relationships with members of the opposite sex.

When you talk with a boy about sexual harassment:

➤ Let him know you understand that playful teasing among boys is different.

➤ Tell him clearly that any unwelcome comment about a girl's or another boy's physical appearance can be considered harassment.

➤ Give him examples. It's all right to say, "That's a nice T-shirt"; it's not all right to make comments (to her or anyone else) about how the shirt fits. Among boys, friends might have affectionate nicknames that refer to size or weight; that's not okay between a boy and a girl.

➤ Sexual harassment can happen between boys, too. Make sure he realizes that any unwanted or hurtful teasing is unacceptable. (For more on bullying and teasing see chapter 6 of this book, "Bullies and Troublemakers.")

Even if he's too young to be "going out" with anyone, this is also a good time to teach your boy to respect the word "no" when he hears it in a sexual encounter of any kind, and to see mutuality as the essence of a romantic relationship. Respecting someone else's wishes in intimate matters is one of the most important habits you can help him form.

"I'm always telling my boy that we can't always get what we want," said Martin. "I figure if I show him that in some areas—like whether I let him use my car, or whether he can go to a concert if it causes someone else in the family a problem—then he'll learn he's not the only one who counts when it comes to girls."

YOUR BOY'S SEXUAL SAFETY

"I've been worried about my boy, Orville," said Lee Ann, the mother of a seventeen-year-old. "He's had a whole string of girlfriends this year, and I get the feeling he's hooked up with more than a couple of them. I finally asked him if he knew about the viruses you can pick up by playing around like that, but he got real huffy with me. No one he knew had that kind of problem, he told me."

Unfortunately, Orville is dead wrong. Viruses don't care how nice someone is, and the chances of contracting something through unprotected sex climbs higher with every sexual partner a boy has. Among the most common conditions that spread through sexual contact are:

- Gonorrhea
- Syphilis
- HIV infection
- Chlamydia
- Genital warts (human papillomavirus, or HPV)
- Herpes

KNOW THE FACTS

- Every year, 3 million teens—and about one in four sexually experienced teens—acquire a sexually transmitted infection.
- Almost 16 percent of urban adolescent women carry the human papillomavirus (HPV)—often acquired soon after they start having sex.
- Chlamydia is more common among teens than among adults; in some settings up to 10 percent of teenage boys tested were found to have chlamydia.
- Yet between 41 percent and 60 percent of sexually active female students said their partners didn't use condoms at their most recent sexual intercourse.

HELPING YOUR BOY MAKE HEALTHY CHOICES

Before your boy hits puberty, make sure he knows the facts about safe sex. If you can't bring yourself to teach him about condoms, ask a doctor or nurse to do it.

Don't worry that giving your boy the facts he needs means you approve of his having sex. Research shows, in fact, that it is more likely to influence him to delay his first sexual intercourse, as well as to raise the likelihood that he will use protection when he does.

Give him the love, warmth, and caring he craves from his immediate family. Don't just be there; be loving. Research shows this delays first intercourse among young people. If he is already having sex, keeping his family connections strong also makes him much more likely to use protection.

Stay alert to problems. If he seems to be having a lot of sexual partners, he may be using sex to counter bad feelings, conflicts, or depression. Make sure he knows that you are on his side when he's in trouble, and then seek out help for him.

HOMOSEXUALITY AND HOMOPHOBIA

While helping her fifteen-year-old son, Jake, clean out his room one day, Emma was unprepared when she came across a tattered copy of a gay men's magazine hidden under the comic books. When she confronted Jake with it, he turned red and stammered, "It's nothing—a friend left it there."

"Then I sort of overreacted," Emma admitted later. "I told him those kinds of people weren't welcome in our house, and if he was going to be friends with them, then he would be seriously punished. I guess I thought if I gave him a good scare, he would drop that kind of behavior and turn out normal." But now Jake won't say a word to her and stays in his room with the door locked after school. Some days he doesn't come home at all. When Emma asks him where he's been, he will only mutter, "What do you care, anyway? You don't even want me here."

"I just don't want Jake to have a terrible life," Emma said. "I know gay people die of AIDS all the time, and they don't have families or children. Shouldn't I try to steer him away from that?"

Emma's pain and worry about her boy are very understandable. If Jake is actually interested in romantic relationships with members of his own sex, she fears he will have to deal with society's fear (and sometimes hatred) of gay people. And of course she wants to protect him from being mistreated by others because of his sexual orientation.

But much of Emma's concern springs not from facts but from society's misconceptions about gay people, which she has absorbed over the years. Without all the facts, she worries about how Jake's decisions about sex will affect his (and her) life as an adult. If Jake is gay, will he be able to have children? Will he be physically and emotionally healthy? Will he be happy?

As more people learn what it really means to be gay, they are increasingly treating people who have same-sex relationships with the respect and love they deserve. And as more gay people live openly in communities throughout America, many are forming lasting committed relationships, having families, and achieving career success with the acceptance of their families, friends, teachers, and clergy. Nationwide, people are realizing that being gay is not a negative, but simply one aspect of who some people are.

KNOW THE FACTS ABOUT HOMOSEXUALITY

> ➤ Five to 10 percent of men of all religions, nationalities, and racial and ethnic backgrounds discover as young or adolescent boys or in early adulthood that they are gay.

> ➤ Homosexuality is a normal variant of human sexuality. It is not something that people choose, but rather an aspect of themselves that they discover.

> ➤ Homosexuality is not a disease. Although homosexuals were once labeled by psychiatrists as "abnormal," and extremely traumatic "cures" were attempted, by 1980 homosexuality was deleted from the *Diagnostic and Statistical Manual of Mental Disorders* by the American Psychiatric Association when psychiatrists decided it could no longer be seen as a behavior disorder.

> ➤ Much of the trauma and inner turmoil many gay people experience stem not from their homosexuality in itself, but from society's reaction to and fear of their homosexuality—*homophobia*.

> ➤ Homosexuality is not usually "caused" by emotional trauma as a child, by an overbearing mother, by an absent father, by playing with "girl toys," by taking dance lessons, or by dressing up in fancy clothing. Many researchers now believe that whether one is gay, straight, or bisexual is mostly genetically determined. Some even think homosexuality may have evolved as a positive, adaptive trait for human social organization.

> ➤ Many gay people, just like many straight people, enter committed relationships, raise children, and lead happy and healthy lives.

When we teach boys these facts about homosexuality—in an age-appropriate way, along with other critical information about sex and reproduction—we are giving them the tools they need to make intelligent, healthy decisions about their sex lives.

All the research now shows that when a boy who is gay becomes lonely, sad, or troubled, his homosexuality is not the cause. Having to cope with teasing and bullying about being or "seeming" gay is actually what pushes many boys to become sad, isolated, anxious, and sometimes dangerously depressed.

Listen to what Jake said later about his inner tumult when his mom found the magazine in his bedroom:

"I didn't even buy that magazine. Some of the guys got it and we were just making fun of the stuff in it. But some of the pictures in it were kind of exciting. . . . If this means nobody is going to like me anymore, I don't know what I'll do—I'd rather kill myself than have people turn on me! And now my mom hates me. I wish I could run away to another country. Maybe I should move out!"

If boys are not told early that being gay is a normal and healthy—though less common—part of human sexuality, many may feel terrified if they discover they are drawn toward others of the same sex. If his parents and teachers have never spoken to him in a warm or loving way about gay people, a boy in this situation may think that there is no safe place to go, and no caring person to whom he can turn. If his shame becomes unbearable, it may lead him to run away from home, get heavily involved in drugs and alcohol, engage in promiscuous or unprotected sex, or attempt suicide.

Homophobia is not a problem easily solved, for it is deeply rooted in our society. But the single most important factor for boys' happiness and well-being, whether they are gay or straight, is that they feel loved and accepted by their families no matter which way their sexual feelings may turn.

➤ The average high-school student hears twenty-five antigay slurs daily, and 97 percent of high-school students regularly hear homophobic remarks. This harassment takes its toll: Gay students are far more likely to skip classes, drop out of school, or commit suicide.

➤ Gay youths account for up to 30 percent of teenage suicides. In a recent study of gay and bisexual adolescent males, nearly one third of them reported having attempted suicide at least once.

During adolescence, many of the boys in our care will wonder at least once whether they might be gay. It is common knowledge that many teenage boys—whether they are primarily gay or straight—have their first sexual experiences with other boys. And many boys, even if they have never had a homosexual fantasy or experience, worry that they are gay simply because others have teasingly called them "queer" or "faggot." Whether they turn out to be straight or gay, boys need steady support as they work through these difficult issues of identity.

Even if our own backgrounds or beliefs make it hard for us to accept homosexuality, our unconditional love and support are absolutely critical to all the boys in our care. They may prove a matter of life and death. So don't wait for a boy you know to announce his sexual orientation. Instead, try to create an understanding that says: "I want to know about who you are. I want to know about whom you feel attracted to and whom you feel you love. I will always be there for you, no matter what."

IF YOUR BOY IS GAY

"My heart almost broke to see how scared Devon was when he told us," said Donna, whose sixteen-year-old son recently came home and told his parents that he was dating another boy. "My husband, Barry, was even more upset than I was, but thank God he didn't come down hard on Devon. Instead, we both sat for a long time with Devon, listening to what he said. He cried, and

we cried, too. I just couldn't bear to think that he would be afraid we wouldn't love him anymore."

Since Devon told his parents that he is gay, Donna and Barry have had many long discussions about how best to support their boy and keep him safe from shame and risk. They struggled to relinquish their own long-held pictures of what his first romantic experiences would look like, and to build new attitudes and expectations. What could they do to feel more comfortable if he brought a boyfriend home for dinner? Would they object if he went with his boyfriend to the prom? How could they deal with prejudices and discrimination from school and community?

"Barry kind of fixated on the AIDS thing," Donna said. "But once he learned that Devon's boyfriend was at school with him—in fact, was the quarterback on the football team—he started to calm down. Devon and Chris, at our insistence, both got tested for HIV. They are both negative, and they've promised to do what it takes to stay that way."

Devon's parents were particularly proud when Devon, despite some of the teasing he faced, decided to create a Gay-Straight Alliance at his school. Devon asked his English teacher, one of the best-liked teachers at the school, to be the group's adult leader. One of the group's first events was a whole-school teach-in about homophobia, with Devon and Chris as invited speakers. When they spoke of how moved they were by the support and protection of other kids and teachers from their school, the entire audience—including the football team and its coach—stood in warm applause.

"We were so impressed with Devon's courage that, in the end, we actually joined PFLAG, a group for parents of gay kids," said Donna. "It really helped a lot—we weren't putting all our anxieties onto Devon all the time, and it made us feel a lot less alone in our worries. A bunch of us decided to start up some activities for our kids so they could get together and share their common experiences. This spring even Barry is going to march in the Gay Pride parade. I never thought I would see the day!"

Besides offering their son loving acceptance and practical help, Barry and Donna have taken an important step for themselves here, too. Especially if they have little experience of gay people, it can be isolating and frightening for parents to discover that a child of theirs is gay. Only through education and open, supportive discussion can the cycle of fear be stopped.

Whether or not you have a gay son, write down the answers to the following questions:

What organizations exist in your area for parents of gay and lesbian youth?

_____

_____

What age-appropriate activities exist in your area for gay teenagers?

_____

_____

_____

In what ways might you help gay children in your community to feel less isolated in their social activities?

_____

_____

_____

WHAT SCHOOLS CAN DO

Schools can also do much to dispel myths about homosexuality and offer support to adolescents who may be questioning their sexual orientation. Gay-Straight Alliances are a very powerful way to do this. Both gay and straight teenagers also benefit from seeing positive adult gay role models, whether they be celebrities like Ian McKellen, Ellen DeGeneres, or Melissa Etheridge, politicians like Congressman Barney Frank of Massachusetts, or a local teacher who is "out."

What Am I Doing to Help?

A REFLECTION FOR TEACHERS

How do you respond when kids at school make homophobic comments or taunt someone for "seeming gay"?

_____

_____

How can you bring awareness of sexual-orientation issues into the curriculum?

_____

_____

If a boy in one of your classes told you he was gay, what would you do to help him?

_____

_____

If you were a student at your school, would you feel safe being honest about your true sexual feelings and experiences?

_____

_____

HOTLINES AND SUPPORT GROUPS

The following organizations offer information about a variety of issues involving sexuality, including support for teachers, students, and parents:

Domestic Violence Hotline:
1-800-799-SAFE (24 hours)
Emergency Contraception Hotline:
1-800-584-9911 (24 hours)
HIV/AIDS Teen Hotline:
1-800-440-TEEN
IYG (peer support for gay, lesbian, and bisexual youth):
1-800-347-TEEN
National Abortion Federation Hotline:
1-800-772-9100
National Child Abuse Hotline:
1-800-4-A-CHILD (24 hours)
National Gay and Lesbian Hotline:
1-888-843-4564
PFLAG (Parents, Families and Friends of Lesbians and Gays):
1-202-467-8180
National HIV/AIDS Hotline:
1-800-342-AIDS (24 hours)
National STD Hotline:
1-800-227-8922
Gay, Lesbian, and Straight Teachers Network (GLSTN):
1-800-727-0135

16

REAL BOYS IN THE REAL WORLD

BOYS AT WORK • A BOY AND HIS MENTORS • SERVICE IN THE COMMUNITY

"For about a year now Alex has worked pumping gas after school and on weekends," said Derrick, the father of a high-school junior. "His mom and I are glad that he's showing some responsibility, but we're also worried. What kind of a place is that to be for twenty hours a week? What kind of people is he with? What's he really learning, and is it worth the time it takes away from his schoolwork? All Alex seems to care about is making money to buy an old car, but we're wondering if we ought to step in."

Whether a boy is shoveling snow for his neighbor or making change at a local market, working for pay or for the satisfaction of helping others, his experience "out in the world" marks a new stage of his life. Work experiences have the potential to change a boy's life in important ways:

➤ He practices in the real world what he learns at home and at school.
➤ He feels valued by others for things he can do well.
➤ He learns to interact with customers and with a boss.
➤ He learns to manage his time.
➤ He decides what to do with his earnings.
➤ He may find new and valuable mentors.

All these experiences contribute to a boy's growing sense of himself as a man. This chapter explores the value and the risks inherent in the world of work and service.

We'll pay particular attention to how a boy's mentors in that world can affect his developing values and self-esteem. And we'll look at how his desire for justice and fairness plays out during these important experiences.

BOYS AT WORK

A boy's first work is usually in the family. When his family recognizes and openly appreciates such actions, a boy begins to connect even "boring" chores with a sense of satisfaction and self-esteem.

Fill out the following exercise to describe your family's situation:

What regular household tasks does your boy usually do?

_____

_____

What unusual household tasks has your boy helped with in the past?

_____

_____

*Does your boy receive an allowance? If so, how much?*_____

*Is the allowance conditional on his helping around the house?*_____

Explain:

_____

_____

If your boy does not receive pay for his work around the house, how do you show your appreciation?

_____

_____

As boys grow older, they start to develop a keen sense of what is fair, and that can connect with new ways to take action outside the home. Something as simple as collecting for UNICEF at Halloween gives a boy the pleasure of using his energy for a cause outside himself.

WHAT A BOY GAINS FROM WORK

What does a boy get from his experience in the "real world" that he doesn't get at home or at school? One clear benefit comes to boys who have somehow received the message that they never measure up at school. At work, as they meet the very clear standards of real-world tasks, they gain valuable motivation and confidence. Let's look at a few examples:

"When we're out on a painting job, we're expected to pay attention to every little detail," says Scott, who works summers for a painting contractor. "You're in someone's home, so you've got to watch how you talk, if it's okay to play music, things like that. The boss says that makes the difference in whether you get word-of-mouth business."

The stakes for Scott's everyday actions have gone up now that he's working for someone whose business success depends on his behavior. With a summer to build these habits of responsibility and respect, he's likely to carry them into his home and school environments, too.

"I know it's just flipping burgers, but I like having the money to save for the things I want," says Warren, who works at a fast-food place after school. "If I keep a good record here for a couple of years, they'll make me a manager by the time I'm eighteen."

Warren is learning persistence in his job, and how to go after his goals even though they may take years to attain. Just showing up on time consistently may be a challenge for a boy who might rather be sleeping late or hanging out with his friends. And working on a team with others develops his ability to collaborate on more ambitious tasks later.

"I started in seventh grade by helping my mom's friends set up their Internet accounts," says Russell, who at sixteen runs his own computer consulting business and is saving for college. "It's fun to be the expert on something that older people have trouble doing. And the guys at school are always asking me to help them, too."

Even though he's no athlete, Russell has won a star's reputation in his community, and he takes real pride in his own abilities. His confidence pays off in social interactions with his peers, too.

"First I was a counselor-in-training at the camp where I went when I was younger, and then I got a job on the waterfront there," said Jon. "I really like working with kids, so during the school year I started taking baby-sitting jobs in my spare time. Now I'm like a big brother to the kids I sit for. I think I'd like to be a teacher someday."

From both his jobs, Jon is learning important things about his talent with kids. And he has the chance to express his caring, nurturing nature in an arena where people admire and appreciate these qualities.

BREAKING DOWN THE STEREOTYPES

In fact, a boy's work is yet another place where he confronts the stereotypes of gender, and an important place where adults can support him in breaking through them.

At sixteen, Hal has the chance at two great summer opportunities—one as an intern in his neighbor's law offices and one as an apprentice at a summer-stock theater. "He loves to act, and he's dying to take the summer-stock job," says his mother, Helene. "But his dad's pushing him to take the law-firm job. He says it's the first step toward the real career that Hal will need to have someday."

Pressured by his father to get a head start on a successful, highly paid career, Hal will need support if he decides to follow his heart into the theater apprenticeship. He is especially vulnerable to his father's opinion that the actor's life isn't "a real career," implying an eventual path toward marriage and support of a family.

Our society still lays these expectations on boys, even though so many women work at careers outside the home. As our boys begin their first explorations into the real world, they need help in imagining their roles as broadly as possible, without feeling shamed by gender stereotypes.

KEEPING WORK IN BALANCE

Cedric started working after school at a fried-chicken takeout place as soon as he was old enough. The boss was perpetually short of help, and what started as eight hours a week soon ballooned to twenty-five. "I'm worried because he doesn't have time for homework anymore," said Cedric's mother, Louann. "I want him to work, but he's got to think about his future, too!"

Sometimes a boy's work becomes so demanding that he has no time left for school, sports, or family activities. If this is happening, talk together about why, listening carefully to the trade-offs he is making. Use the following worksheet to record what you learn:

How Much Is Too Much?

AN EXERCISE FOR PARENTS AND BOYS

*How many hours per week does the boy work?*_____

His work takes place mainly:
___ Before school
___ After school
___ On weekends
___ A combination:_____

The boy spends so much time at his job because:

___ He needs or wants the money.

___ His boss really needs him and he wants to help.

___ If he doesn't work this many hours, he can't have the job.

___ He is much more interested in the job than in other activities.

___ Other_____

On the following list, check any area to which the boy would like to be giving more time if it weren't for the demands of the job. Use the space after each item to explain what he'd like to be doing, and how much time it would take:

___ School_____

___ Sports_____

___ Family_____

___ Extracurricular activities_____

___ Other_____

Can either of you imagine ways to adjust the boy's schedule to make room for other activities? If so, write your ideas here:

_____

_____

_____

_____

A BOY AND HIS MENTORS

*"Our boy Jesse got interested in doing magic when he was about eleven,"
said John, the father of a fifteen-year-old. "A friend's grandfather, who used
to be an amateur magician, was visiting one week and showed Jesse a few
tricks when he was there." Before long Jesse was seeking out the retired man
for practice sessions, and his new friend introduced him to professional
conferences where he could learn even more. "Last week, at fifteen, Jesse
got his first paying gig at a child's birthday party," said his father. "I think
his friend's grandfather sees more of my boy than I do!"*

Like Jesse's father, many parents feel wistful as they see their growing boys form strong relationships with other adults. It may be a coach or a teacher, a friend's parent or an older relative, who wins your boy's confidence as he seeks models away from his immediate family circle. Or he may find a mentor through his job, his hobby, or his volunteer work.

As a boy's admiration for this expert friend grows, he can find in his mentor—whether male or female—an important testing ground for his newly emerging sense of male identity. What can he gain from such a mentor that he can't learn from his parents?

➤ He learns that admired adults can have many different voices, backgrounds, approaches, and attitudes.
➤ He learns how to learn from and connect with an adult in the real world.
➤ He learns practical or technical matters that a parent may not know about.
➤ He learns to take correction and strive to meet the mentor's standards of excellence.
➤ He learns that he can earn the confidence of an adult in the outside world.

Who Was My Mentor?

A REFLECTION FOR PARENTS

Outside your immediate family, was there anyone who served as an important model or mentor to you during your growing-up years? If so, what did you learn from that person? How did your relationship with that person differ from your family relationships?

_____

_____

_____

APPRECIATE A BOY'S MENTORS

"When this Democrat who was running for Congress visited the high school, my son Larry got involved with politics for the first time—and I have

to admit it kind of bugs me," said Steve, a lifelong Republican. "He started working for this fellow, passing out flyers and holding up signs at intersections. I tried not to let arguments about politics ruin our family dinners—but I put my foot down when Larry wanted to put a bumper sticker on our car. I wish he had never met the guy!"

Though his boy's mentor doesn't share Steve's opinions, he still serves an important function in Larry's development. Thinking back to his own youth, for example, Steve began to calm down after he asked himself:

➤ How old was I when I first took an interest in politics?
➤ Who particularly influenced me in my political opinions?
➤ What role did my parents play in developing my opinions?
➤ Did my opinions change as I grew older?

"In the end, I decided it was more important not to disparage Larry's candidate than it was for him to share my views," said Steve. "When we got into political arguments, I tried to stick to the issues and show respect for what Larry had to say. We even talked about putting both candidates' stickers on the car—but that seemed too weird to me, so we decided to let the whole thing go."

Do you know who serves as a mentor—or might do so—in your boy's life? Describe the person(s) here:

_____

_____

What could you do to foster, strengthen, or show respect for that relationship?

_____

_____

SERVICE IN THE COMMUNITY

Ramon grew up reading to his grandmother, who was blind, and by the time he was ten he regularly wrote letters in Spanish for her to her relatives in Mexico. "I think that experience had a big effect on him in lots of ways," said his mother, Luisa. "He's at the top of his class in reading and writing—but even more, he has a sense that what he does really matters to someone."

Ramon's family is giving him a chance to express his love and desire for justice through action, starting at an early age. Activities like this can reach beyond the home as a boy grows older and prove an important bond within the family as he begins to find his own identity.

SOME WAYS A FAMILY CAN ENCOURAGE BOYS TO SERVE OTHERS:
- ➤ Volunteer in a soup kitchen once a month.
- ➤ Hold family meetings to decide which charities to donate to.
- ➤ Walk in a fund-raising march for a cause you believe in (cancer research, etc.).
- ➤ Wrap toys for children living in shelters at the holidays.

What opportunities does your boy have for service to your community?

_____

_____

_____

What could you do to foster situations in which that could occur?

_____

_____

WHEN SCHOOLS TEACH SERVICE
Throughout the fall term, students in one high school's elective service-learning class paid weekly visits to residents of a local nursing home. "I'm glad I'm involved with this project," wrote William, sixteen, in his service journal. "I've learned that I can help people and it makes me feel good. I

am less nervous around older people and happy to have made new friends from a different generation. I've enjoyed hearing their stories."

Schools can teach boys the habit of active participation in the outside world. Though it takes considerable effort to organize courses like William's, schools that do so find new strengths and attitudes growing in the students who participate.

As with any work in the "real world," community service can build strong connections between a boy's experience and interests and his academic learning.

In appealing to his impulses toward action and toward social justice, it also teaches him that what he does can make a difference in the world.

SOME WAYS SCHOOLS MIGHT FOSTER COMMUNITY SERVICE:

➤ Give every student a job that contributes to the school (washing the blackboard, helping to sort mail in the office). Make sure boys and girls get all kinds of tasks.

➤ Have homerooms or advisory groups take rotating responsibility for lunchroom duty.

➤ End classes a few minutes early so that everyone can go outside and pick up litter. Designate one period each week to service (helping in the kindergarten, visiting a nursing home, working with handicapped children).

➤ Match older boys with younger children for reading and writing activities, math help, games, and activities. Have the older ones keep journals of what they are learning.

➤ Start a high-school service club or class that plans schoolwide community-service projects (like a clothes drive) or assemblies about community issues (like homelessness or the environment).

➤ Use part of the senior year for individual community-based projects.

What opportunities does your school offer for service to the community?

_____

_____

What could you do to foster situations in which that could occur?

_____

_____

KNOW THE FACTS

Young people who help others are 50 percent less likely to use drugs, join gangs, or get pregnant. Their dropout rate is lower, and they achieve higher grades throughout high school.

EPILOGUE

Real Men: A New Vision for Tomorrow

"I've been thinking a lot about my own childhood because Lisa and I are expecting a baby boy next month," said Ted, a thirty-year-old teacher. "I realized how much my parents were there for me when I was growing up, even though they were pretty busy running a copy shop together. I think that's one reason I went into teaching—I want to have a schedule where I have time off when my kids do."

"My mom always listened to me as if what I felt was the most important thing she wanted to hear," said Michael, a young doctor just beginning his medical residency in a major cancer treatment center. "I remember her sometimes, when I'm talking with a patient. Mom gave me a place where I felt safe if I was scared, or if I didn't know what to do. Now I feel like I can do the same thing for other people."

"I really look forward to the time I spend with my Little Brother in the mentoring program I belong to," said Barton, a graphic artist with his own studio in a downtown loft. "I'm probably not going to have children of my own, but I feel really protective of Conrad. I'm determined that he'll get the same chances my folks made sure I had, even though his background is so different from mine. And I want to help him make good decisions, because he's going to face some hard choices if he wants to stay away from trouble in that neighborhood."

Ted, Michael, and Barton all entered manhood with a legacy that has continued to affect the way they live their lives. From their stories, it's easy to imagine the ways their parents built that legacy through their everyday actions with their boys:

- ➤ They spent time with their boys, even when they were really busy.
- ➤ They genuinely listened to their boys and let them know that all their feelings were important.
- ➤ They accepted and supported their boys just the way they were, even if it was different from the norm.

What would our world be like if all of us gave our boys those things? It's a powerful question, and one that every chapter in this workbook has aimed to explore with you.

In these final pages you'll look back on what you've written in this book, and reflect on how your own experiences affect the way you understand your boy. And you'll look ahead, imagining how you'd like your boy to remember his years with you.

HOW HAVE YOU CHANGED?

Take some time to look back through your notes and comments in the exercises throughout this book. Then, write your responses to the questions below:

Was there any one exercise that was particularly important to you?

_____

_____

_____

Do you have more thoughts on any one topic, now that you've come to the end of the workbook?

_____

_____

_____

_____
_____
_____

Have you changed your mind about anything you wrote earlier in the book?

_____
_____
_____
_____
_____

Do you have questions about your life with your boy that you'd like to explore further?

_____
_____
_____

Are there areas in which you particularly hope to grow?

_____
_____
_____
_____
_____

Are there specific changes you want to make in the way you are with the boys in your life?

_____
_____
_____
_____
_____

Are there specific changes you want to make for boys in the school with which you are associated?

_____

_____

_____

_____

_____

_____

Are there specific changes you want to make for boys in the organized sports activities that you're involved with?

_____

_____

_____

_____

_____

_____

WRITE A LETTER TO YOURSELF

Throughout this book, you've been recollecting your own experiences and connecting them to the ways you understand boys. As you've done so, you may have come to understand new things about your own growing-up years.

➤ Were you placed in a gender straitjacket, or were you free to be the person you yearned to be?
➤ Did your feelings seem important or were they something to hide away?
➤ Did you have someone who believed in you, accepted you, and guided you?

In the space that follows, write a letter to the young child you once were. Tell that child—yourself—what you now understand about her or him. Say what you wish someone had said to you back then. Take as much time as you want, and use additional pages if necessary:

_____

_____

_____

_____

_____

_____

_____

_____

_____

_____

_____

_____

_____

_____

WRITE A LETTER TO THE BOYS IN YOUR LIFE

Now think about the boys you care about. What would you like to say to them—about their past, about their future, about their time with you now? In the space that follows, write those thoughts down as a letter.

You may want to show it some day to the boy or boys you care about, or you may prefer to keep it private—it's up to you. Write about your deepest feelings, wishes, fears, and hopes.

_____

_____

_____

_____

_____

_____

_____

_____

_____

_____

_____

_____

_____

_____

_____

_____

_____

_____

FROM NOW ON

Our time with our boys is short. If we use it well, we will be helping to create a different, better world—a world of Real Boys who grow into the Real Men we hope for. Both strong and emotionally connected, they will change the world—not just for boys but for girls, not just for men and women, but for the children they guide.

We want this workbook to help make that possible, by continuing the dialogue about rescuing our boys from the myths of boyhood. If you have questions or stories that would enrich the next edition of this book, we hope you will write them down and send them to us. At the Real Boys Workshops® website (*www.realboysworkshops.com* or *www.williampollack.com*) you can also access more information about activities and workshops that can help both parents and teachers in their everyday work with boys. If you want to write to us, e-mail your questions or letters to *info@williampollack. com*. We look forward to continuing this important conversation with you as we build a new world together in which all of us can be most fully ourselves.

ABOUT THE AUTHORS

William S. Pollack, Ph.D., a clinical psychologist, is an assistant clinical professor of psychiatry at Harvard Medical School, the director of the Center for Men and Young Men at McLean Hospital, and a founding member and fellow of the American Psychological Association's Society for the Psychological Study of Men and Masculinity. He is the bestselling author of *Real Boys* and *Real Boys' Voices*. He and his family live in Massachusetts.

Kathleen Cushman writes about education and family issues for a national audience. She is a coauthor of *Schooling for the Real World* and several other books, and her articles and essays have appeared in *Parents*, *The Atlantic Monthly*, and *American Educator*, among many other publications. She is currently the story director of What Kids Can Do, Inc.

NOTES